ARTEMIS™
& THE ASSASSIN

STEPHANIE PHILLIPS

MEGHAN HETRICK

FRANCESCA FANTINI

LAUREN AFFE

TROY PETERI

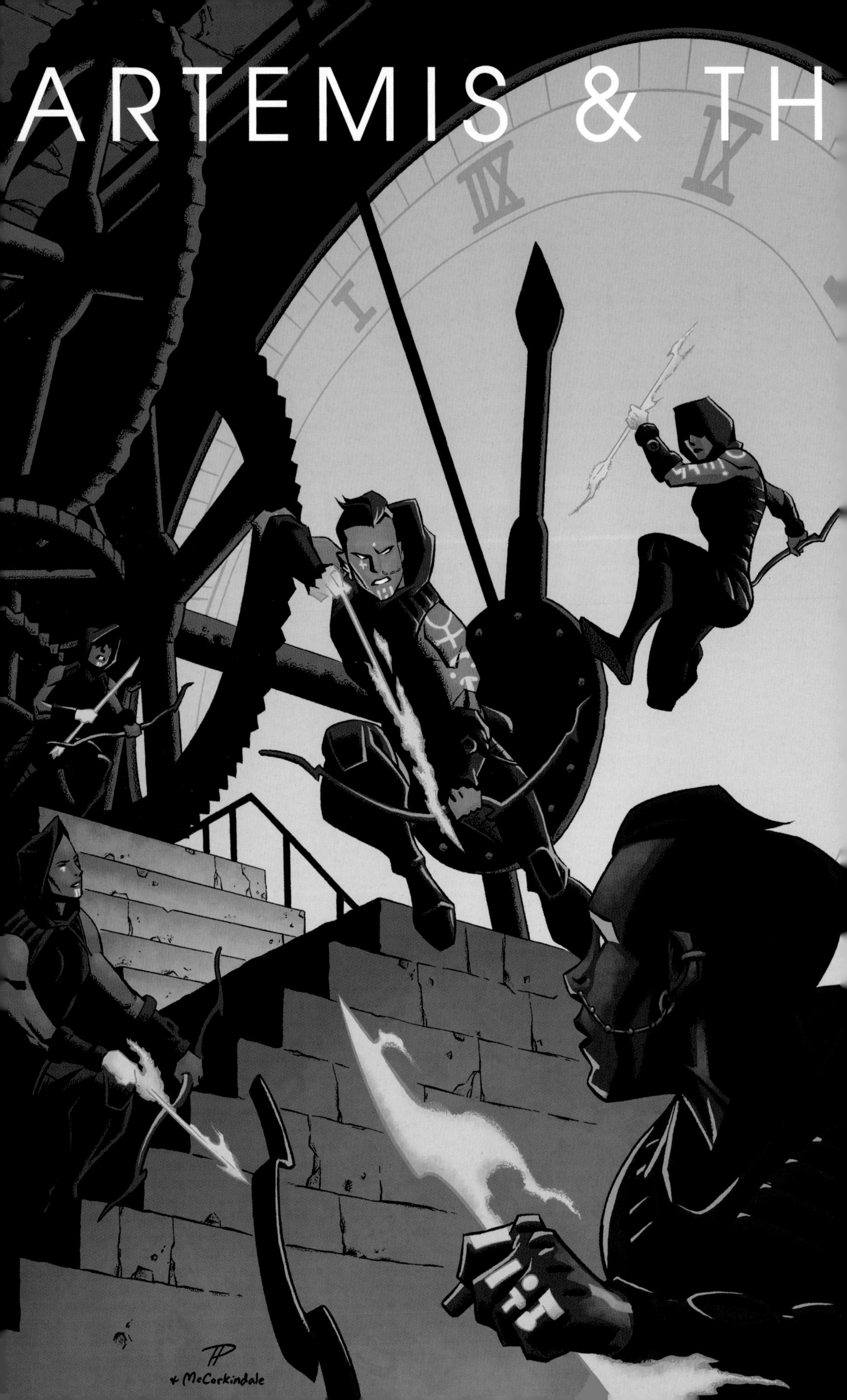
ARTEMIS & TH
TP
+ McCorkindale

E ASSASSIN

STEPHANIE PHILLIPS writer
MEGHAN HETRICK artist (issues #1-2)
FRANCESCA FANTINI artist (issues #3-5)

LAUREN AFFE colorist

A LARGER WORLD'S TROY PETERI letterer

PHIL HESTER w/ BRUCE McCORKINDALE,
ERIC GAPSTUR and MARK EGLERT front & original covers

TIM BRADSTREET, BUTCH GUICE and DAVE JOHNSON variant covers

CHARLES PRITCHETT logo designer

COREY BREEN book designer

CHRISTINA HARRINGTON editor

created by STEPHANIE PHILLIPS

AFTERSHOCK™

MIKE MARTS - Editor-in-Chief • JOE PRUETT - Publisher/CCO • LEE KRAMER - President • JON KRAMER - Chief Executive Officer
STEVE ROTTERDAM - SVP, Sales & Marketing • DAN SHIRES - VP, Film & Television UK • CHRISTINA HARRINGTON - Managing Editor
MARC HAMMOND - Sr. Retail Sales Development Manager • RUTHANN THOMPSON - Sr. Retailer Relations Manager
KATHERINE JAMISON - Marketing Manager • KELLY DIODATI - Ambassador Outreach Manager • BLAKE STOCKER - Director of Finance
AARON MARION - Publicist • LISA MOODY - Finance • RYAN CARROLL - Development Coordinator • JAWAD QURESHI - Technology Advisor/Strategist
RACHEL PINNELAS - Social Community Manager • CHARLES PRITCHETT - Design & Production Manager • COREY BREEN - Collections Production
TEDDY LEO - Editorial Assistant • STEPHANIE CASEBIER & SARAH PRUETT - Publishing Assistants

AfterShock Logo Design by COMICRAFT
Publicity: contact AARON MARION (aaron@publichausagency.com) & RYAN CROY (ryan@publichausagency.com) at PUBLICHAUS
Special thanks to: ATOM! FREEMAN, IRA KURGAN, MARINE KSADZHIKYAN, KEITH MANZZELLA, STEPHANIE MEADOR, ANTONIA LIANOS & ED ZAREMBA

PRINTED IN KOREA. First Printing: January 2021. 10 9 8 7 6 5 4 3 2 1

AFTERSHOCKCOMICS.COM Follow us on social media

I N T R O D U C T I O N

Growing up, I was always a fan of unusual and unexpected comic book team-ups. When I decided to approach AfterShock with my own take on an action/adventure team comic, I decided to take this lens one step further—fictional, time-traveling assassin named Maya teaming up with real-life WWII spy, Virginia Hall.

As much as ARTEMIS & THE ASSASSIN is a story about two dissimilar heroines forced to work together as they're thrown through time, it's also about fact versus fiction, something I work with often as I write historical fiction. Asking, where do I draw the line on reality and allow fiction to take over? And, conversely, where do I impose reality on the fictitious elements of time travel and super-powered assassins? As a writer, playing with the push and pull of fiction and reality was one of the most exciting elements of writing this story.

Maya and Virginia have become some of my favorite characters to write. In their respective time periods and realities, Maya and Virginia are both female heroines. Maya is from an ancient protectorate society trained in martial arts and with supernatural abilities, while Virginia is literally one of the most decorated spies in US history, trained in espionage and combat skills. They have competing missions and interests in the story yet learn how best to complement one another if they hope to survive.

That dynamic, which is often biting or sarcastic, was tons of fun to script, and both Meghan Hetrick and Francesca Fantini brought these characters to life beautifully on the page, alongside Lauren Affe's colors and Troy Peteri's letters.

I sincerely hope you have as much fun reading this story as we did creating it. The saying goes that "truth is stranger than fiction." But they forgot to tell you how much fun it can be when truth and fiction meet.

STEPHANIE PHILLIPS
November 2020

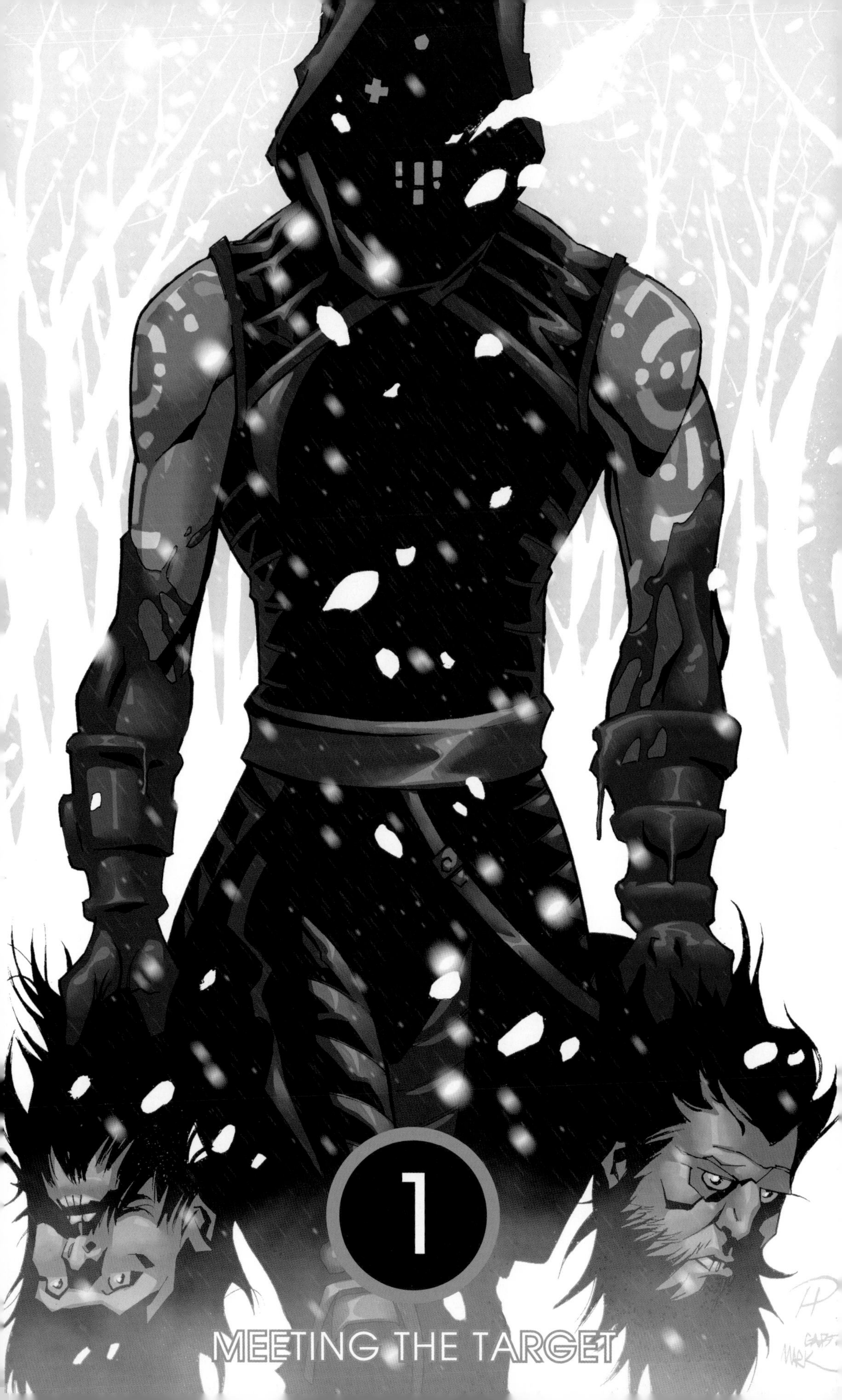

1

MEETING THE TARGET

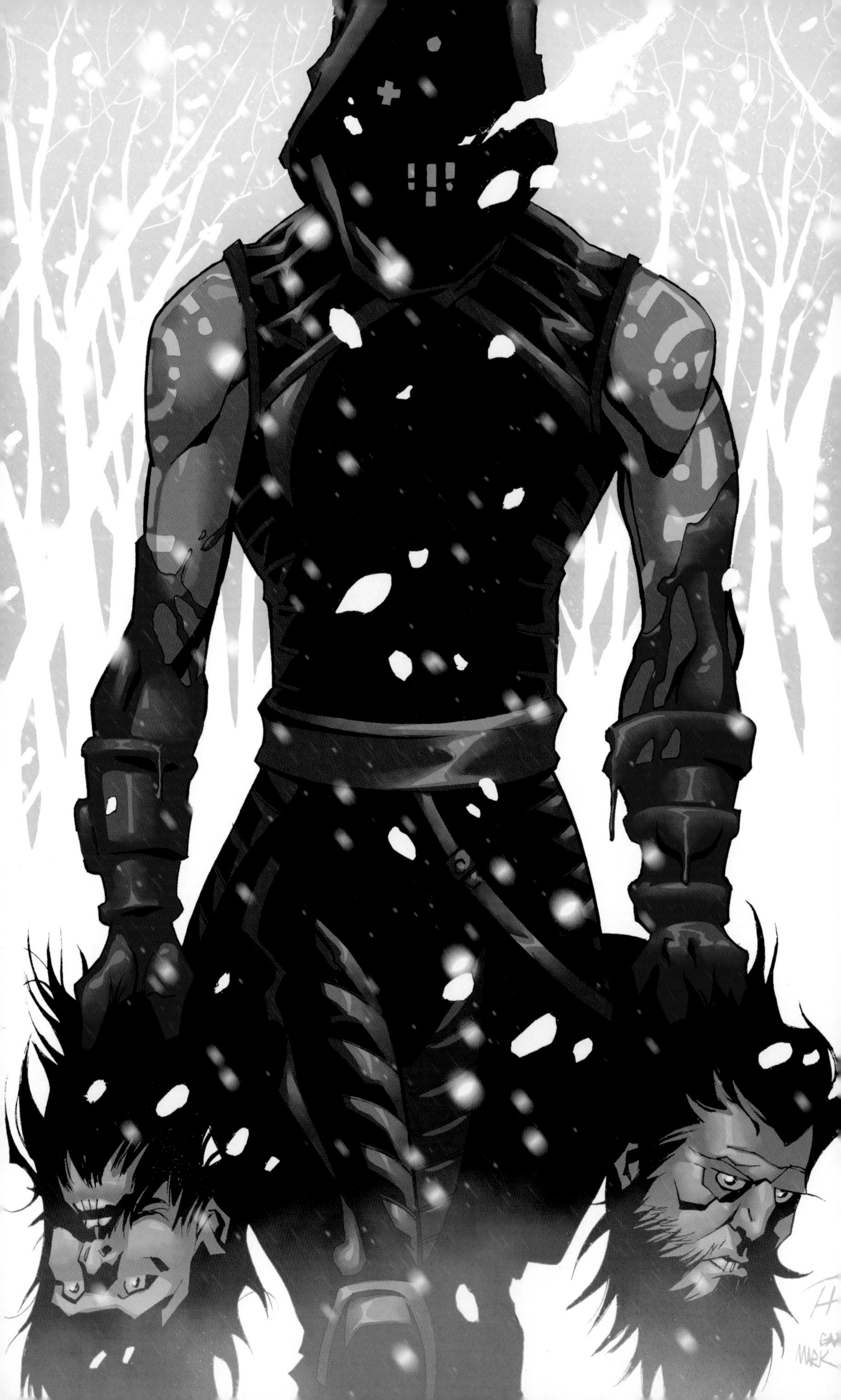

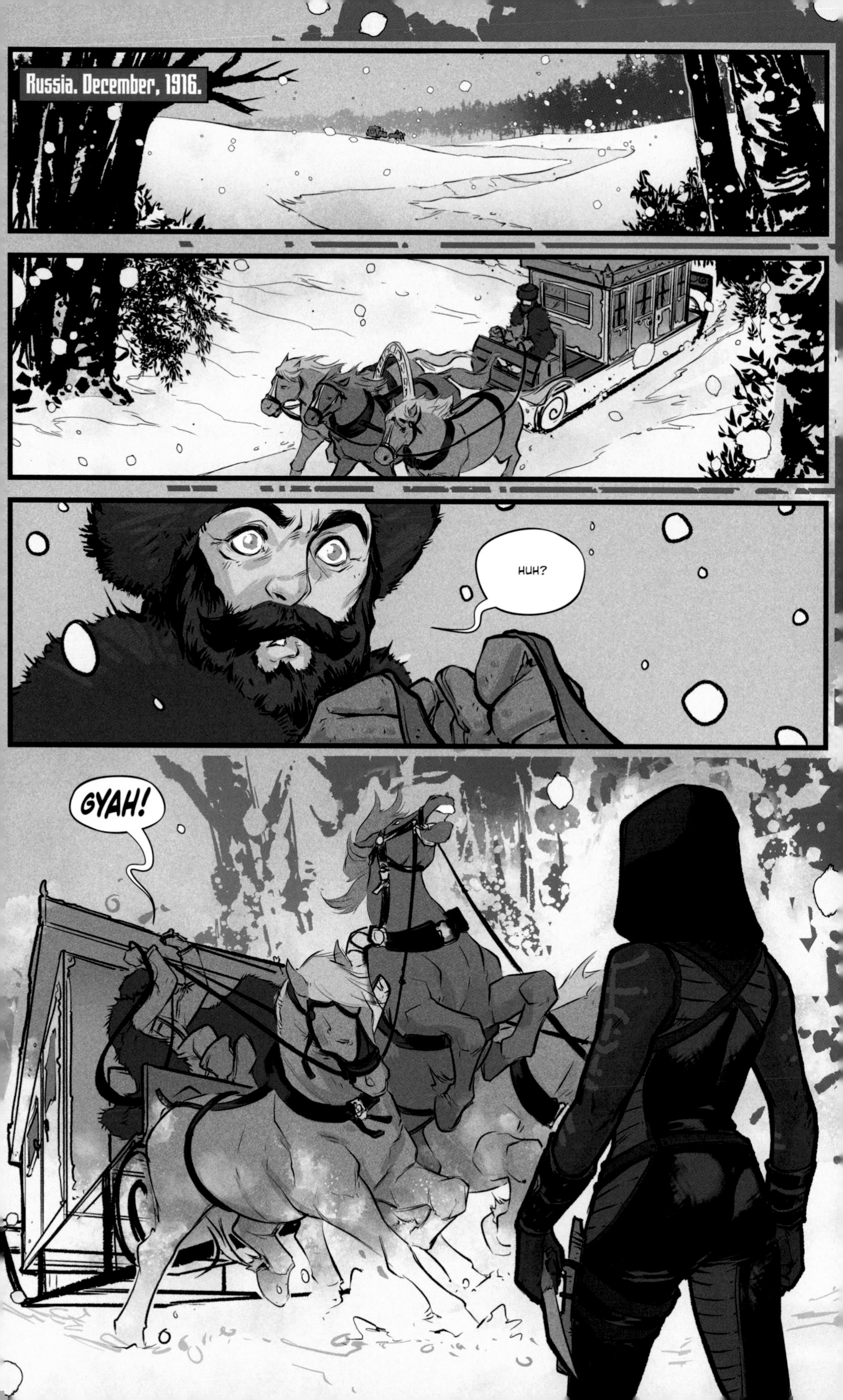
Russia. December, 1916.
HUH?
GYAH!

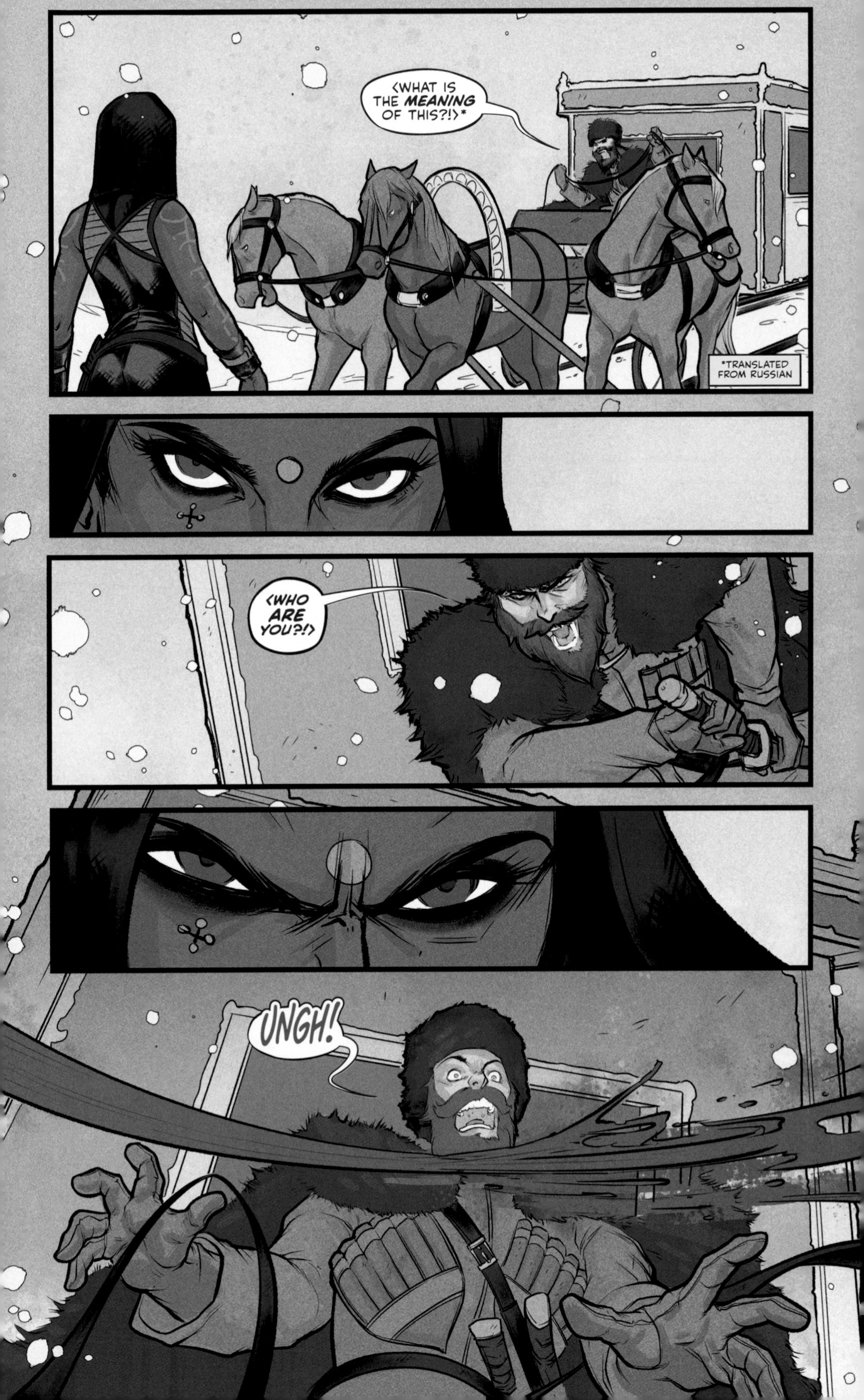

‹WHAT IS THE *MEANING* OF THIS?!›*
*TRANSLATED FROM RUSSIAN
‹WHO ARE YOU?!›
UNGH!

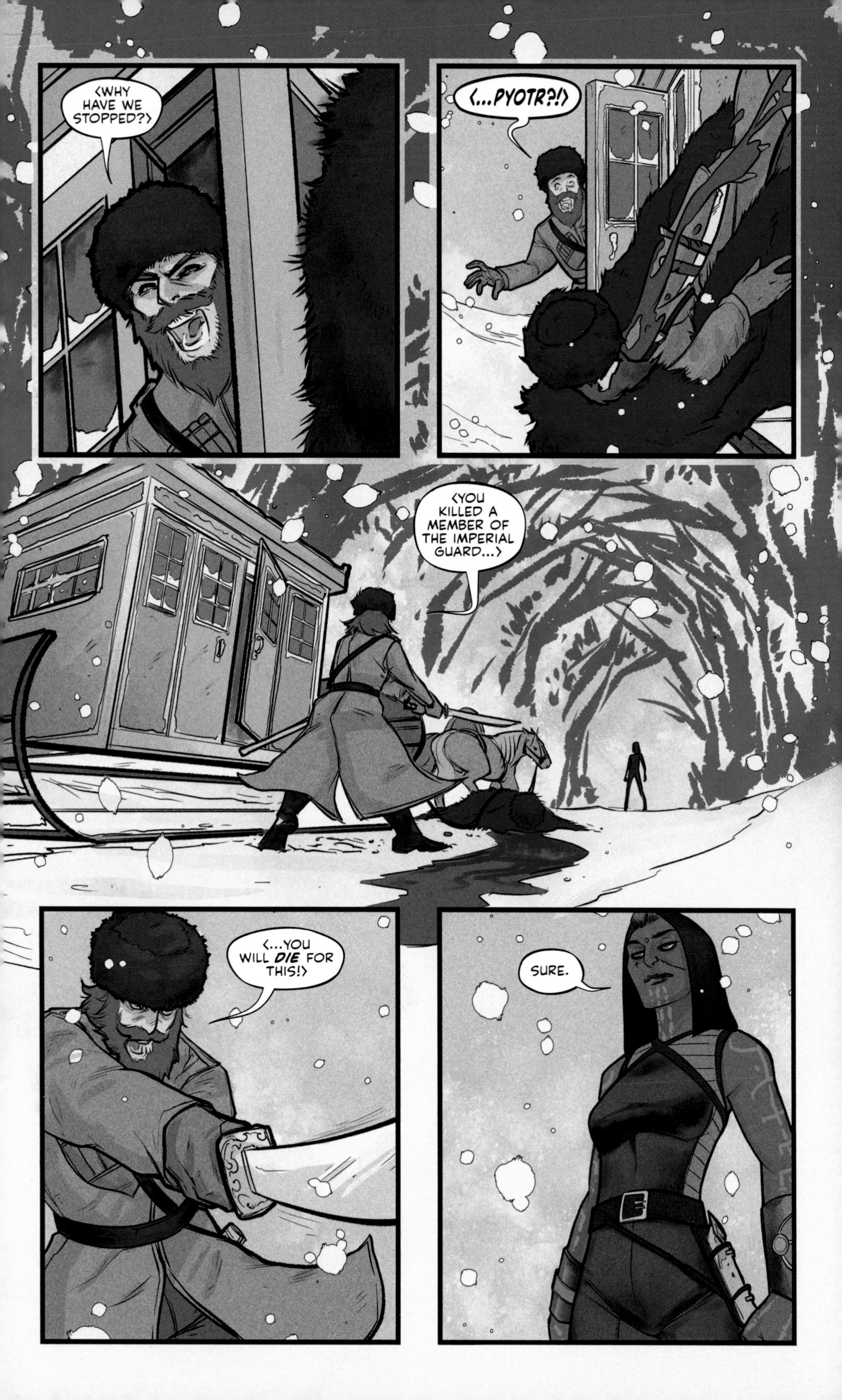
<WHY HAVE WE STOPPED?>
<...PYOTR?!>
<YOU KILLED A MEMBER OF THE IMPERIAL GUARD...>
<...YOU WILL DIE FOR THIS!>
SURE.

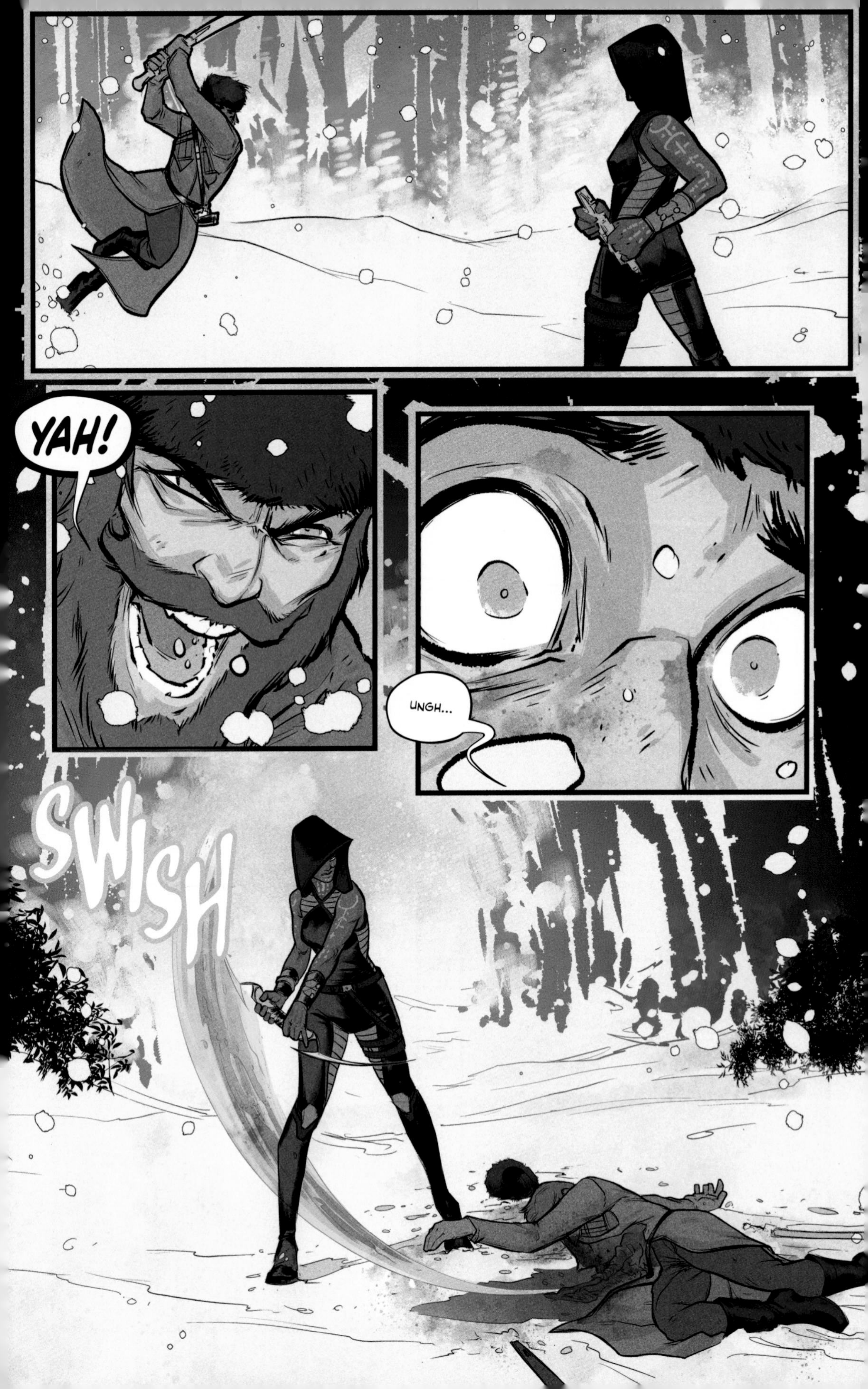
YAH!
UNGH...
SWISH

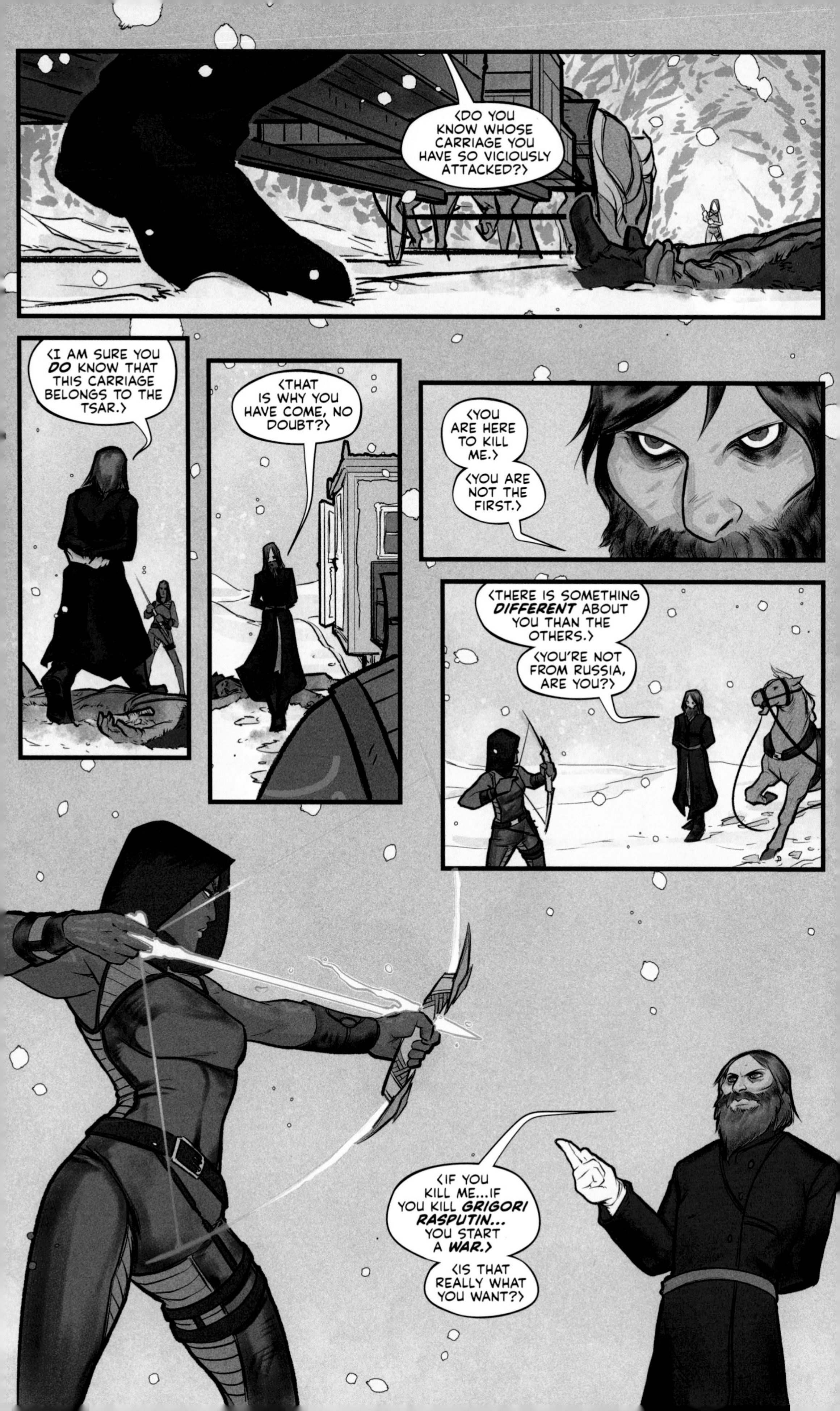

<DO YOU KNOW WHOSE CARRIAGE YOU HAVE SO VICIOUSLY ATTACKED?>
<I AM SURE YOU DO KNOW THAT THIS CARRIAGE BELONGS TO THE TSAR.>
<THAT IS WHY YOU HAVE COME, NO DOUBT?>
<YOU ARE HERE TO KILL ME.>
<YOU ARE NOT THE FIRST.>
<THERE IS SOMETHING DIFFERENT ABOUT YOU THAN THE OTHERS.>
<YOU'RE NOT FROM RUSSIA, ARE YOU?>
<IF YOU KILL ME...IF YOU KILL GRIGORI RASPUTIN... YOU START A WAR.>
<IS THAT REALLY WHAT YOU WANT?>

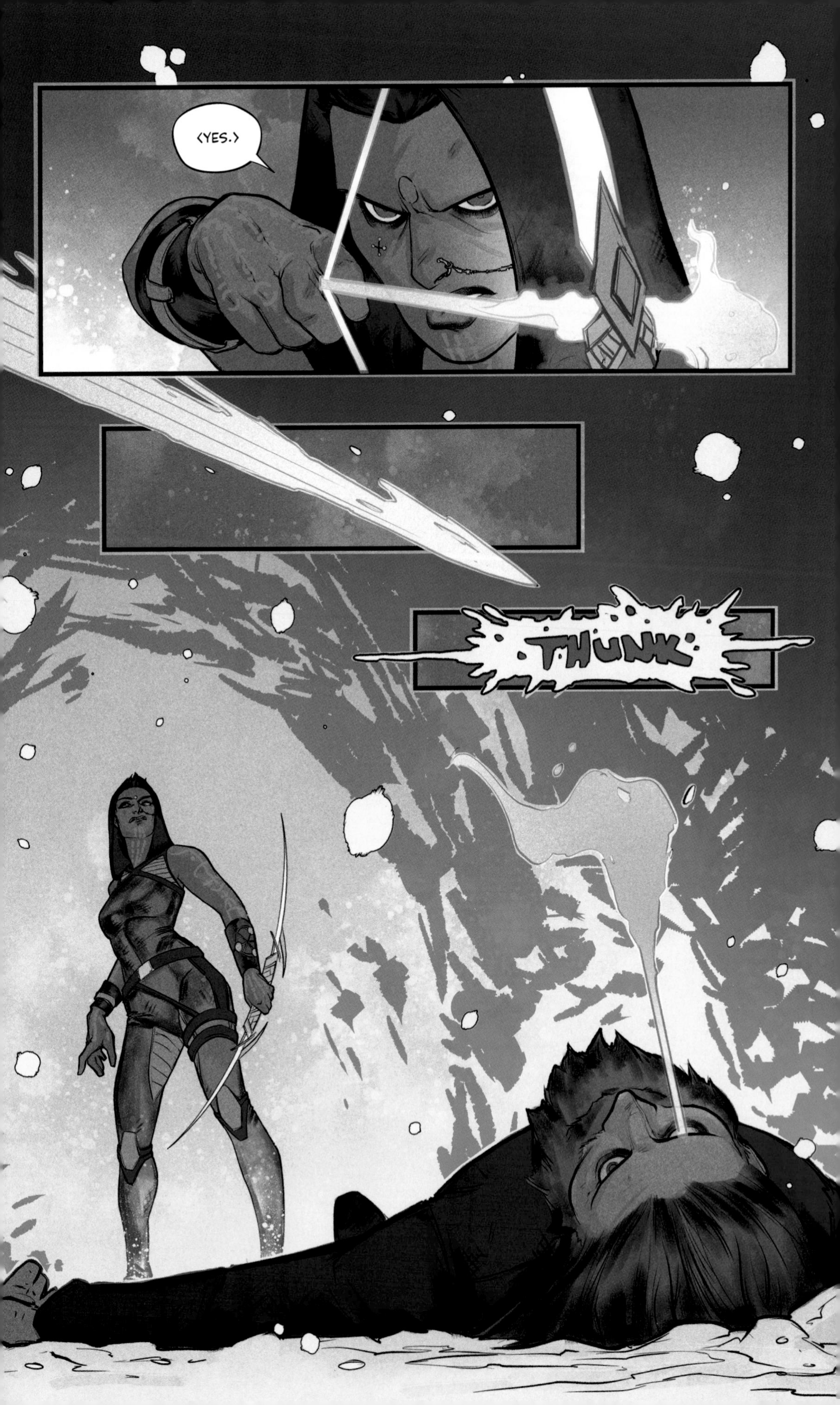
‹YES.›
THUNK

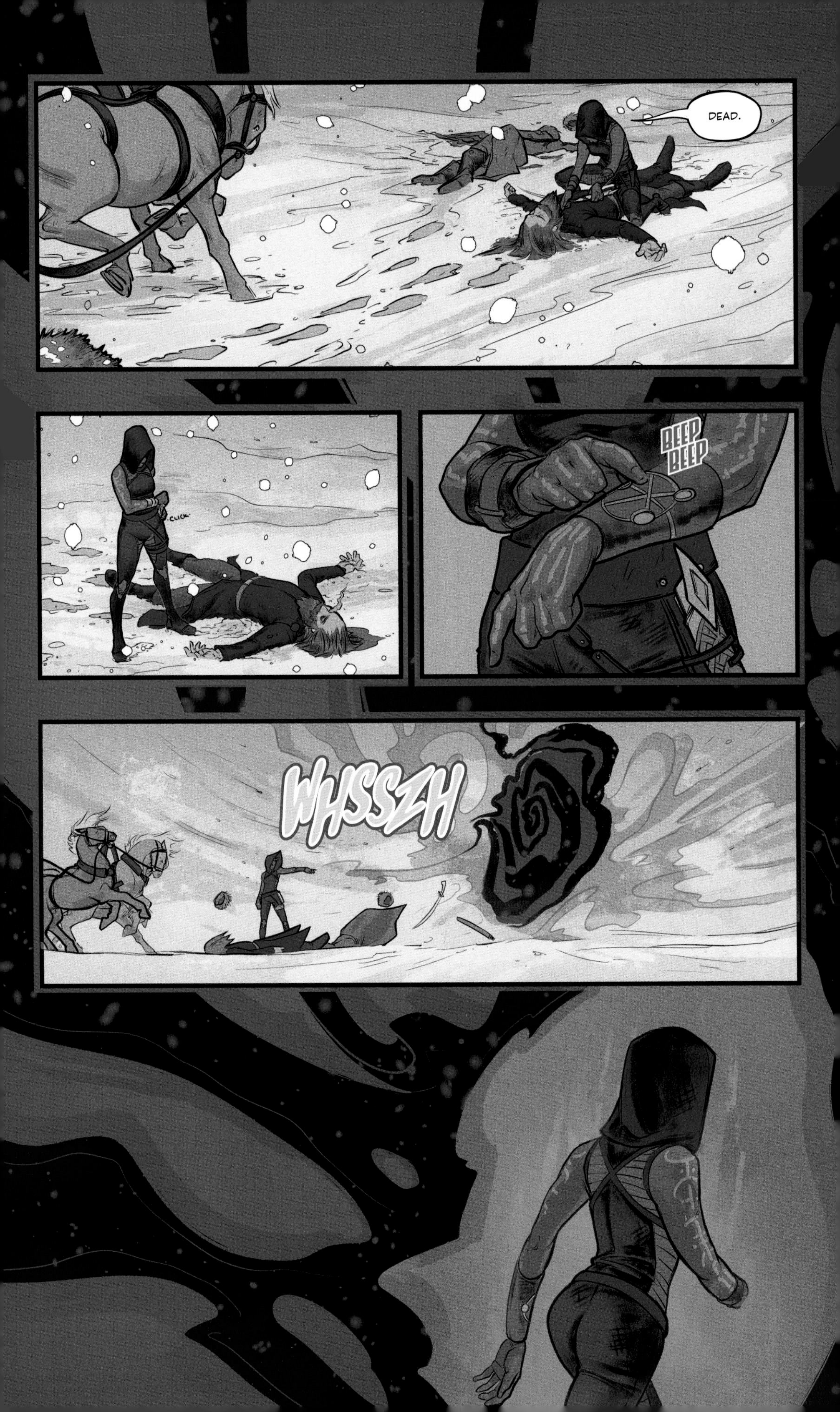
DEAD.
-CLICK-
BEEP BEEP
WHSSZH

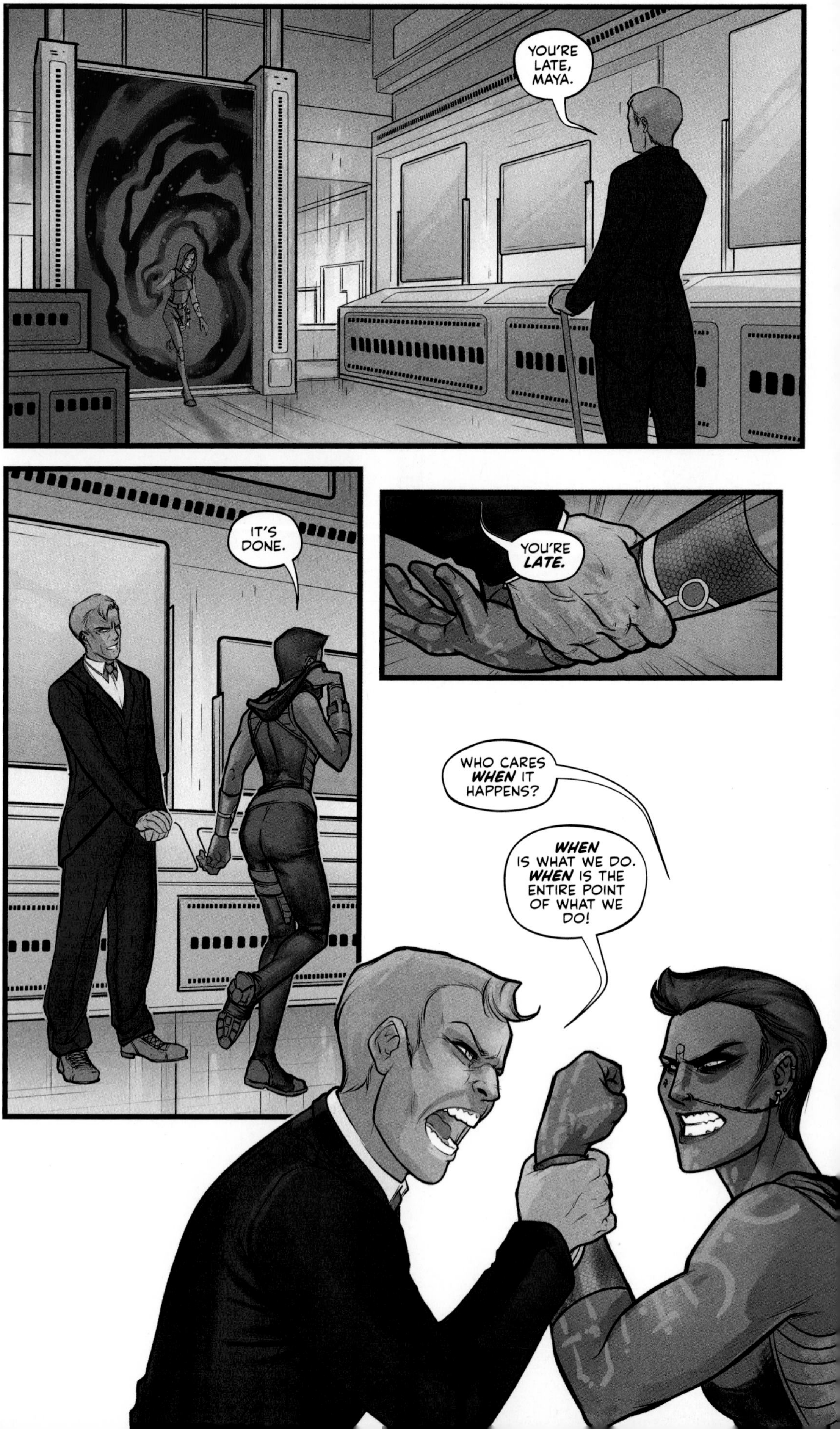
YOU'RE LATE, MAYA.
IT'S DONE.
YOU'RE LATE.
WHO CARES WHEN IT HAPPENS?
WHEN IS WHAT WE DO. WHEN IS THE ENTIRE POINT OF WHAT WE DO!

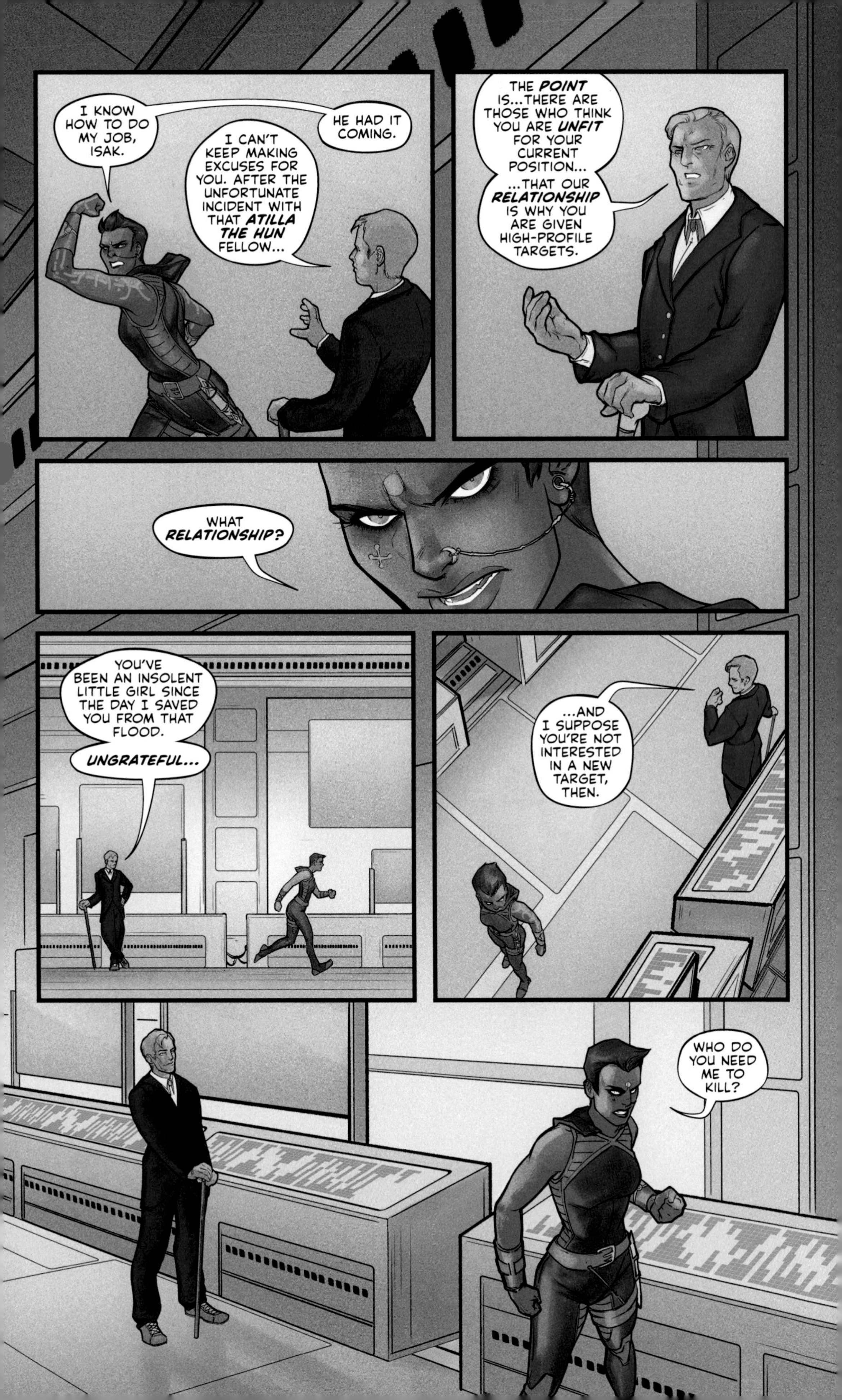
I KNOW HOW TO DO MY JOB, ISAK.
HE HAD IT COMING.
I CAN'T KEEP MAKING EXCUSES FOR YOU. AFTER THE UNFORTUNATE INCIDENT WITH THAT ATILLA THE HUN FELLOW...
THE POINT IS...THERE ARE THOSE WHO THINK YOU ARE UNFIT FOR YOUR CURRENT POSITION...
...THAT OUR RELATIONSHIP IS WHY YOU ARE GIVEN HIGH-PROFILE TARGETS.
WHAT RELATIONSHIP?
YOU'VE BEEN AN INSOLENT LITTLE GIRL SINCE THE DAY I SAVED YOU FROM THAT FLOOD.
UNGRATEFUL...
...AND I SUPPOSE YOU'RE NOT INTERESTED IN A NEW TARGET, THEN.
WHO DO YOU NEED ME TO KILL?

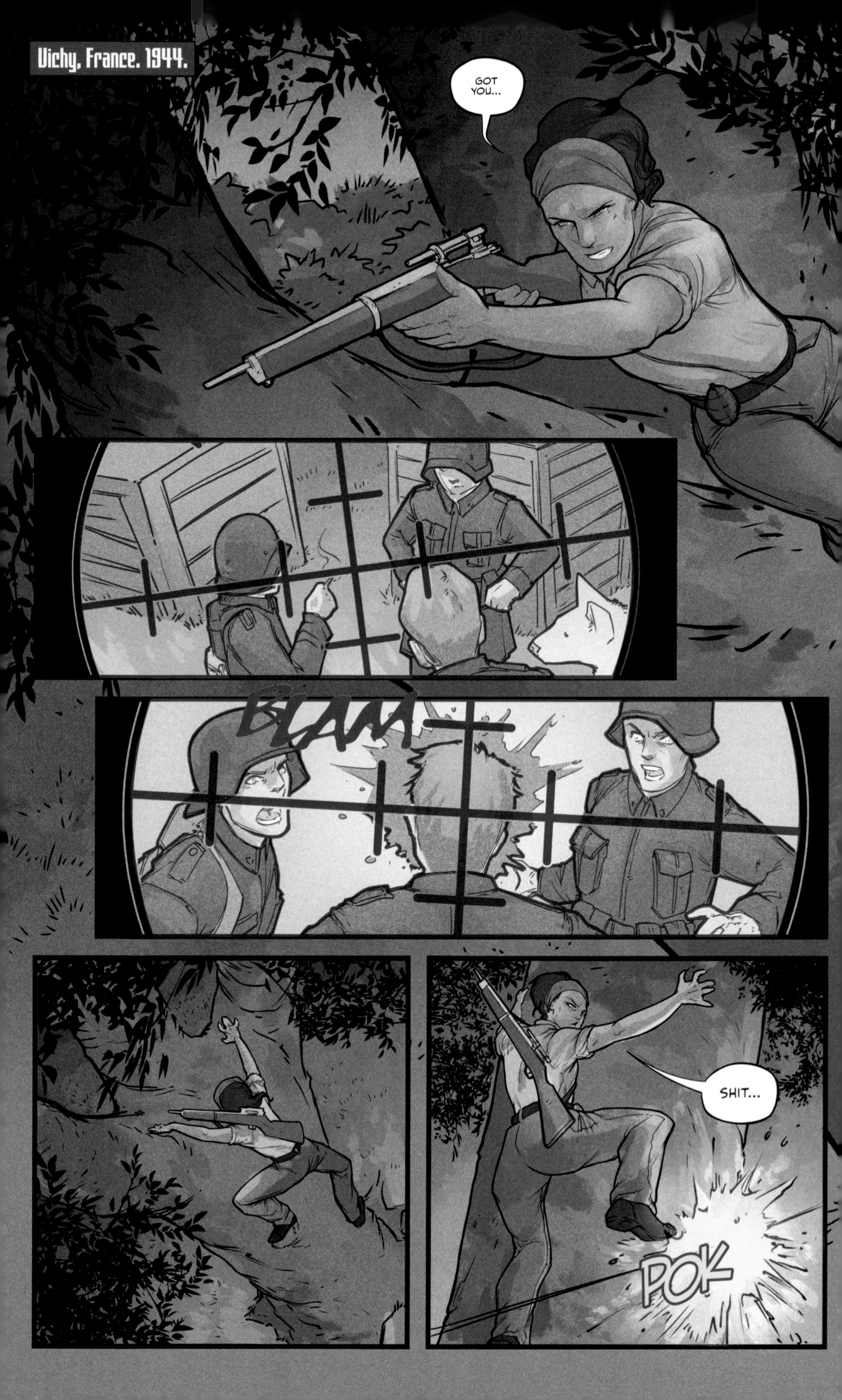

Vichy, France. 1944.
GOT YOU...
BLAM
SHIT...
POK

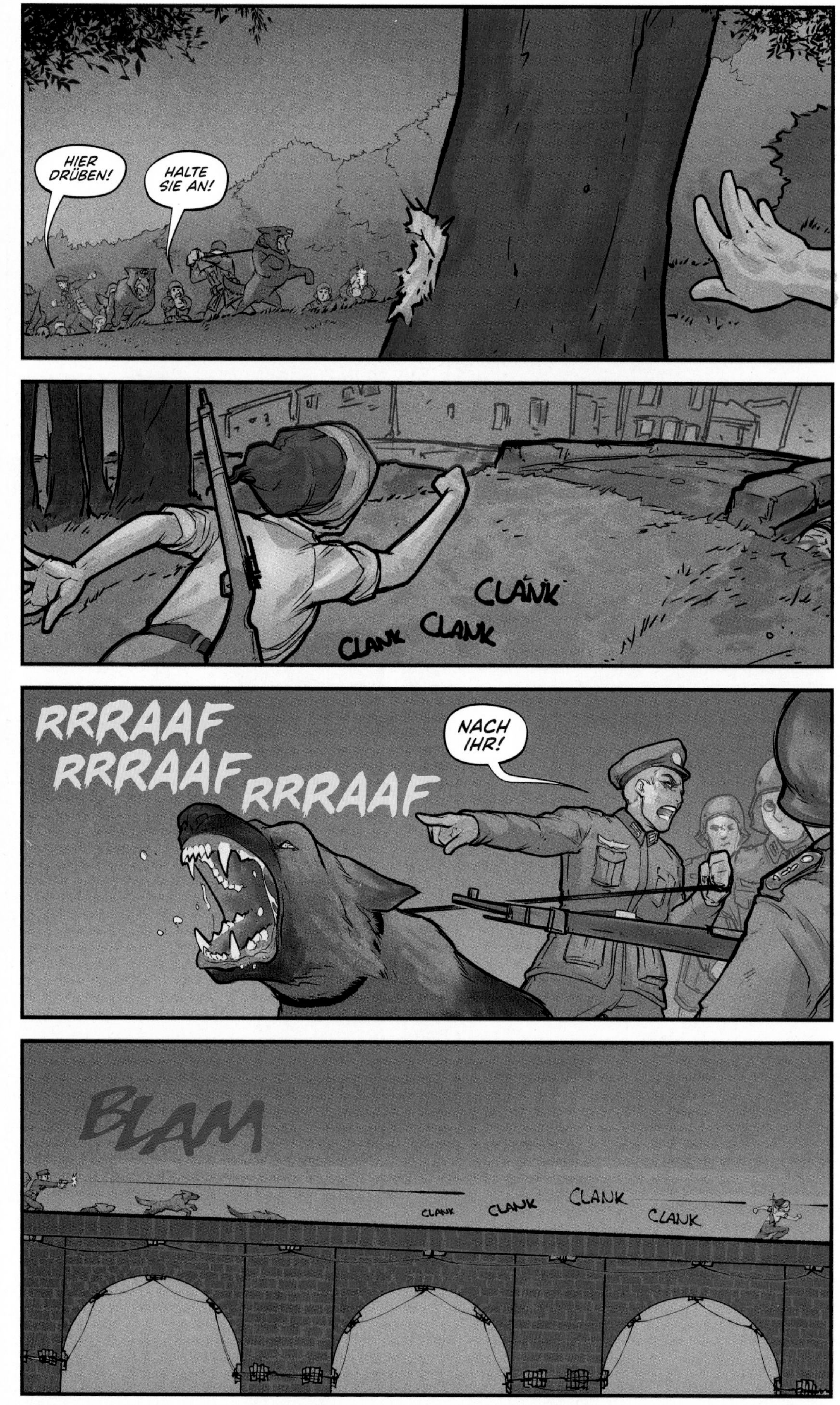
HIER DRÜBEN!
HALTE SIE AN!
CLANK
CLANK CLANK
CLANK
RRRAAF
RRRAAF RRRAAF
NACH IHR!
BLAM
CLANK
CLANK
CLANK
CLANK

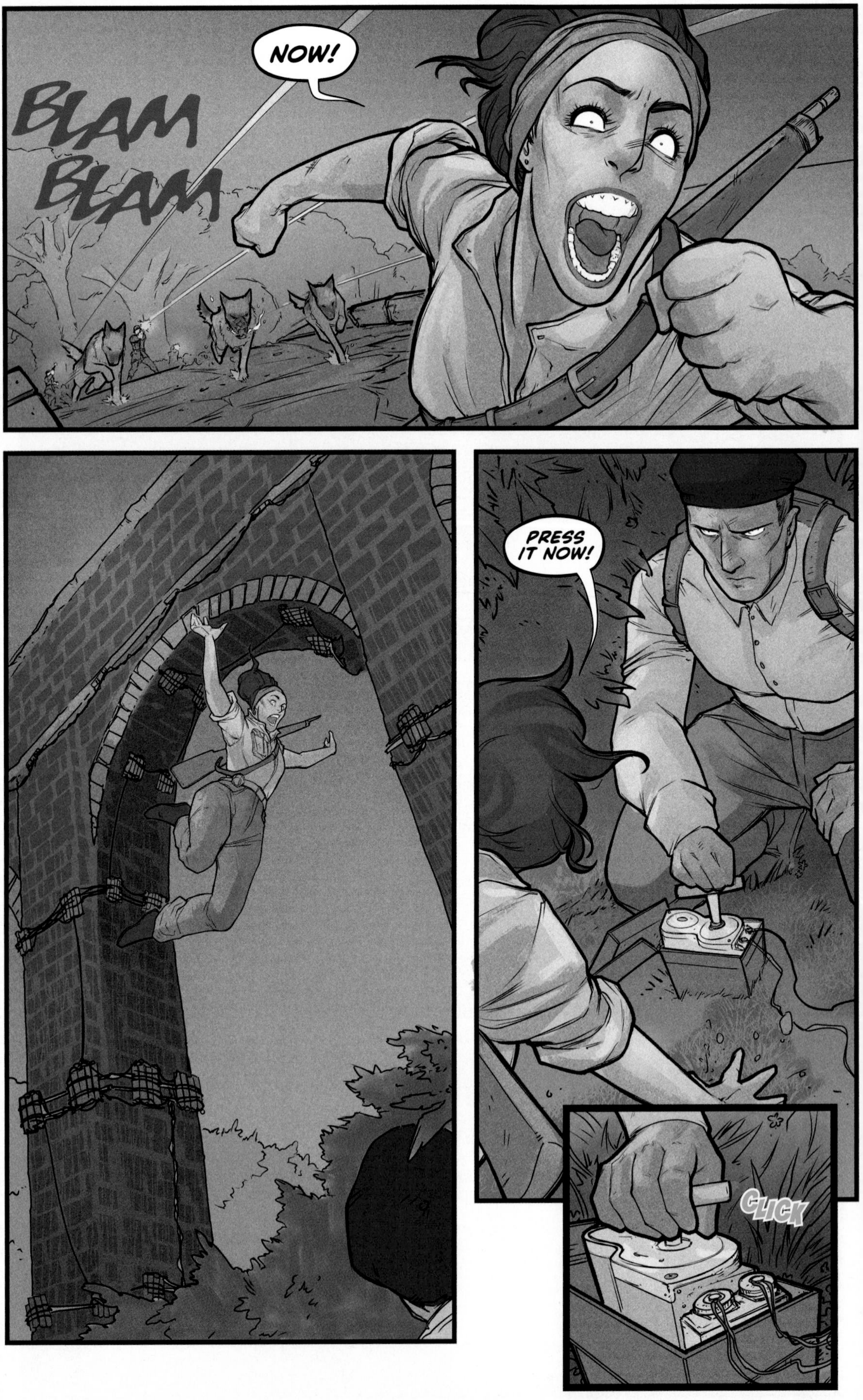
BLAM
BLAM
NOW!
PRESS IT NOW!
CLICK

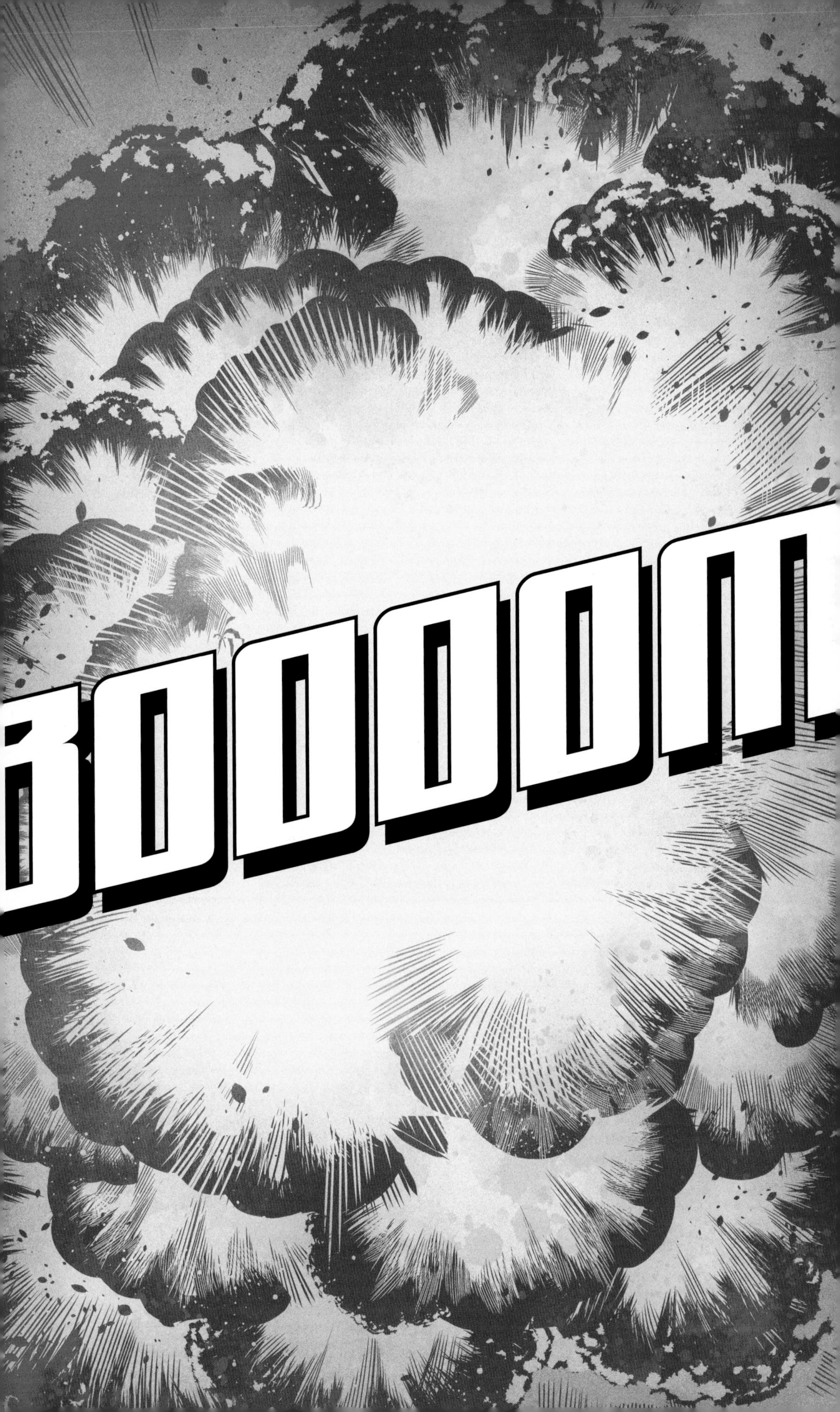
BOOOOM

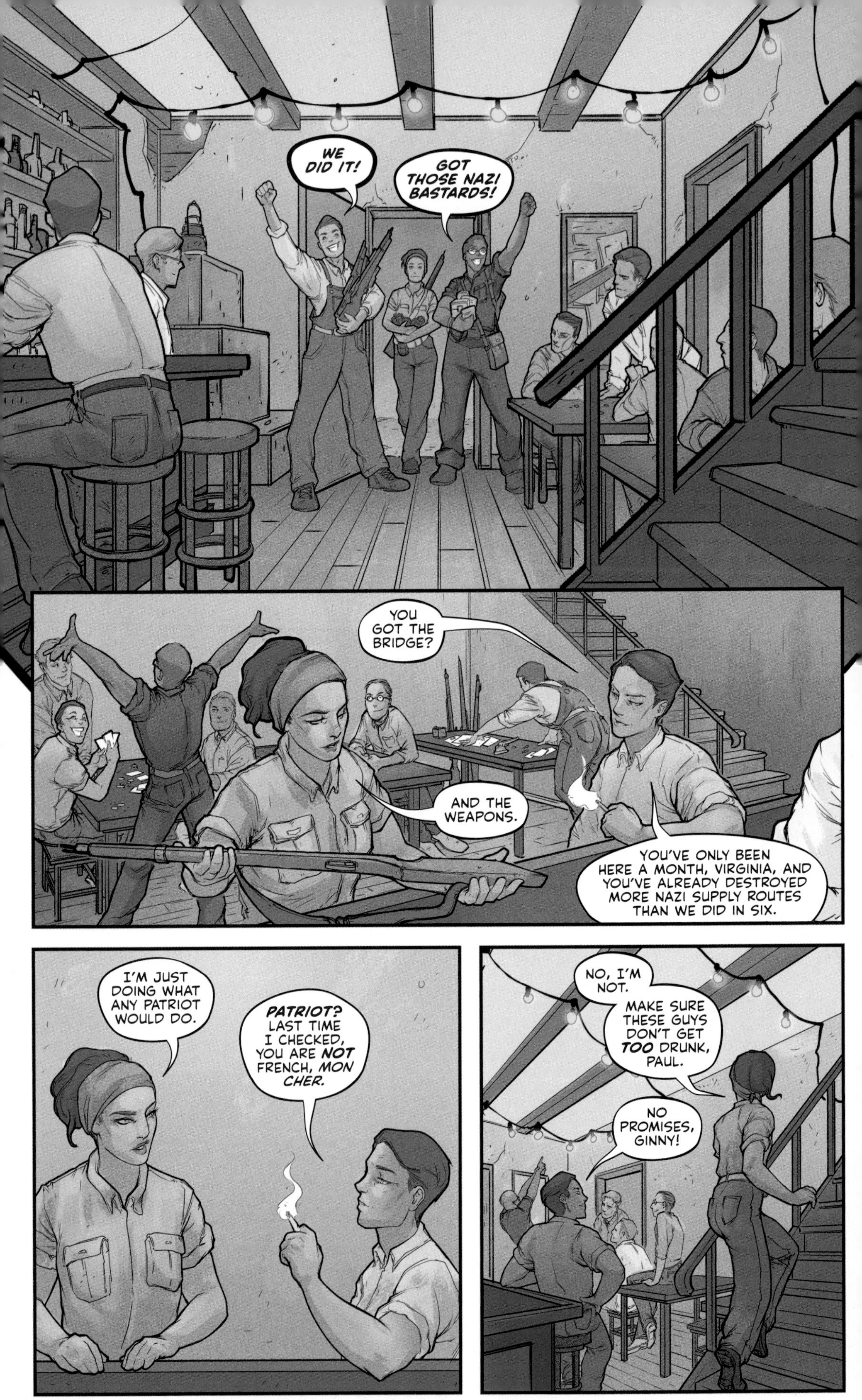
WE DID IT!
GOT THOSE NAZI BASTARDS!
YOU GOT THE BRIDGE?
AND THE WEAPONS.
YOU'VE ONLY BEEN HERE A MONTH, VIRGINIA, AND YOU'VE ALREADY DESTROYED MORE NAZI SUPPLY ROUTES THAN WE DID IN SIX.
I'M JUST DOING WHAT ANY PATRIOT WOULD DO.
PATRIOT? LAST TIME I CHECKED, YOU ARE NOT FRENCH, MON CHER.
NO, I'M NOT.
MAKE SURE THESE GUYS DON'T GET TOO DRUNK, PAUL.
NO PROMISES, GINNY!

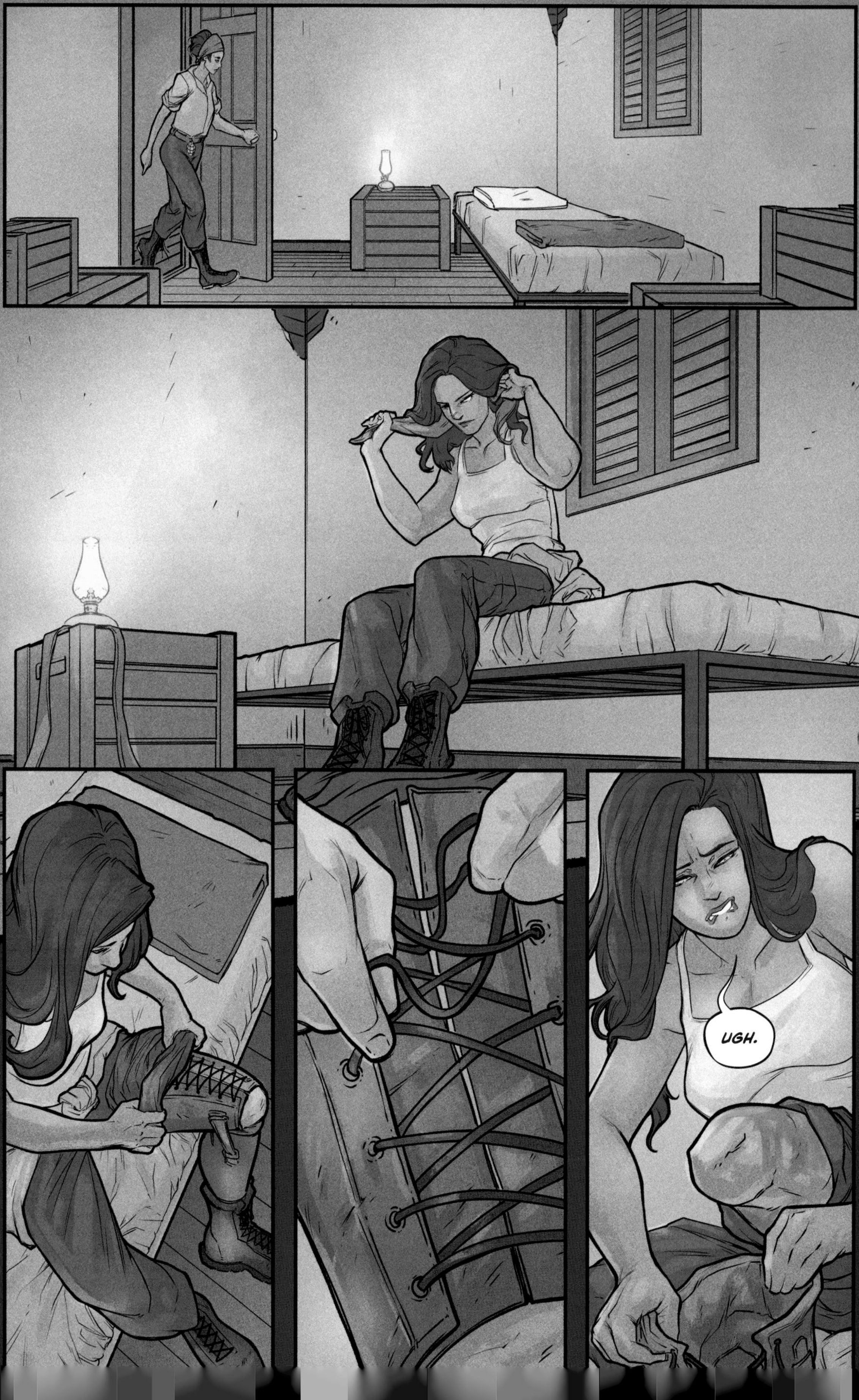
UGH.

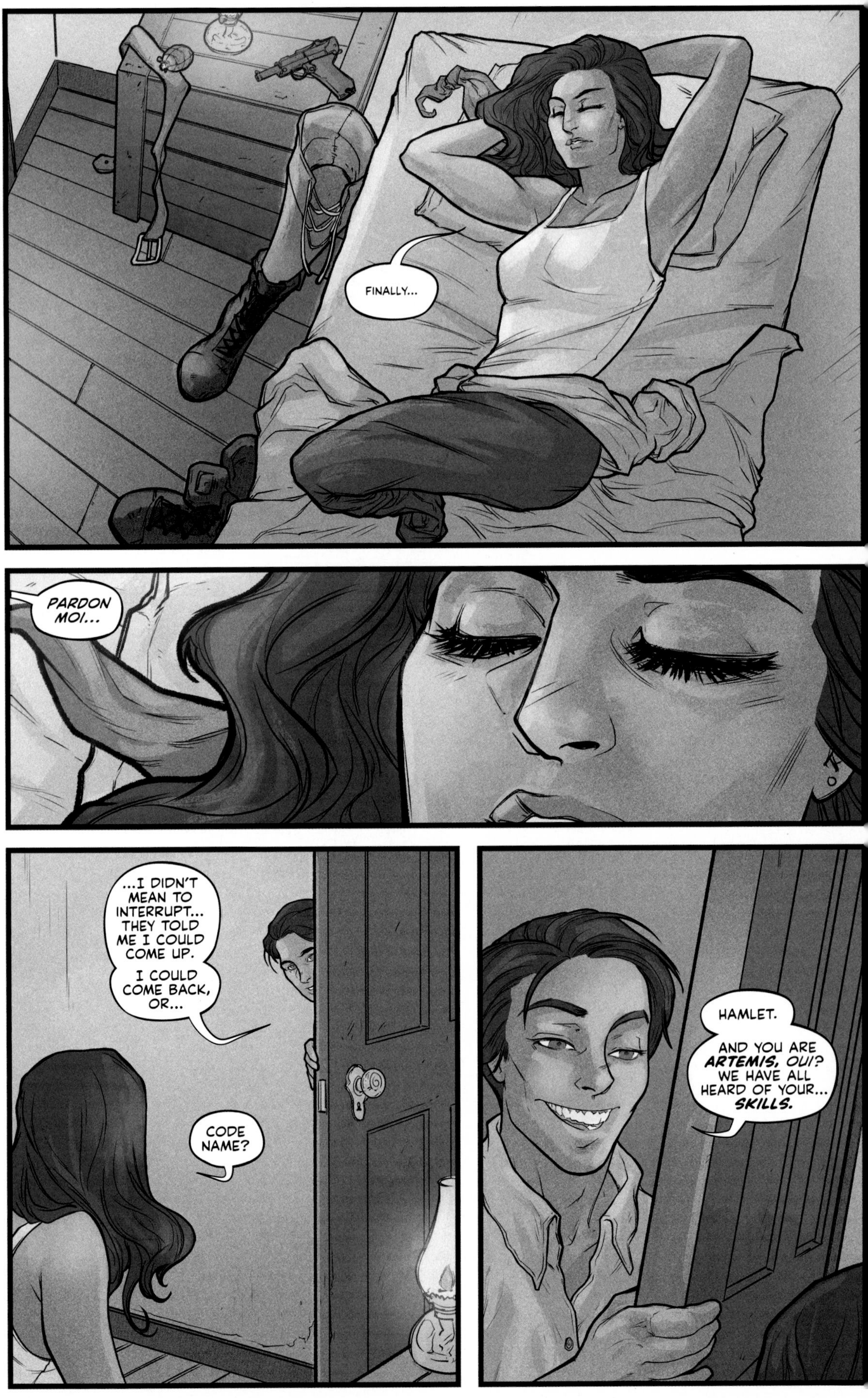
FINALLY...
PARDON MOI...
...I DIDN'T MEAN TO INTERRUPT... THEY TOLD ME I COULD COME UP.
I COULD COME BACK, OR...
CODE NAME?
HAMLET.
AND YOU ARE ARTEMIS, OUI? WE HAVE ALL HEARD OF YOUR... SKILLS.

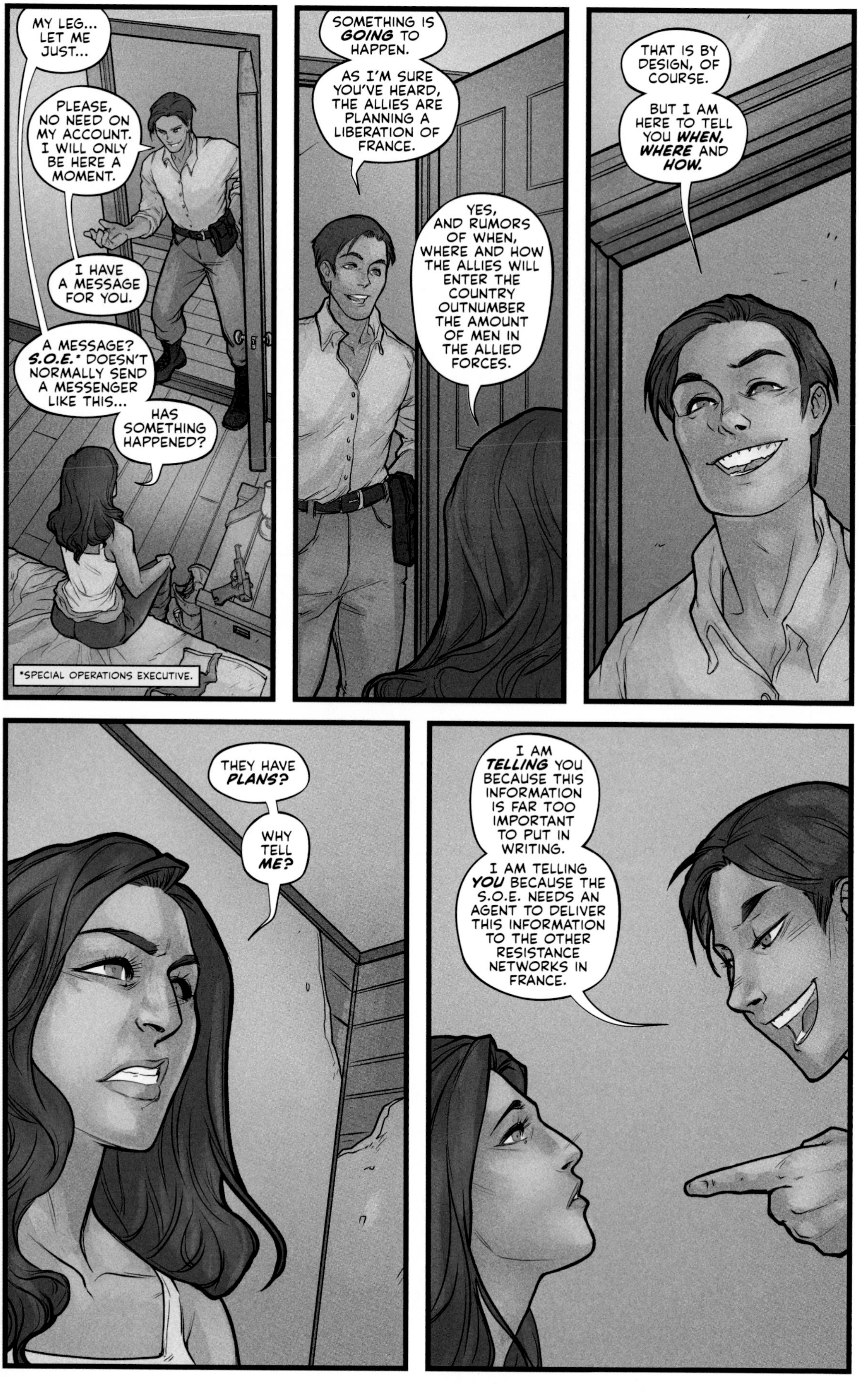

MY LEG... LET ME JUST...
PLEASE, NO NEED ON MY ACCOUNT. I WILL ONLY BE HERE A MOMENT.
I HAVE A MESSAGE FOR YOU.
A MESSAGE? S.O.E.* DOESN'T NORMALLY SEND A MESSENGER LIKE THIS...
HAS SOMETHING HAPPENED?
*SPECIAL OPERATIONS EXECUTIVE.
SOMETHING IS GOING TO HAPPEN.
AS I'M SURE YOU'VE HEARD, THE ALLIES ARE PLANNING A LIBERATION OF FRANCE.
YES, AND RUMORS OF WHEN, WHERE AND HOW THE ALLIES WILL ENTER THE COUNTRY OUTNUMBER THE AMOUNT OF MEN IN THE ALLIED FORCES.
THAT IS BY DESIGN, OF COURSE.
BUT I AM HERE TO TELL YOU WHEN, WHERE AND HOW.
THEY HAVE PLANS?
WHY TELL ME?
I AM TELLING YOU BECAUSE THIS INFORMATION IS FAR TOO IMPORTANT TO PUT IN WRITING.
I AM TELLING YOU BECAUSE THE S.O.E. NEEDS AN AGENT TO DELIVER THIS INFORMATION TO THE OTHER RESISTANCE NETWORKS IN FRANCE.

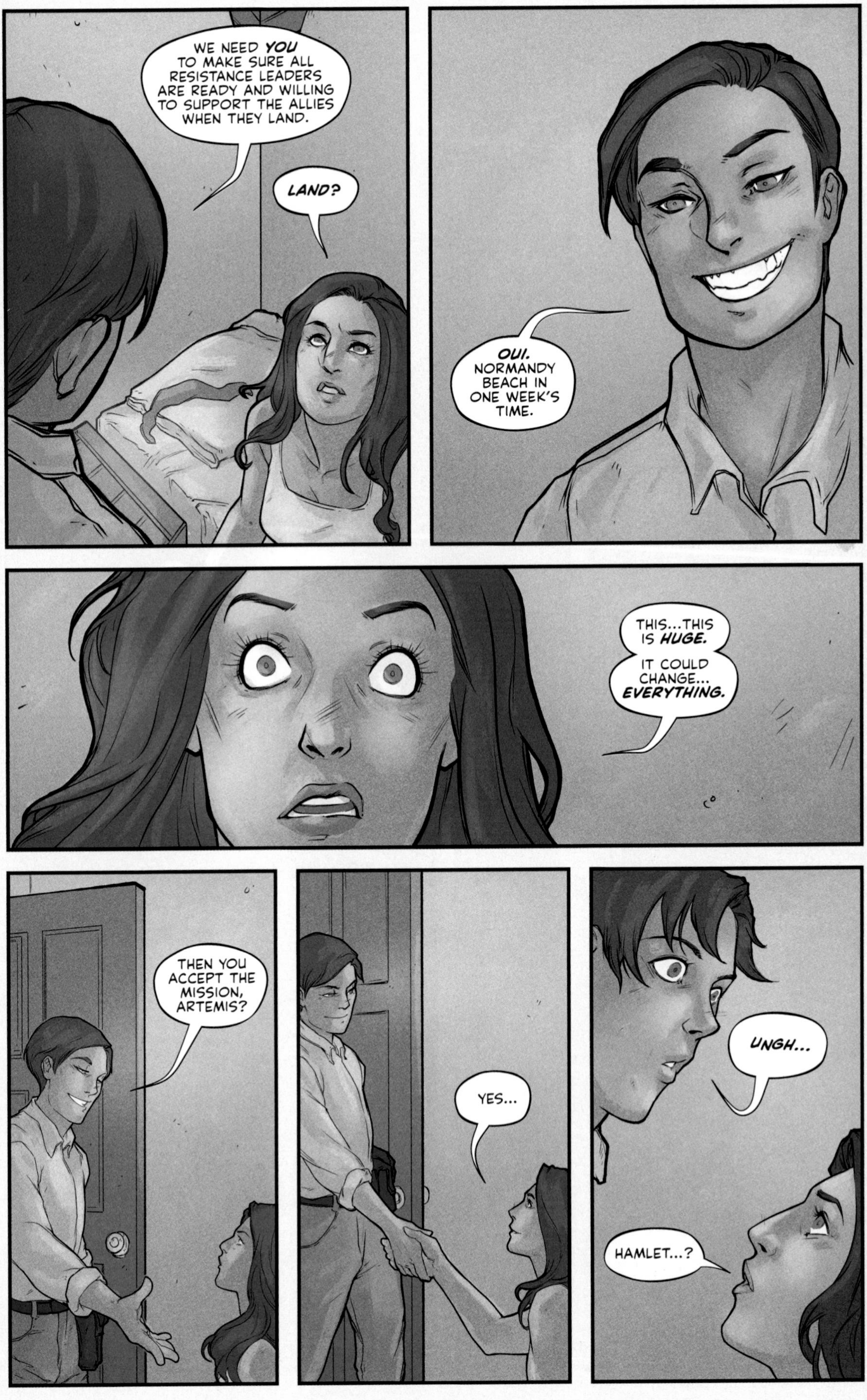
WE NEED YOU TO MAKE SURE ALL RESISTANCE LEADERS ARE READY AND WILLING TO SUPPORT THE ALLIES WHEN THEY LAND.
LAND?
OUI. NORMANDY BEACH IN ONE WEEK'S TIME.
THIS...THIS IS HUGE.
IT COULD CHANGE... EVERYTHING.
THEN YOU ACCEPT THE MISSION, ARTEMIS?
YES...
UNGH...
HAMLET...?

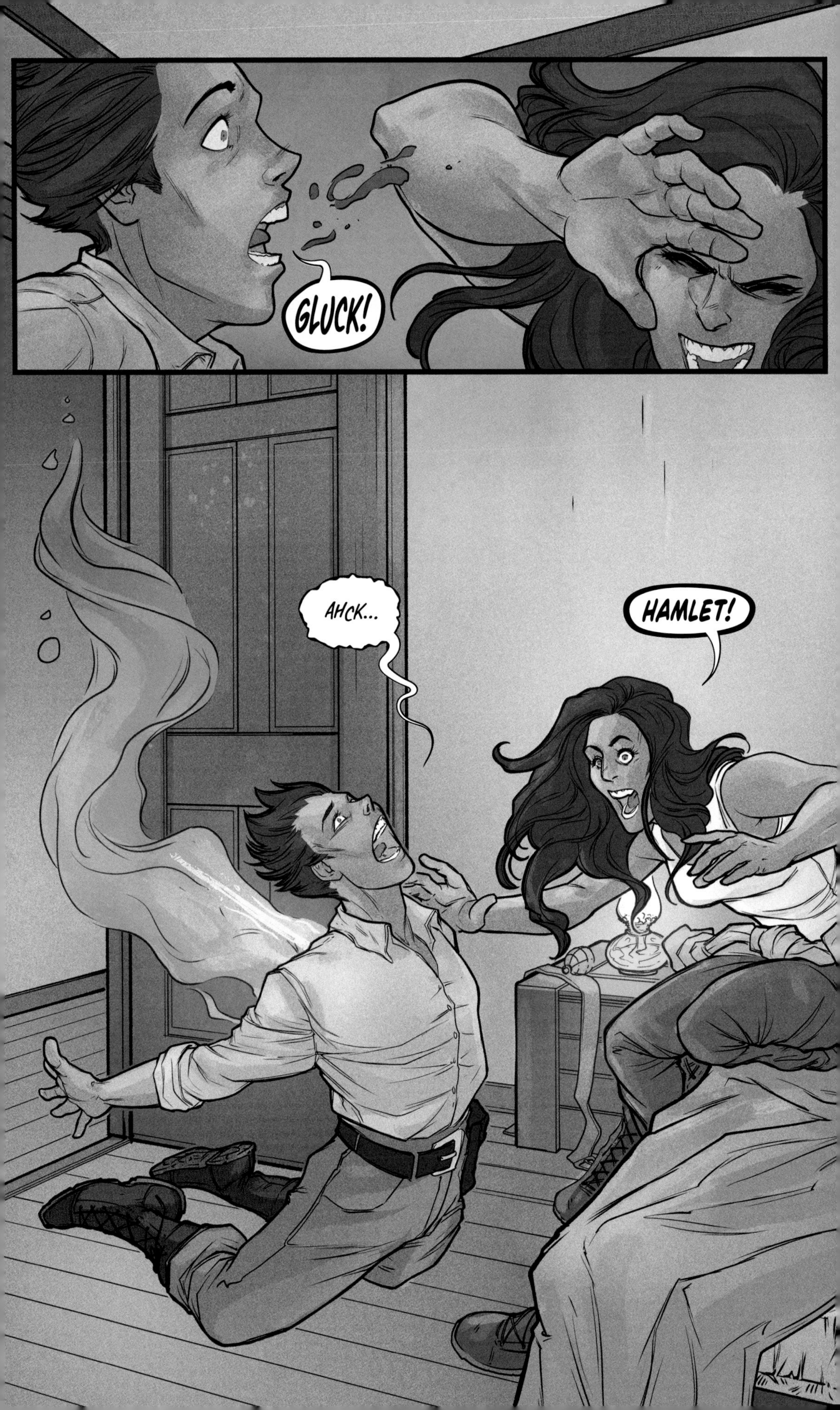
GLUCK!
AHCK...
HAMLET!

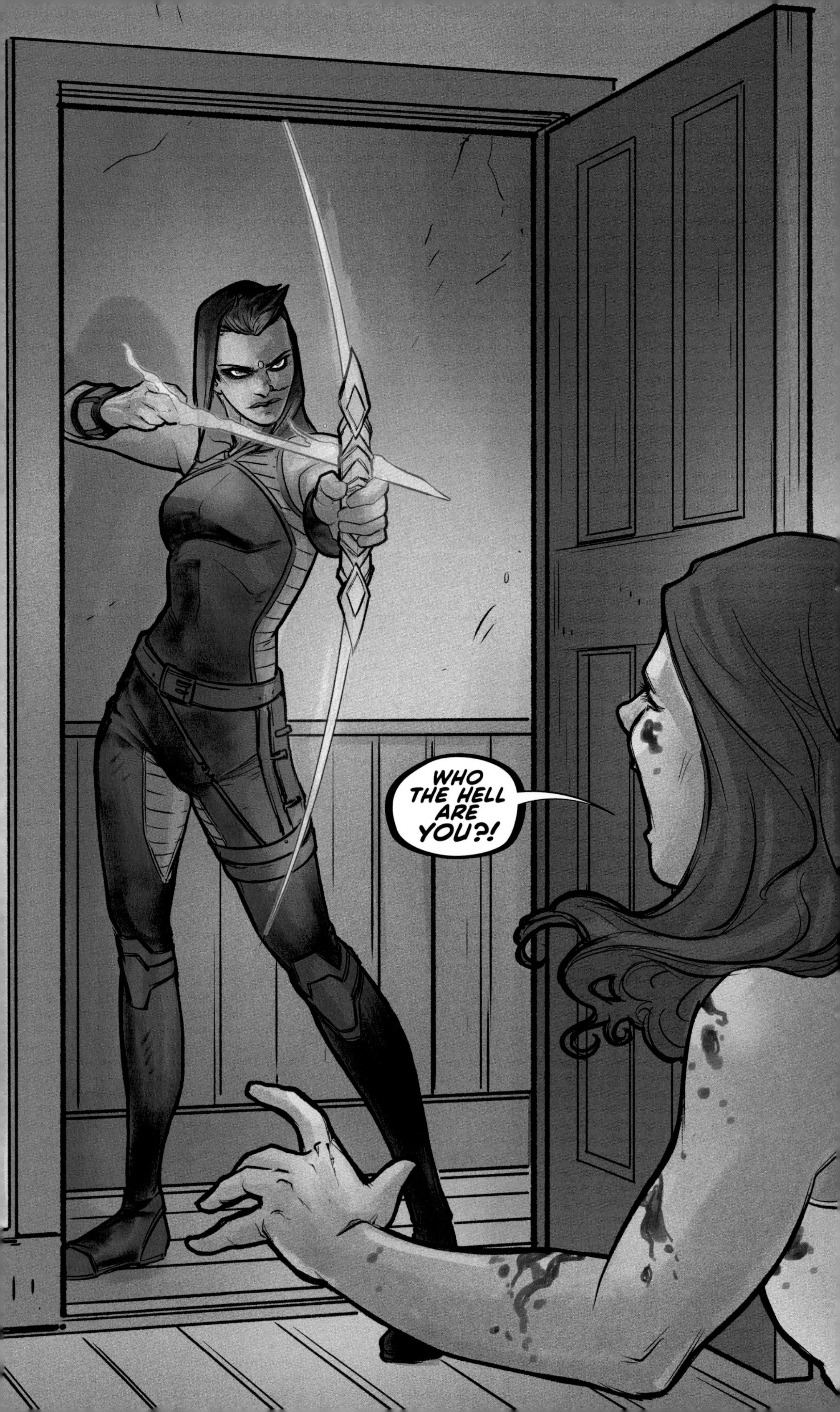
WHO THE HELL ARE YOU?!

2

THIS DOESN'T LOOK LIKE FRANCE

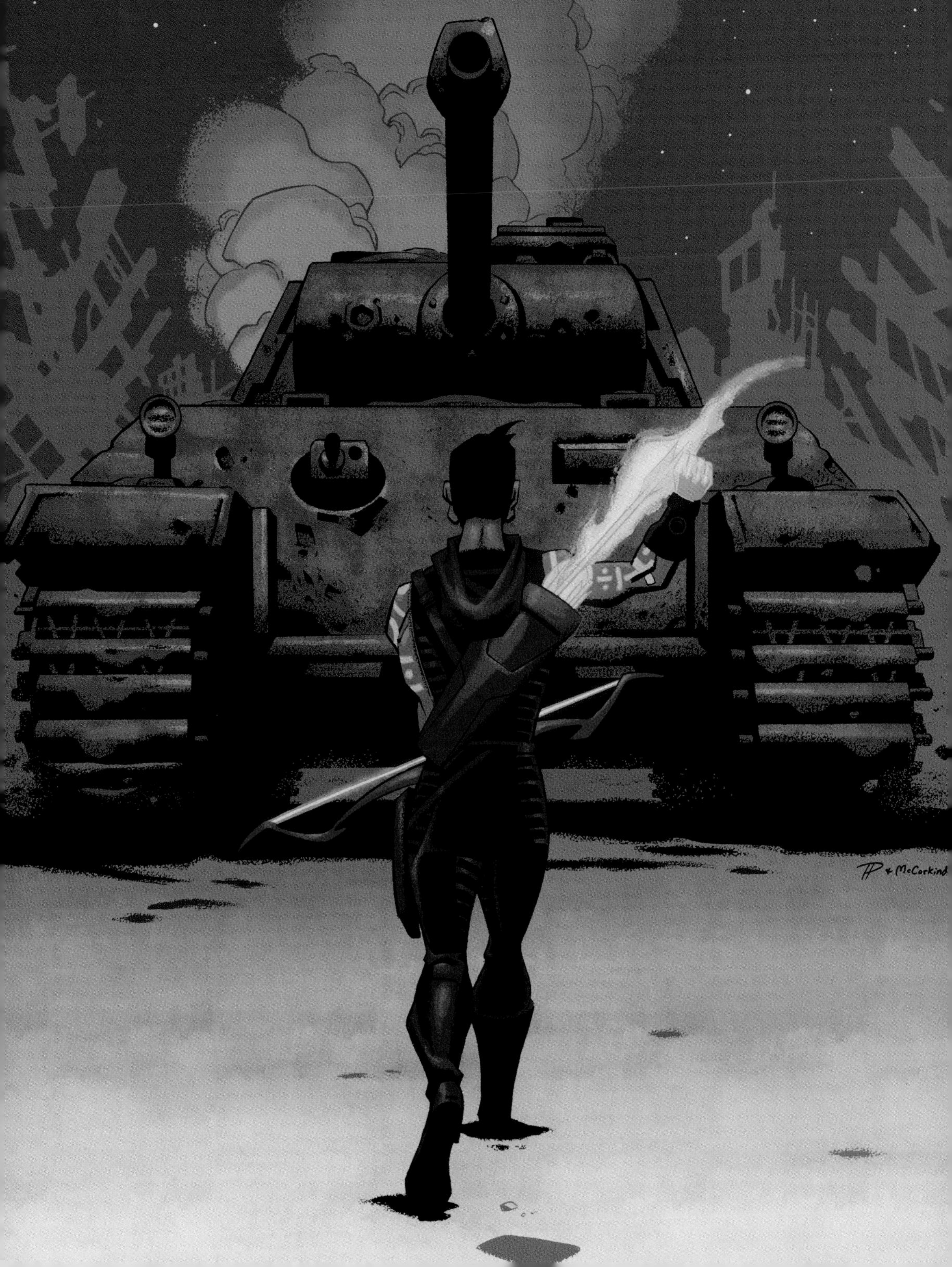

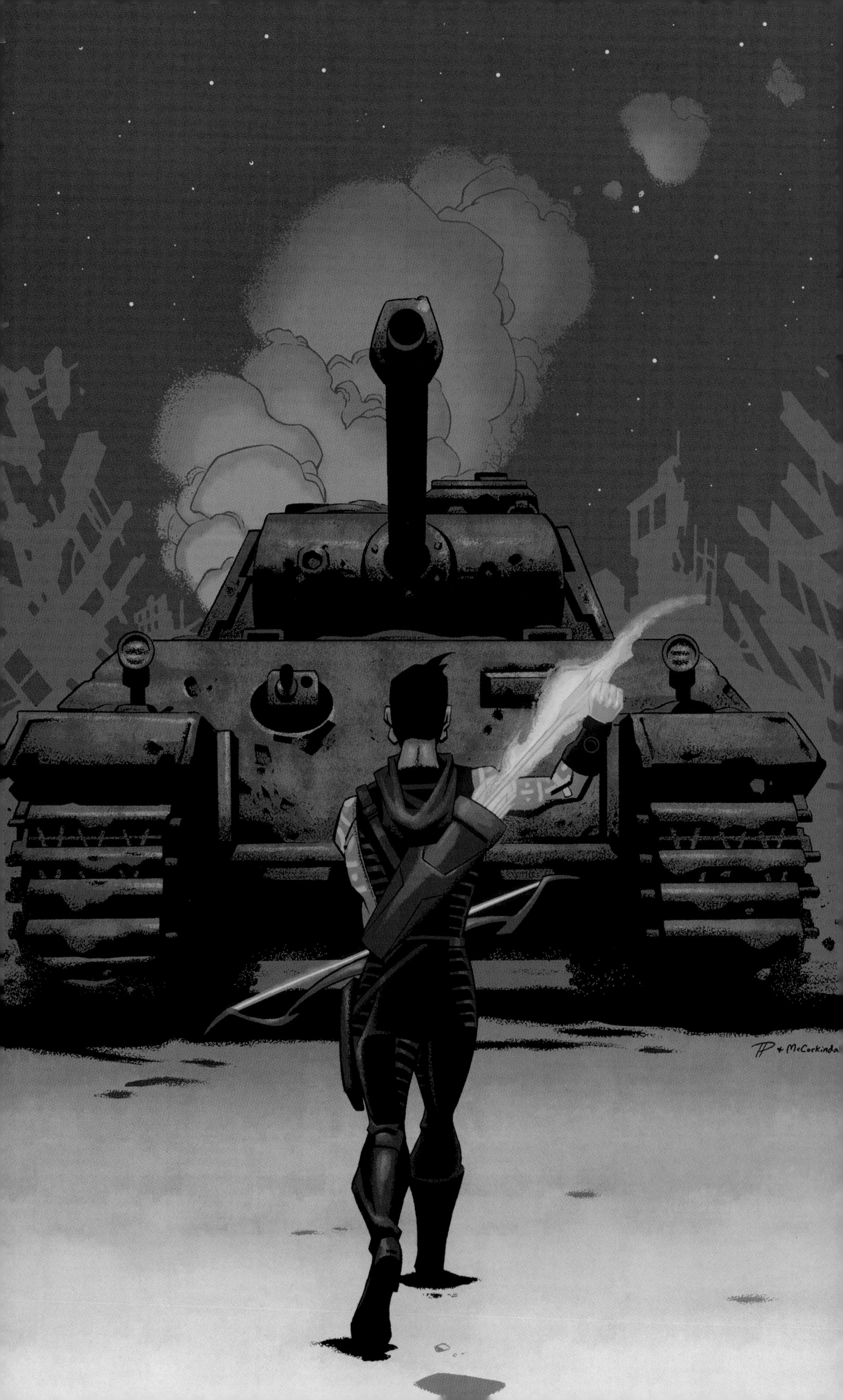
TP & McCorkinda

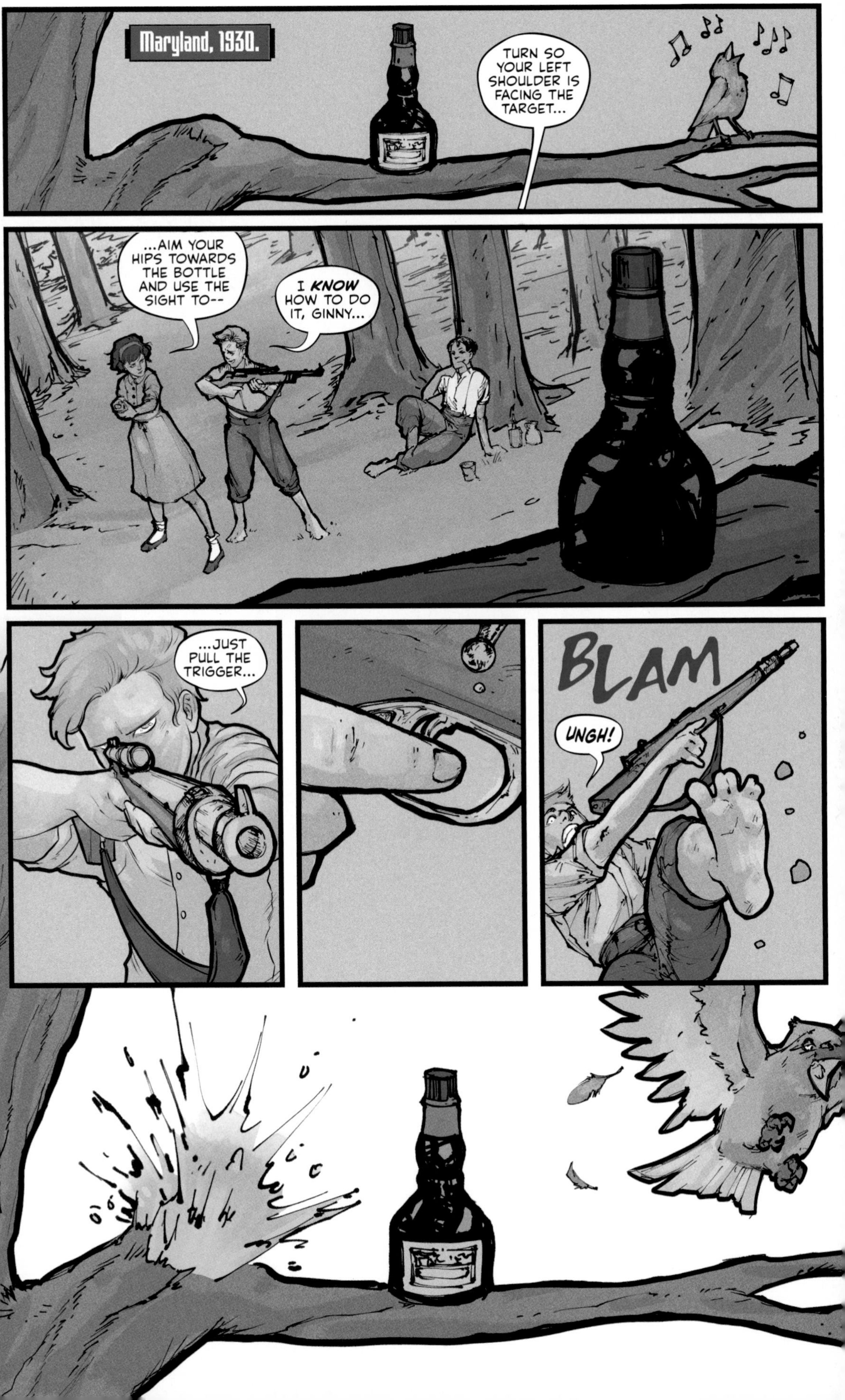

Maryland, 1930.
TURN SO YOUR LEFT SHOULDER IS FACING THE TARGET...
...AIM YOUR HIPS TOWARDS THE BOTTLE AND USE THE SIGHT TO--
I KNOW HOW TO DO IT, GINNY...
...JUST PULL THE TRIGGER...
BLAM
UNGH!

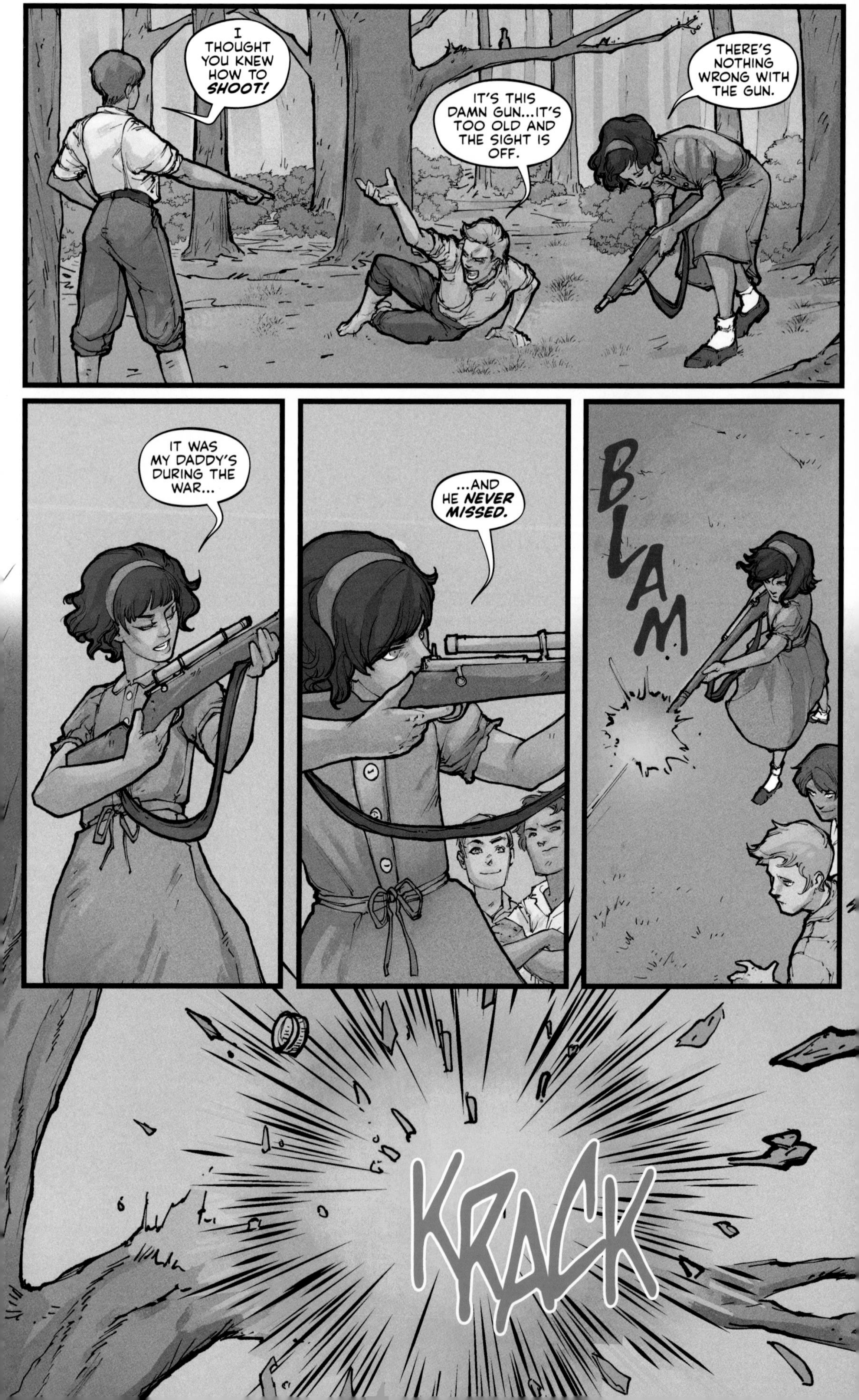

I THOUGHT YOU KNEW HOW TO ***SHOOT!***
IT'S THIS DAMN GUN...IT'S TOO OLD AND THE SIGHT IS OFF.
THERE'S NOTHING WRONG WITH THE GUN.
IT WAS MY DADDY'S DURING THE WAR...
...AND HE ***NEVER MISSED.***
BLAM
KRACK

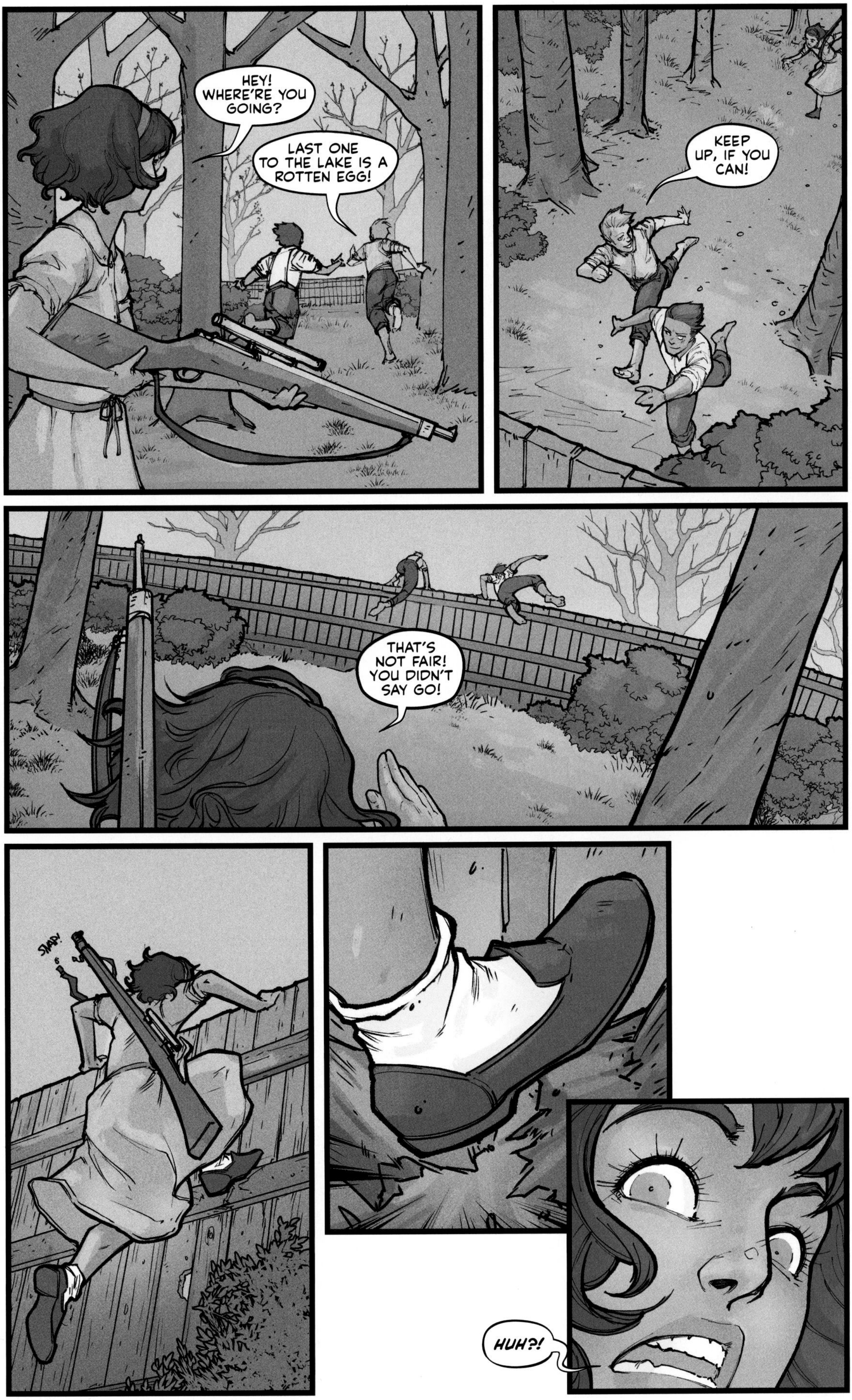
HEY! WHERE'RE YOU GOING?
LAST ONE TO THE LAKE IS A ROTTEN EGG!
KEEP UP, IF YOU CAN!
THAT'S NOT FAIR! YOU DIDN'T SAY GO!
SNAP!
HUH?!

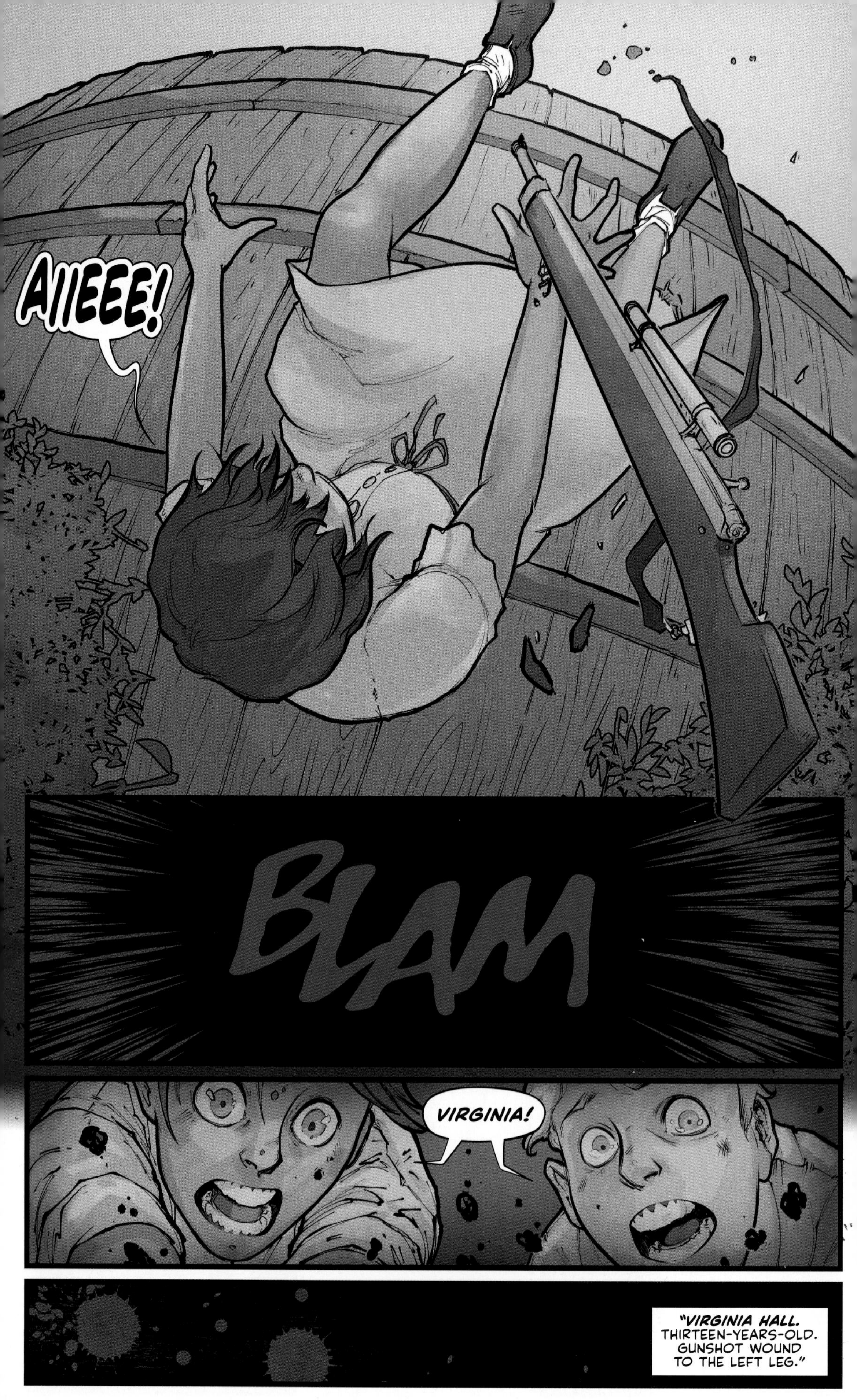
AIIEEE!
BLAM
VIRGINIA!
"VIRGINIA HALL.
THIRTEEN-YEARS-OLD.
GUNSHOT WOUND
TO THE LEFT LEG."

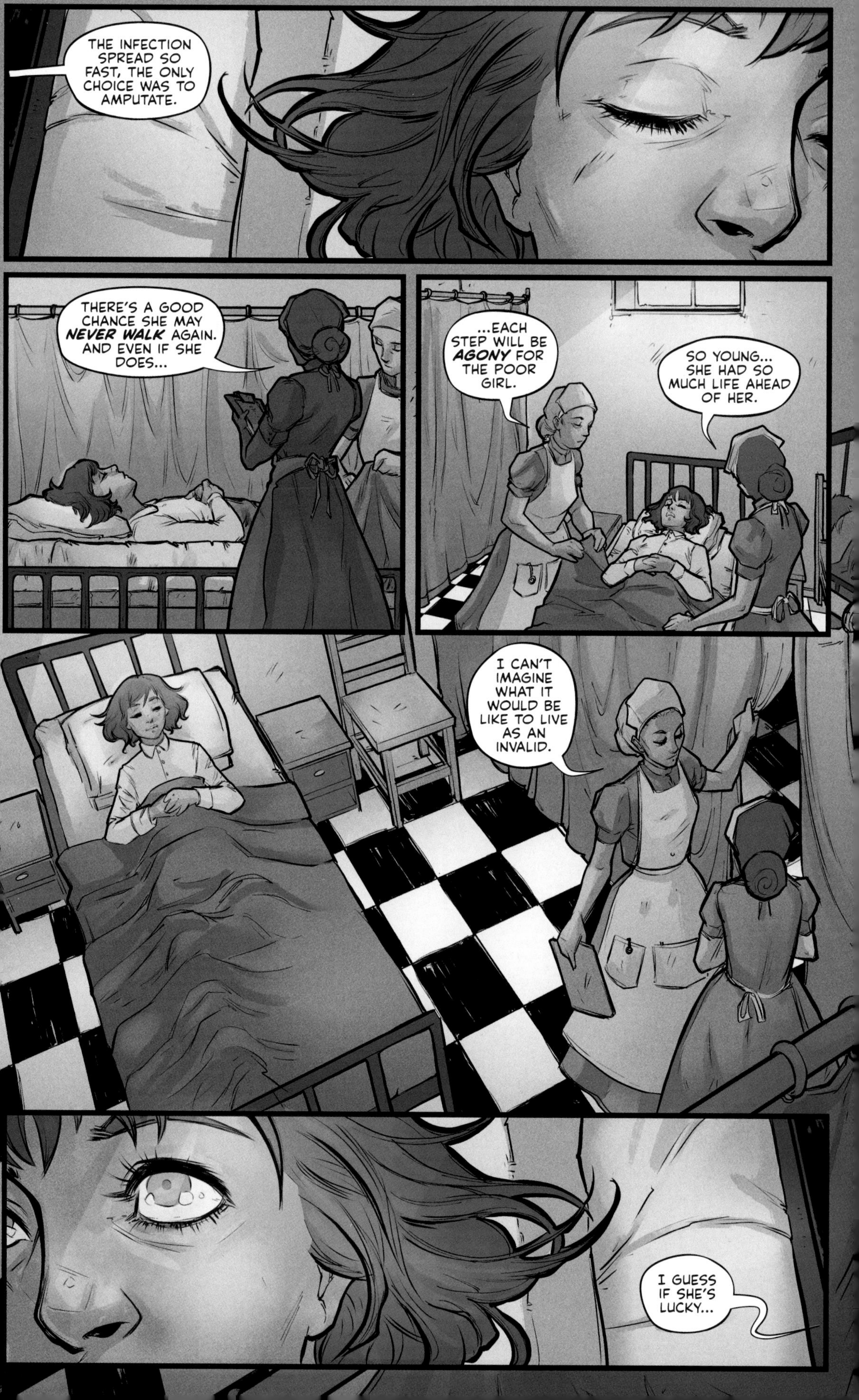
THE INFECTION SPREAD SO FAST, THE ONLY CHOICE WAS TO AMPUTATE.
THERE'S A GOOD CHANCE SHE MAY NEVER WALK AGAIN. AND EVEN IF SHE DOES...
...EACH STEP WILL BE AGONY FOR THE POOR GIRL.
SO YOUNG... SHE HAD SO MUCH LIFE AHEAD OF HER.
I CAN'T IMAGINE WHAT IT WOULD BE LIKE TO LIVE AS AN INVALID.
I GUESS IF SHE'S LUCKY...

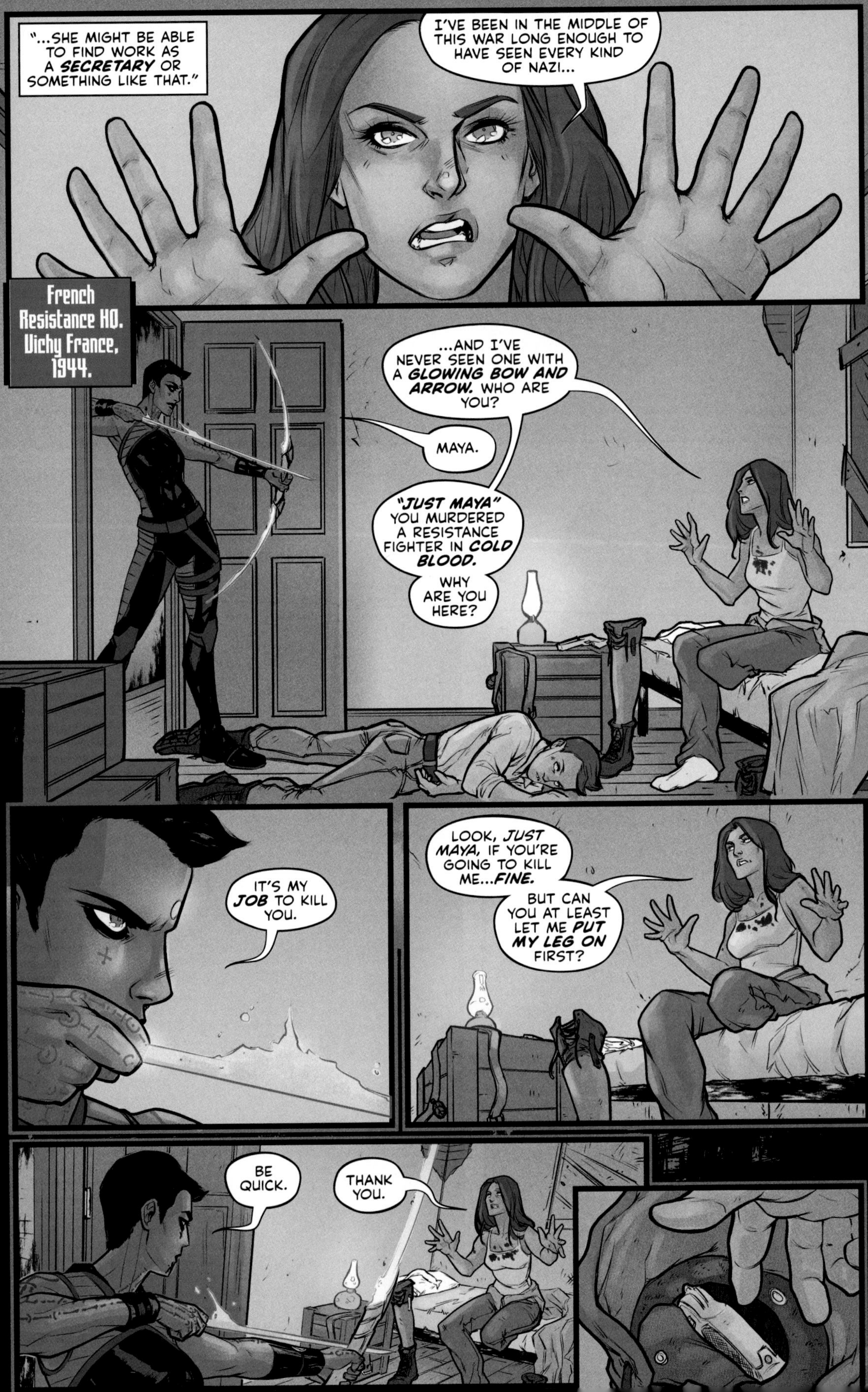
"...SHE MIGHT BE ABLE TO FIND WORK AS A SECRETARY OR SOMETHING LIKE THAT."
I'VE BEEN IN THE MIDDLE OF THIS WAR LONG ENOUGH TO HAVE SEEN EVERY KIND OF NAZI...
French Resistance HQ. Vichy France, 1944.
...AND I'VE NEVER SEEN ONE WITH A GLOWING BOW AND ARROW. WHO ARE YOU?
MAYA.
"JUST MAYA" YOU MURDERED A RESISTANCE FIGHTER IN COLD BLOOD.
WHY ARE YOU HERE?
IT'S MY JOB TO KILL YOU.
LOOK, JUST MAYA, IF YOU'RE GOING TO KILL ME...FINE.
BUT CAN YOU AT LEAST LET ME PUT MY LEG ON FIRST?
BE QUICK.
THANK YOU.

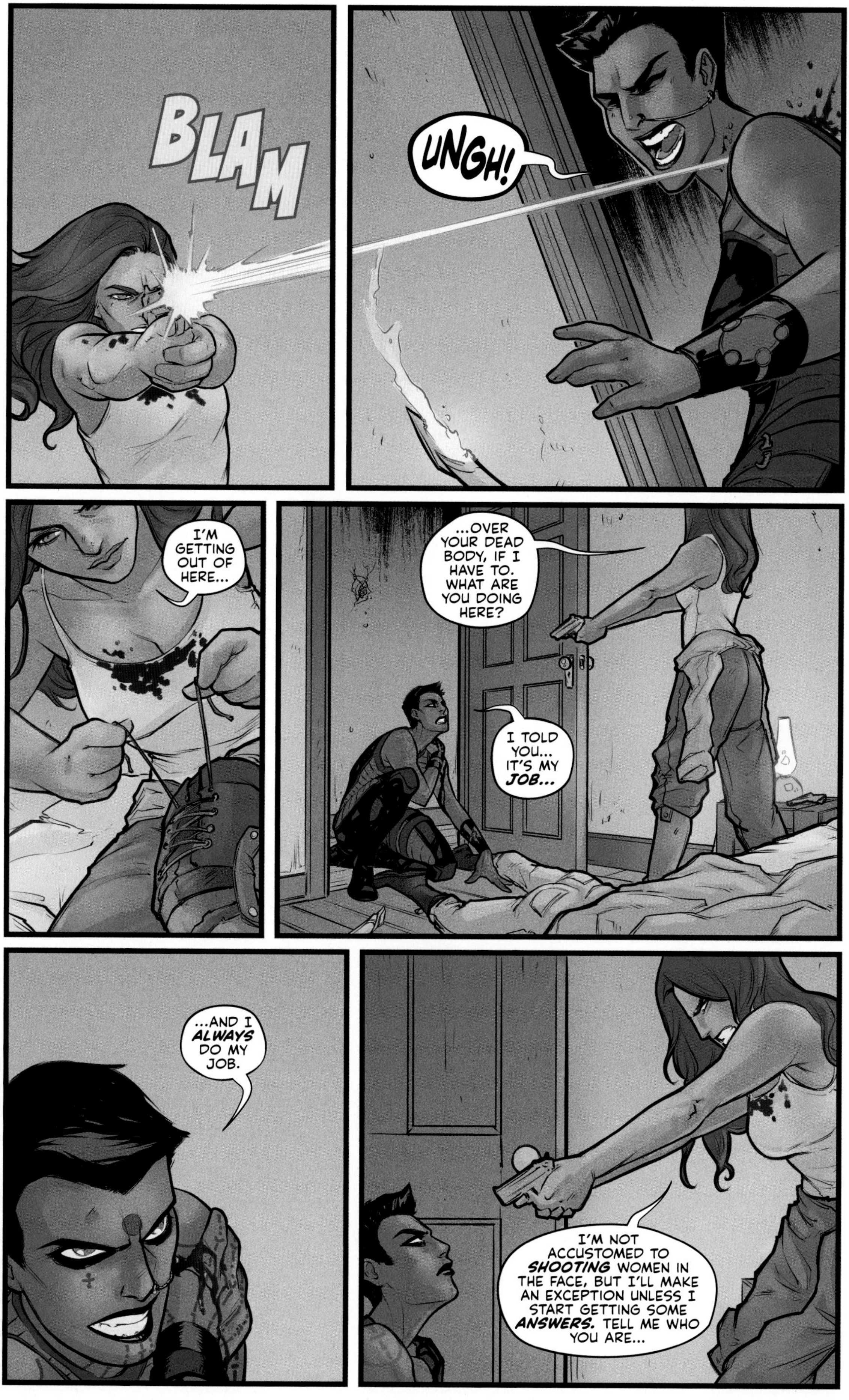
BLAM
UNGH!
I'M GETTING OUT OF HERE...
...OVER YOUR DEAD BODY, IF I HAVE TO. WHAT ARE YOU DOING HERE?
I TOLD YOU... IT'S MY JOB...
...AND I ALWAYS DO MY JOB.
I'M NOT ACCUSTOMED TO SHOOTING WOMEN IN THE FACE, BUT I'LL MAKE AN EXCEPTION UNLESS I START GETTING SOME ANSWERS. TELL ME WHO YOU ARE...

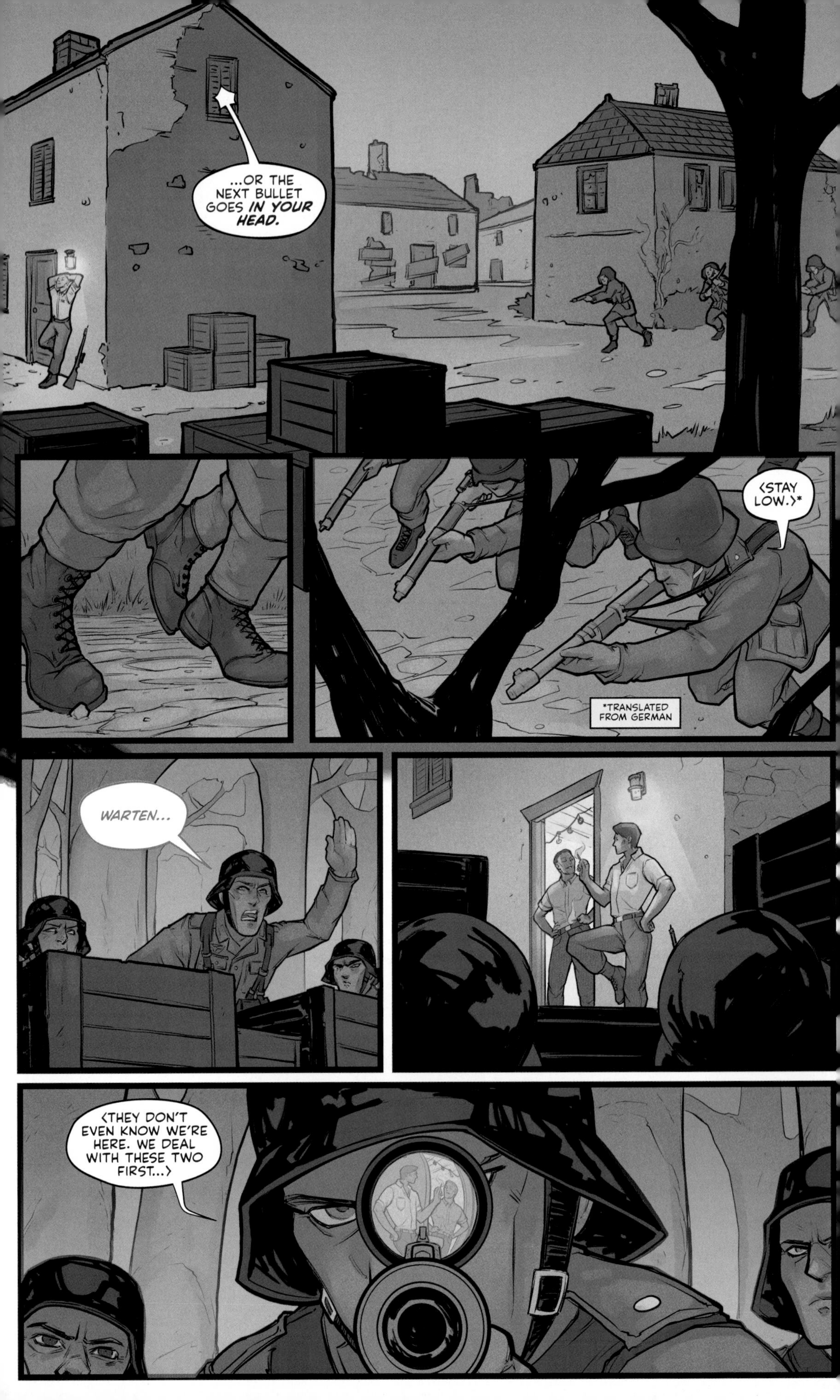
...OR THE NEXT BULLET GOES IN YOUR HEAD.
‹STAY LOW.›*
*TRANSLATED FROM GERMAN
WARTEN...
‹THEY DON'T EVEN KNOW WE'RE HERE. WE DEAL WITH THESE TWO FIRST...›

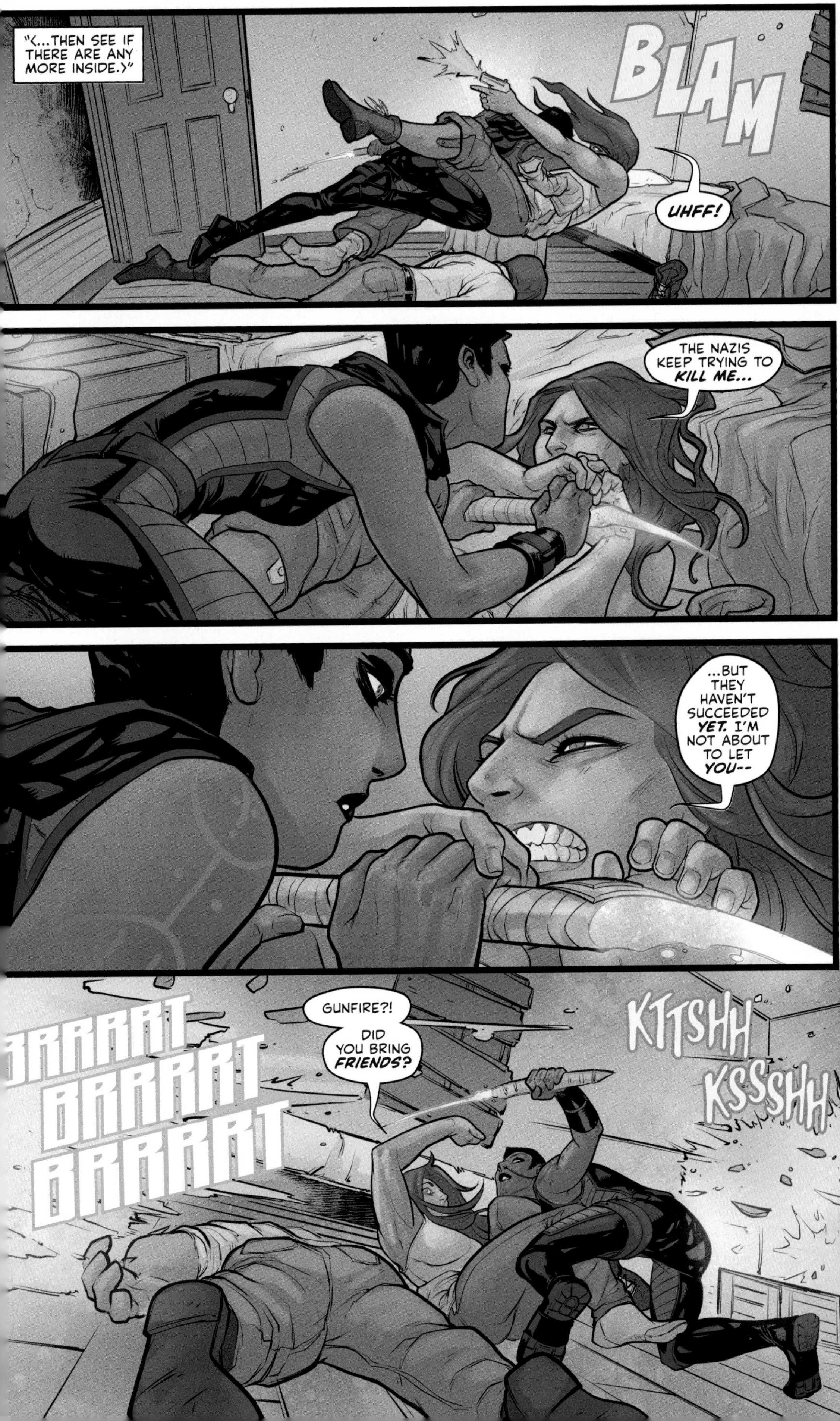

"<...THEN SEE IF THERE ARE ANY MORE INSIDE.>"
BLAM
UHFF!
THE NAZIS KEEP TRYING TO KILL ME...
...BUT THEY HAVEN'T SUCCEEDED YET. I'M NOT ABOUT TO LET YOU--
BRRRRT BRRRRT BRRRRT
GUNFIRE?!
DID YOU BRING FRIENDS?
KTTSHH KSSSHH

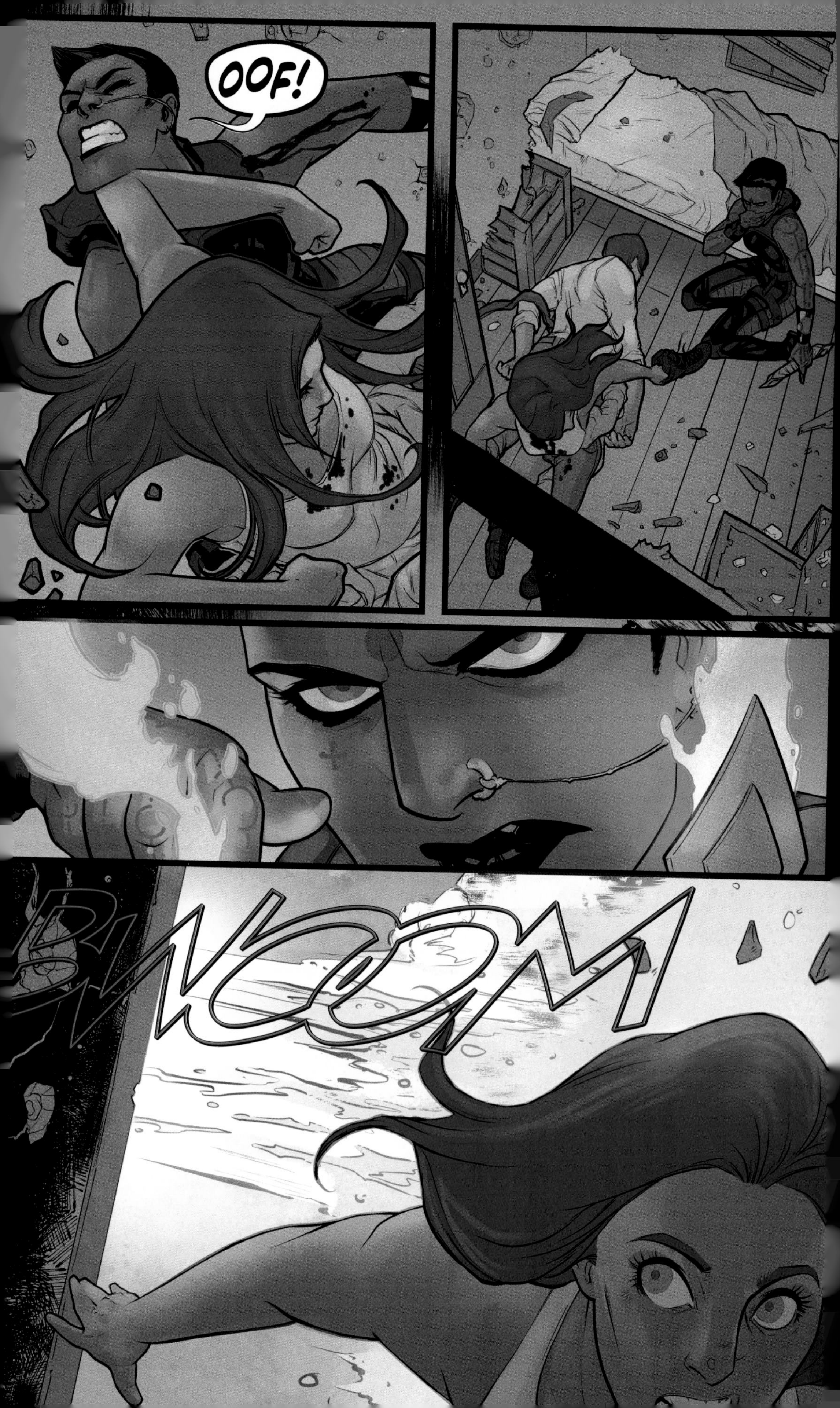
OOF!
BWOOM

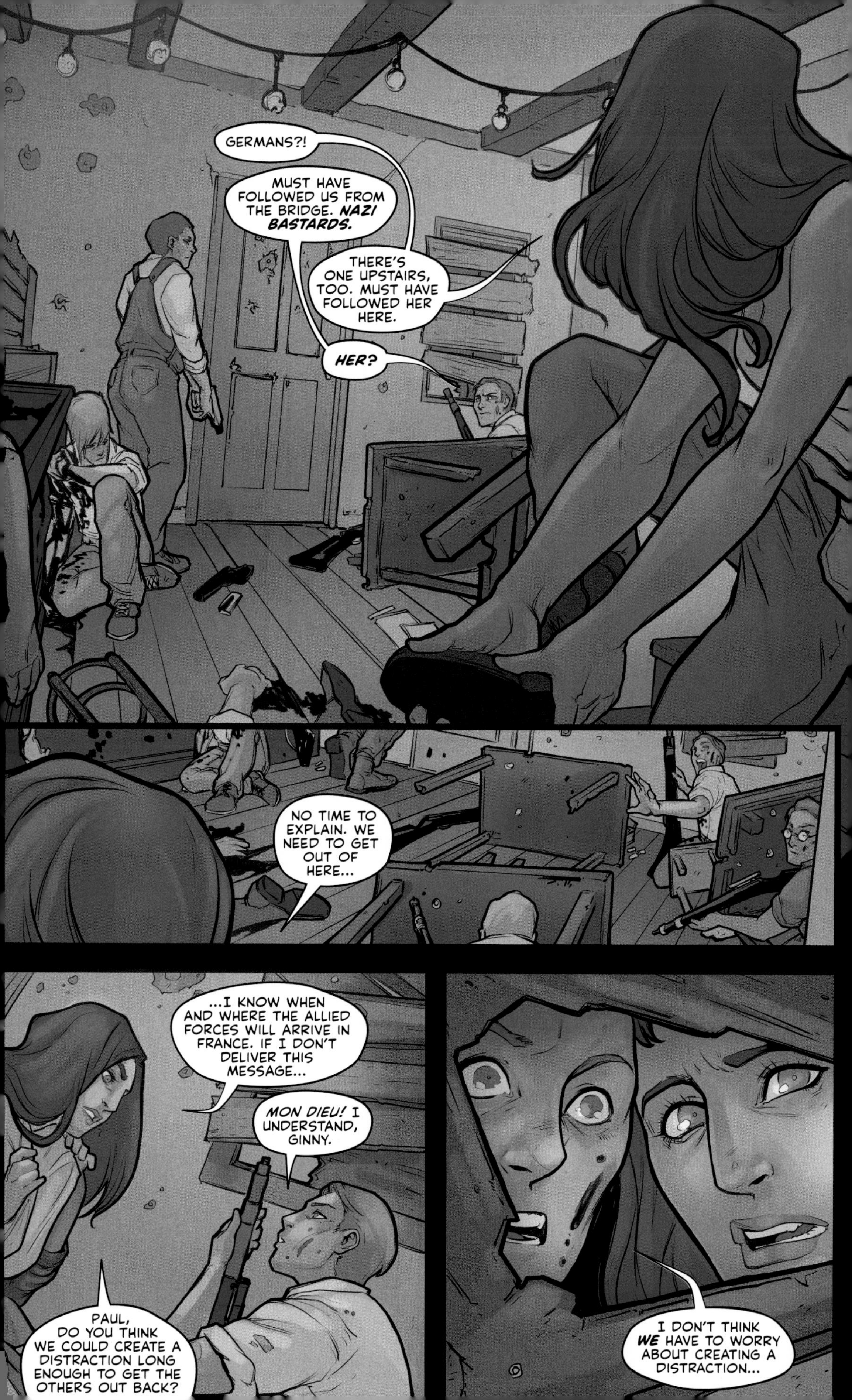
GERMANS?!
MUST HAVE FOLLOWED US FROM THE BRIDGE. *NAZI BASTARDS.*
THERE'S ONE UPSTAIRS, TOO. MUST HAVE FOLLOWED HER HERE.
HER?
NO TIME TO EXPLAIN. WE NEED TO GET OUT OF HERE...
...I KNOW WHEN AND WHERE THE ALLIED FORCES WILL ARRIVE IN FRANCE. IF I DON'T DELIVER THIS MESSAGE...
MON DIEU! I UNDERSTAND, GINNY.
PAUL, DO YOU THINK WE COULD CREATE A DISTRACTION LONG ENOUGH TO GET THE OTHERS OUT BACK?
I DON'T THINK *WE* HAVE TO WORRY ABOUT CREATING A DISTRACTION...

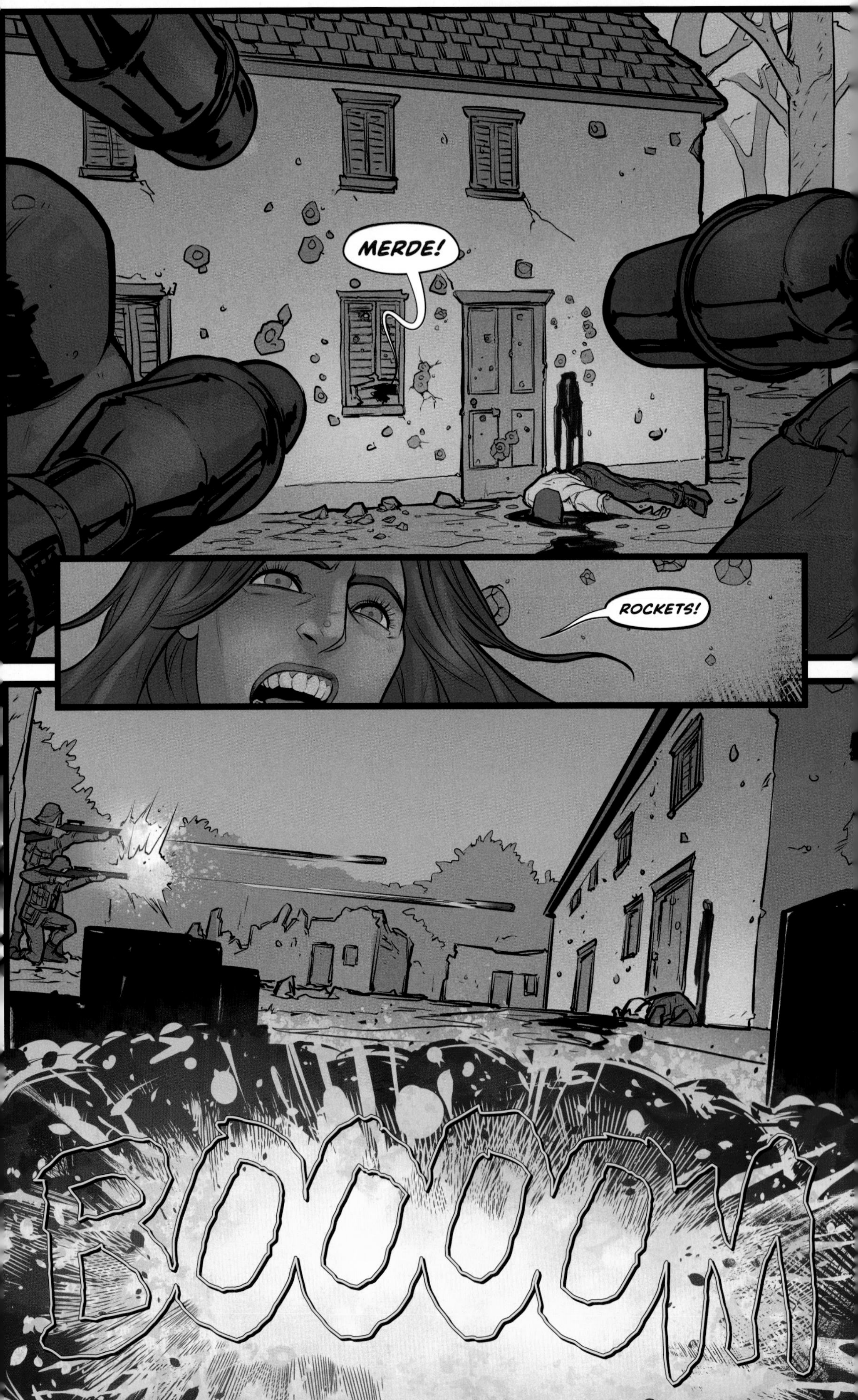
MERDE!
ROCKETS!
BOOOOOM

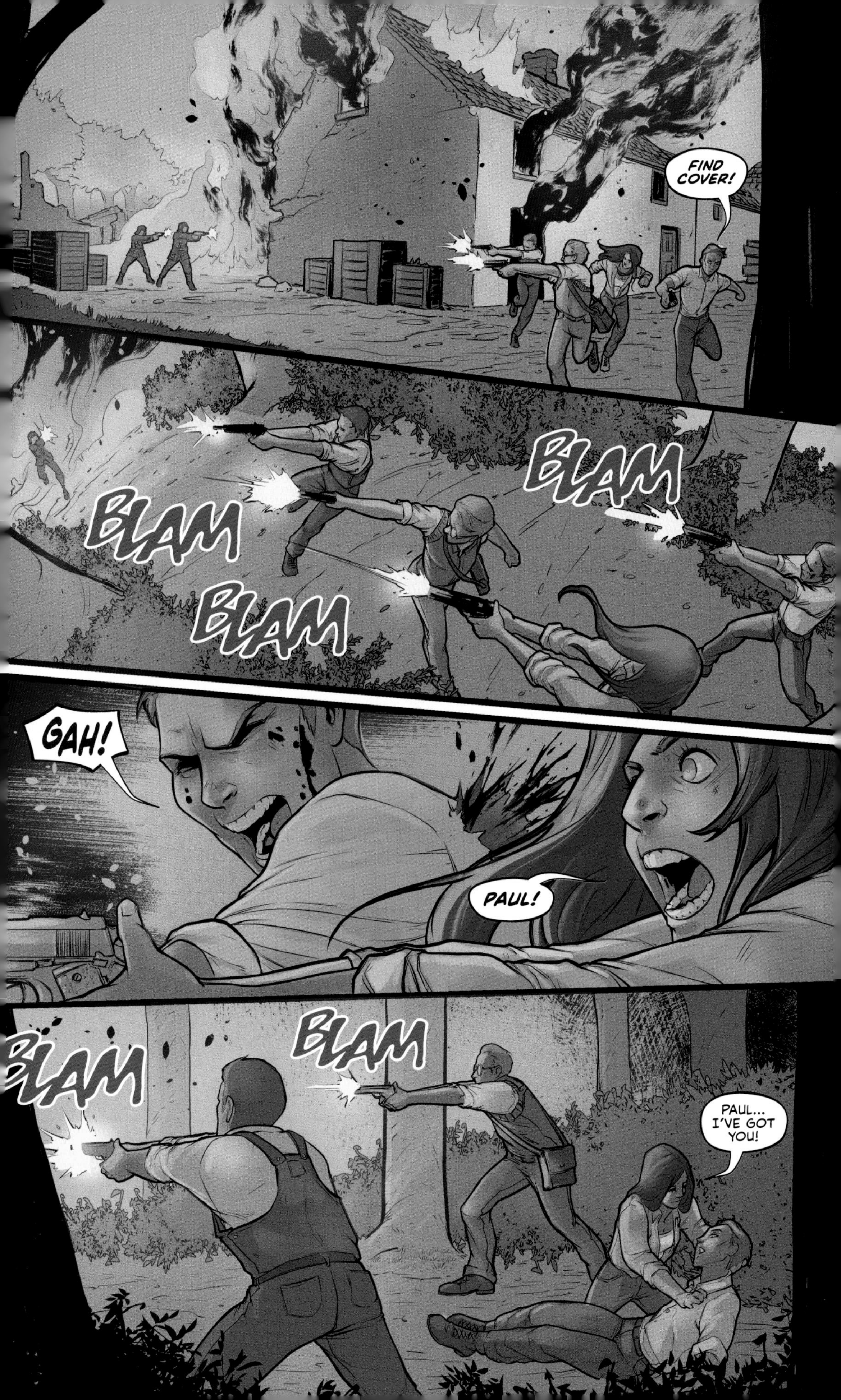

FIND COVER!
BLAM
BLAM
BLAM
GAH!
PAUL!
BLAM
BLAM
PAUL... I'VE GOT YOU!

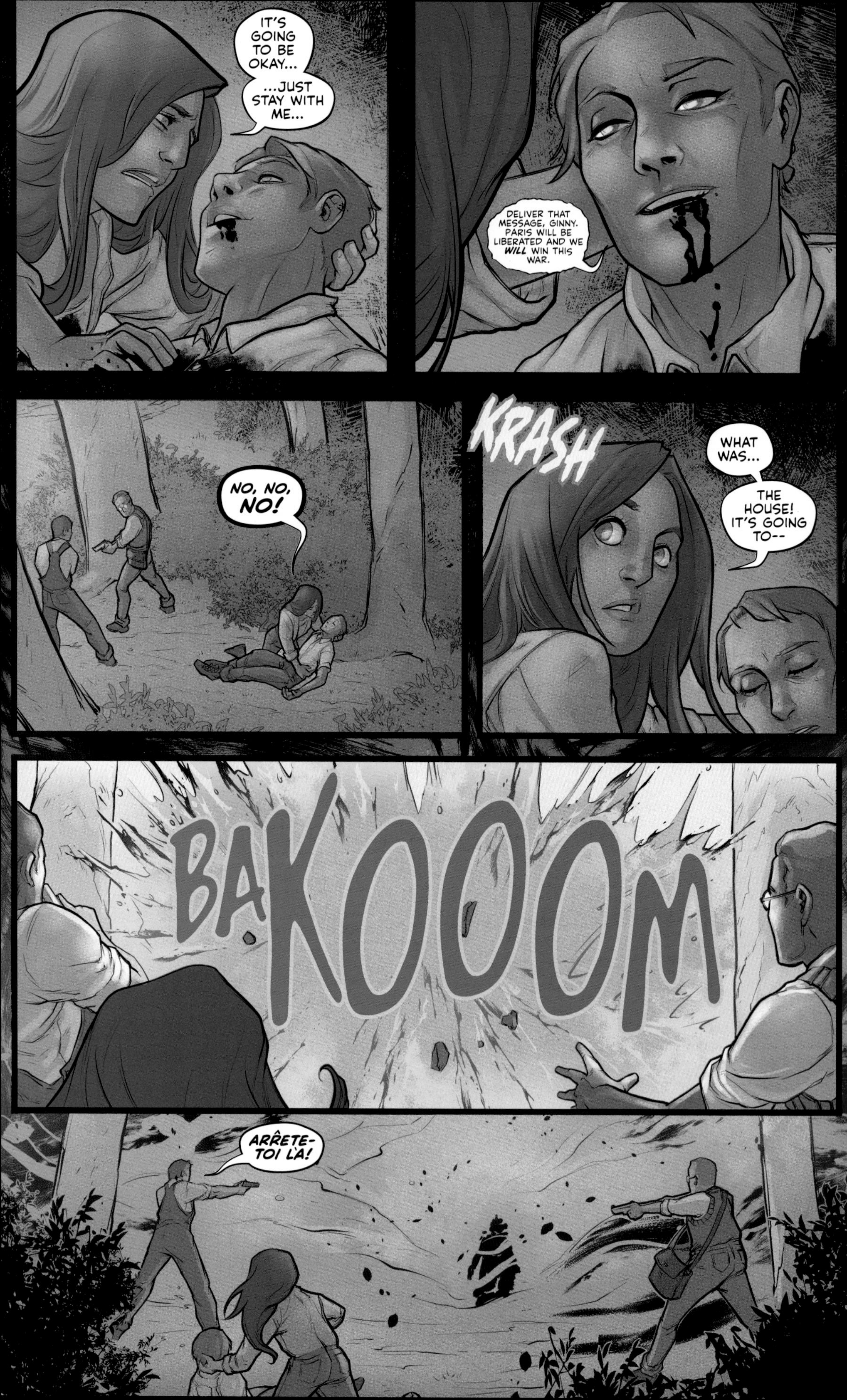
IT'S GOING TO BE OKAY...
...JUST STAY WITH ME...
DELIVER THAT MESSAGE, GINNY. PARIS WILL BE LIBERATED AND WE WILL WIN THIS WAR.
NO, NO, NO!
KRASH
WHAT WAS...
THE HOUSE! IT'S GOING TO--
BAKOOOM
ARRÊTE-TOI LÀ!

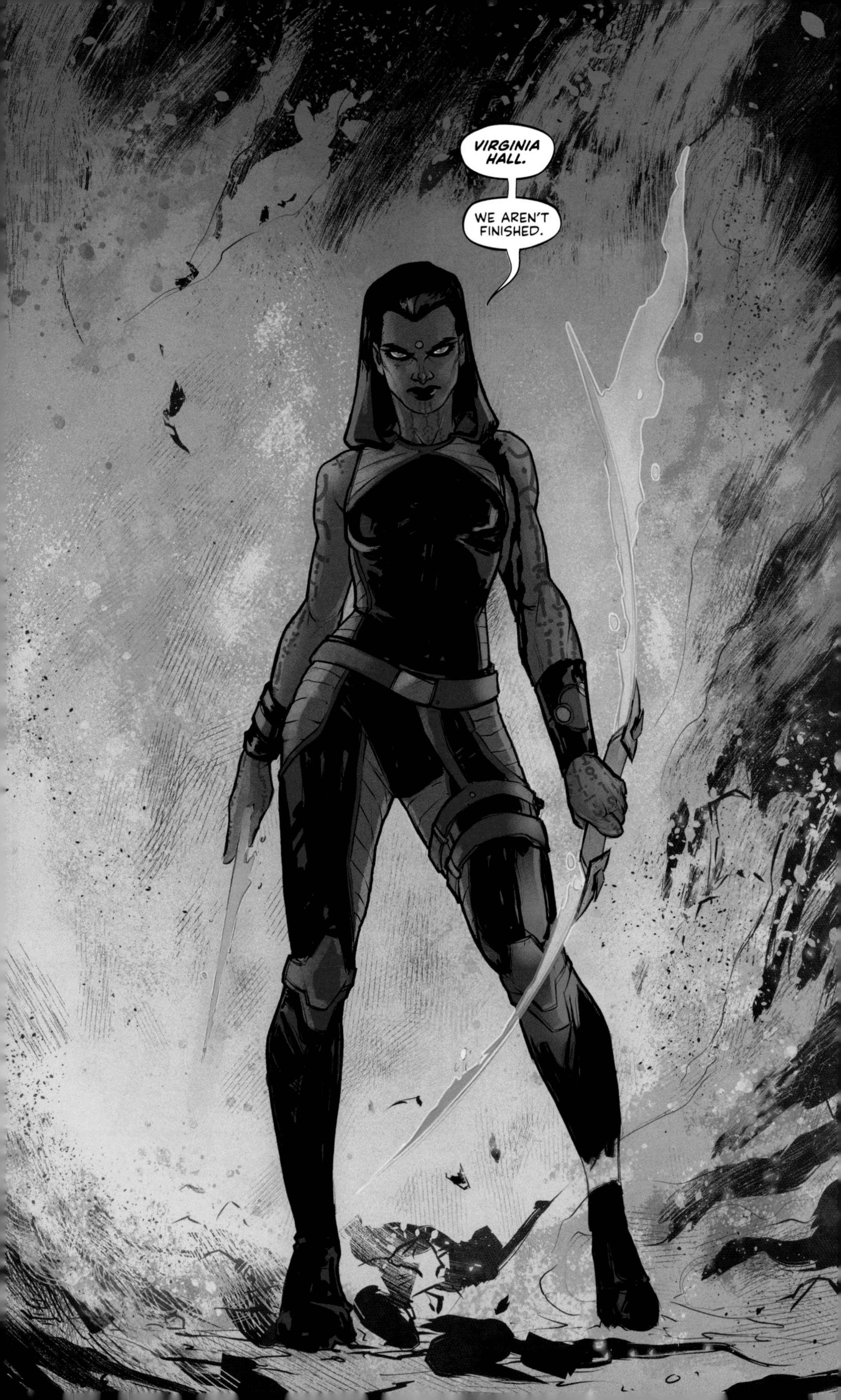
VIRGINIA HALL.
WE AREN'T FINISHED.

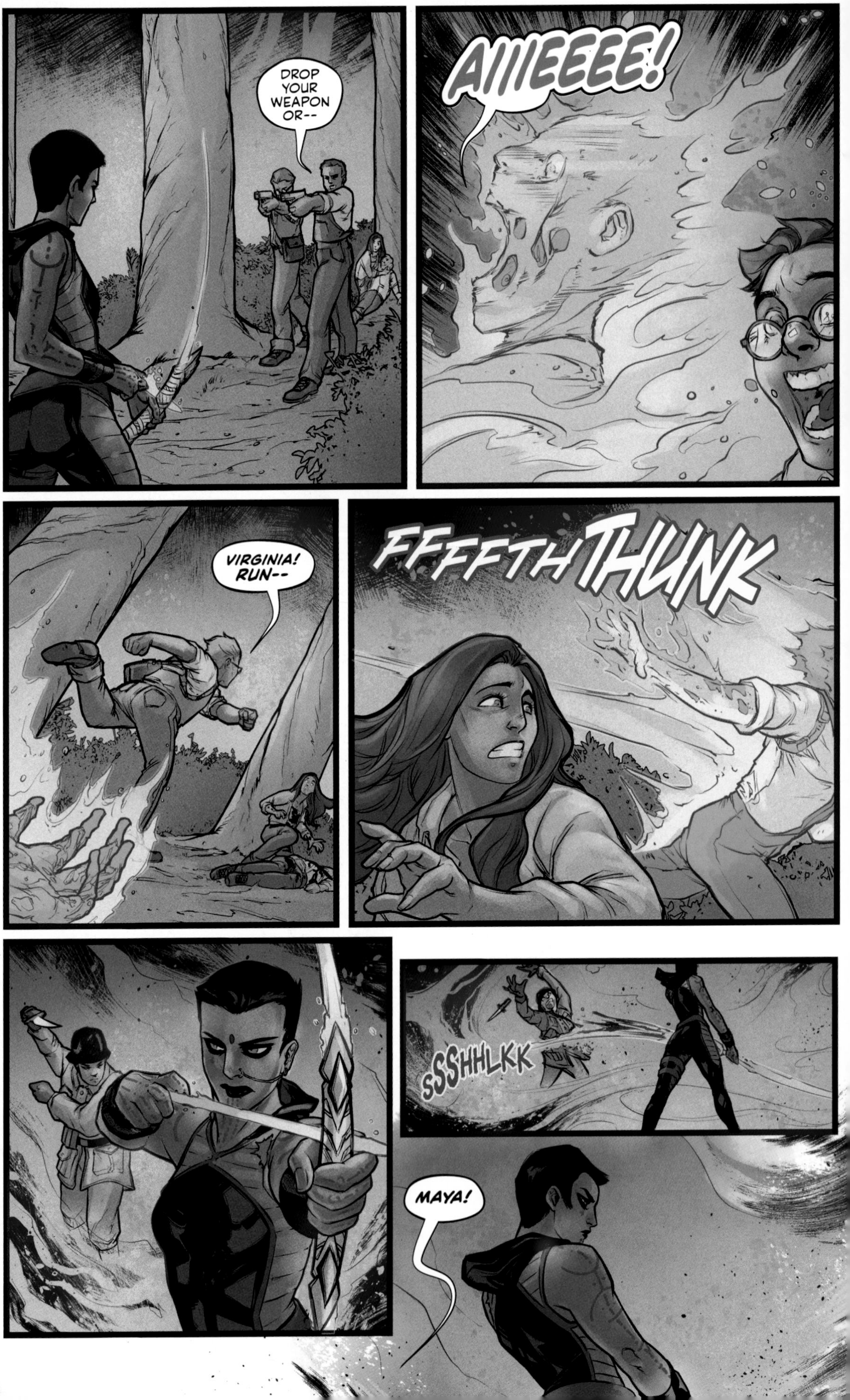
DROP YOUR WEAPON OR--
AIIIEEEEE!
VIRGINIA! RUN--
FFFFTHTHUNK
sSSHHLKK
MAYA!

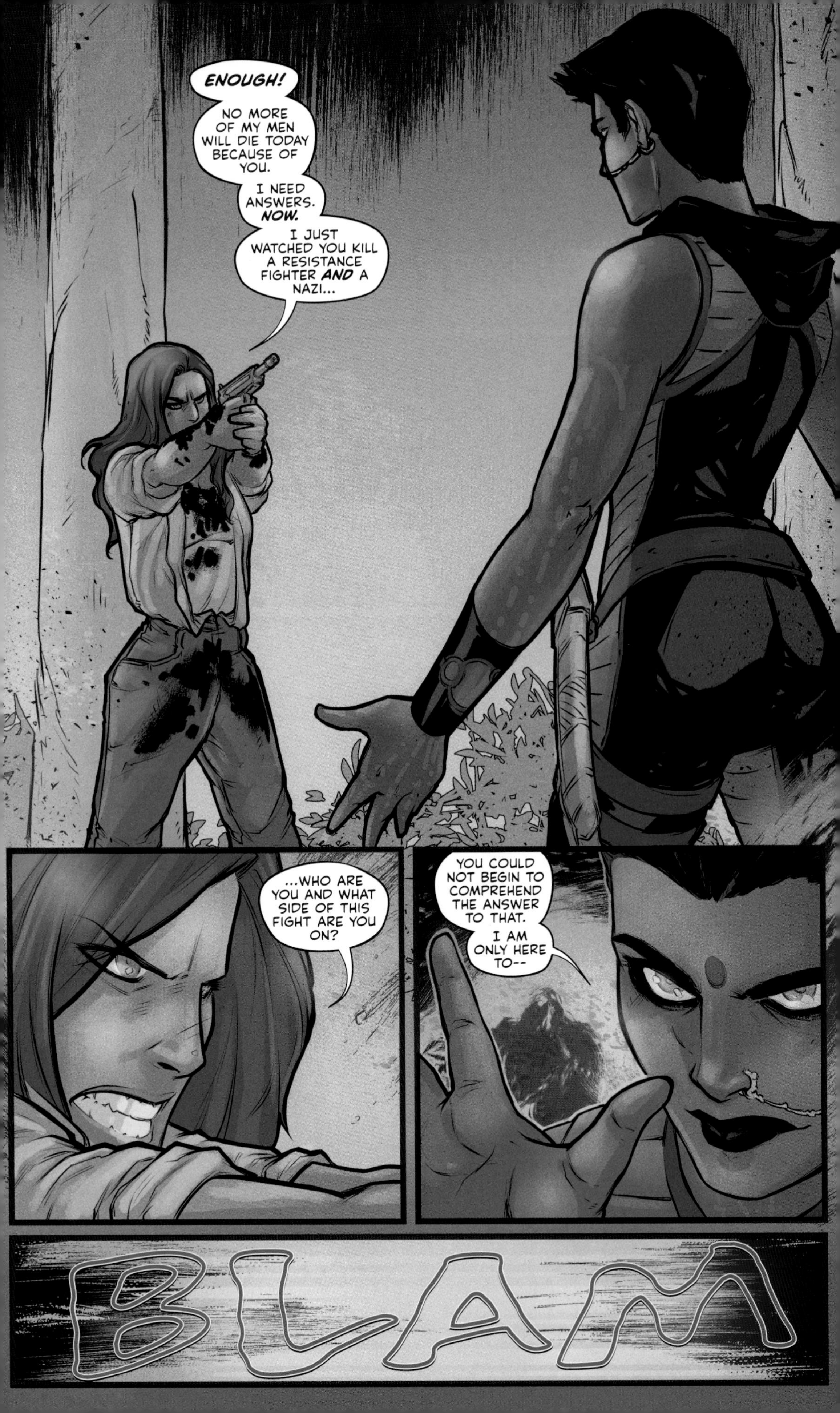
ENOUGH!
NO MORE OF MY MEN WILL DIE TODAY BECAUSE OF YOU.
I NEED ANSWERS. NOW.
I JUST WATCHED YOU KILL A RESISTANCE FIGHTER AND A NAZI...
...WHO ARE YOU AND WHAT SIDE OF THIS FIGHT ARE YOU ON?
YOU COULD NOT BEGIN TO COMPREHEND THE ANSWER TO THAT.
I AM ONLY HERE TO--
BLAM

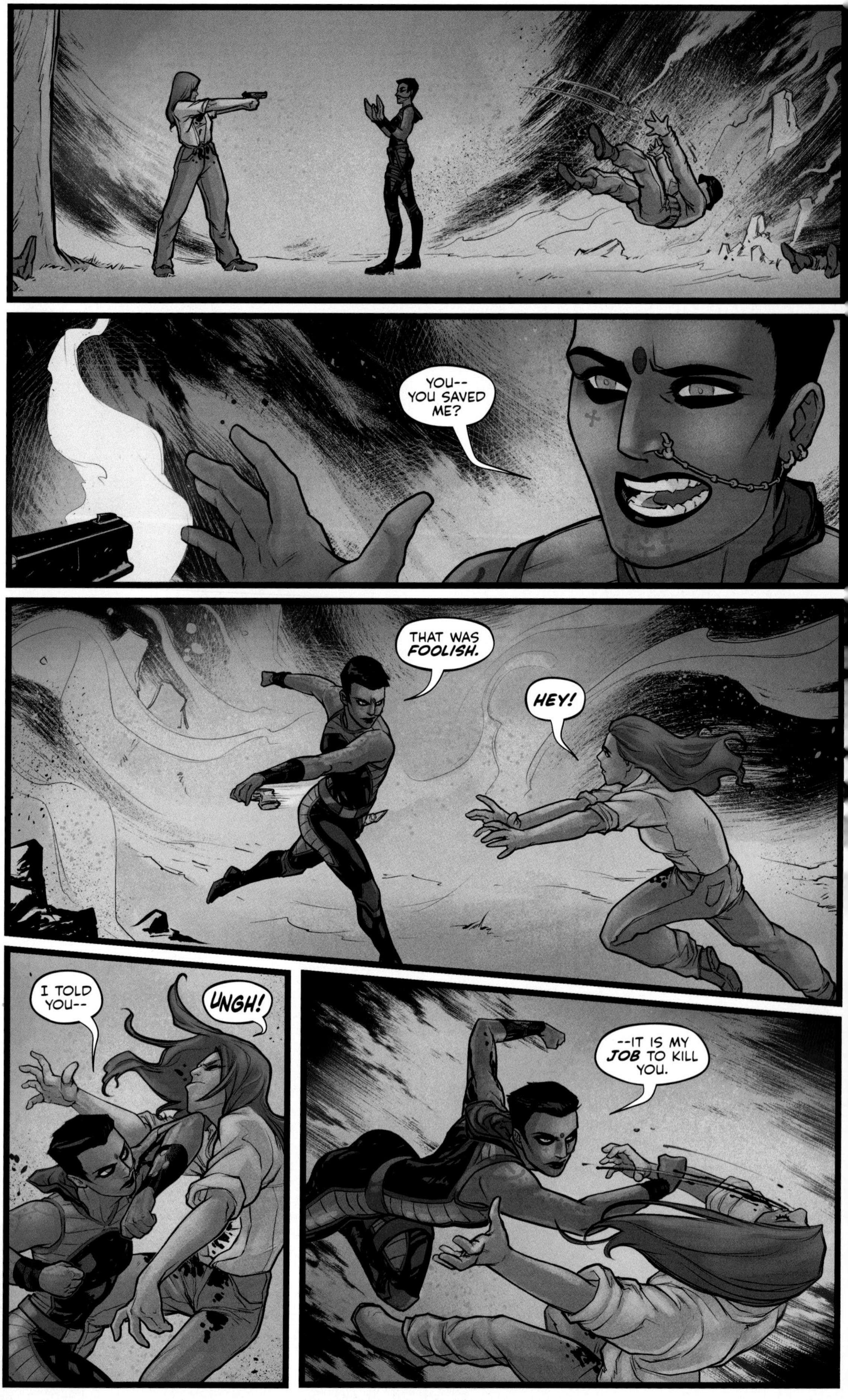
YOU--
YOU SAVED ME?
THAT WAS *FOOLISH.*
HEY!
I TOLD YOU--
UNGH!
--IT IS MY *JOB* TO KILL YOU.

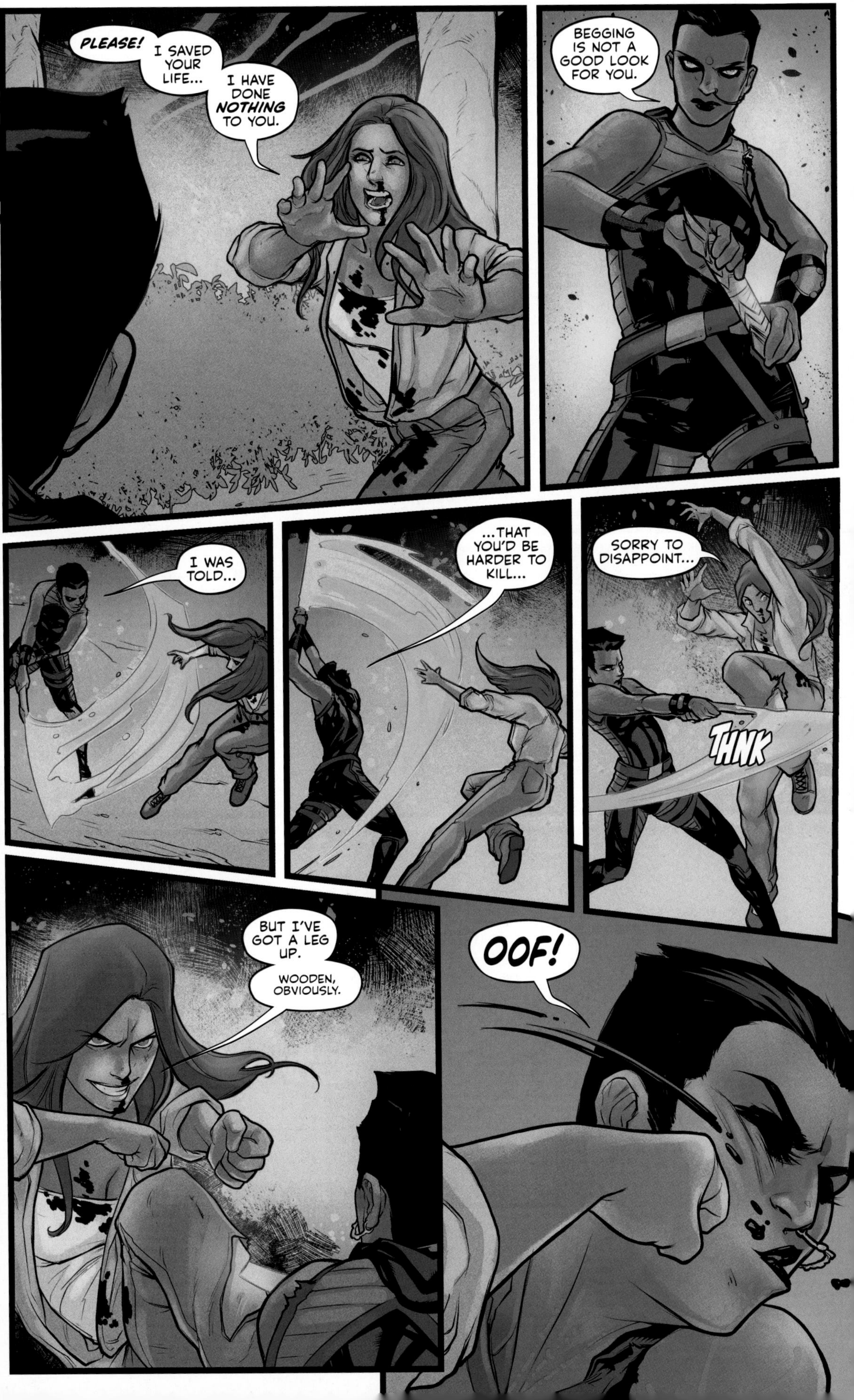
PLEASE!
I SAVED YOUR LIFE...
I HAVE DONE NOTHING TO YOU.
BEGGING IS NOT A GOOD LOOK FOR YOU.
I WAS TOLD...
...THAT YOU'D BE HARDER TO KILL...
SORRY TO DISAPPOINT...
THNK
BUT I'VE GOT A LEG UP.
WOODEN, OBVIOUSLY.
OOF!

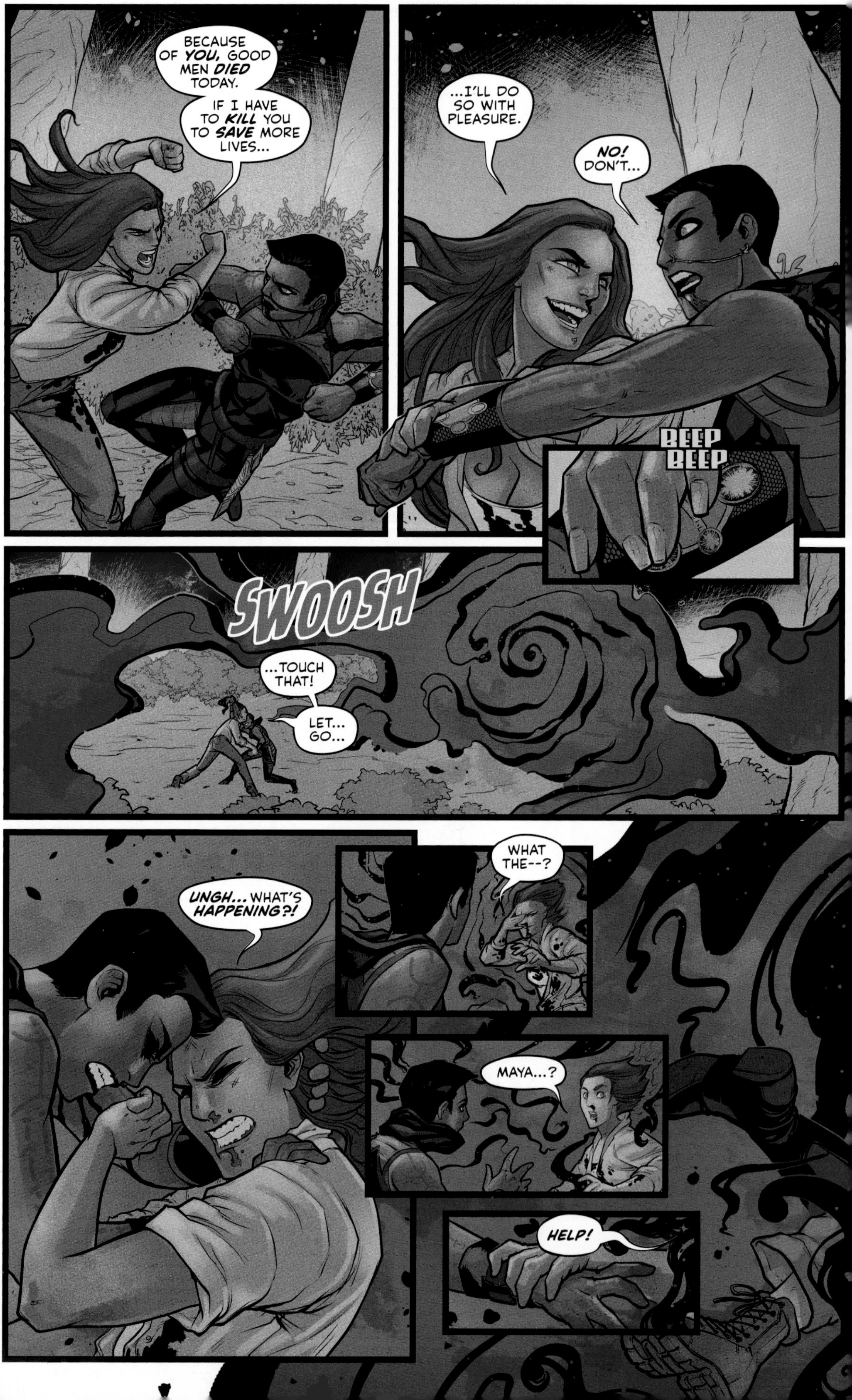
BECAUSE OF YOU, GOOD MEN DIED TODAY.
IF I HAVE TO KILL YOU TO SAVE MORE LIVES...
...I'LL DO SO WITH PLEASURE.
NO! DON'T...
BEEP BEEP
SWOOSH
...TOUCH THAT!
LET... GO...
UNGH... WHAT'S HAPPENING?!
WHAT THE--?
MAYA...?
HELP!

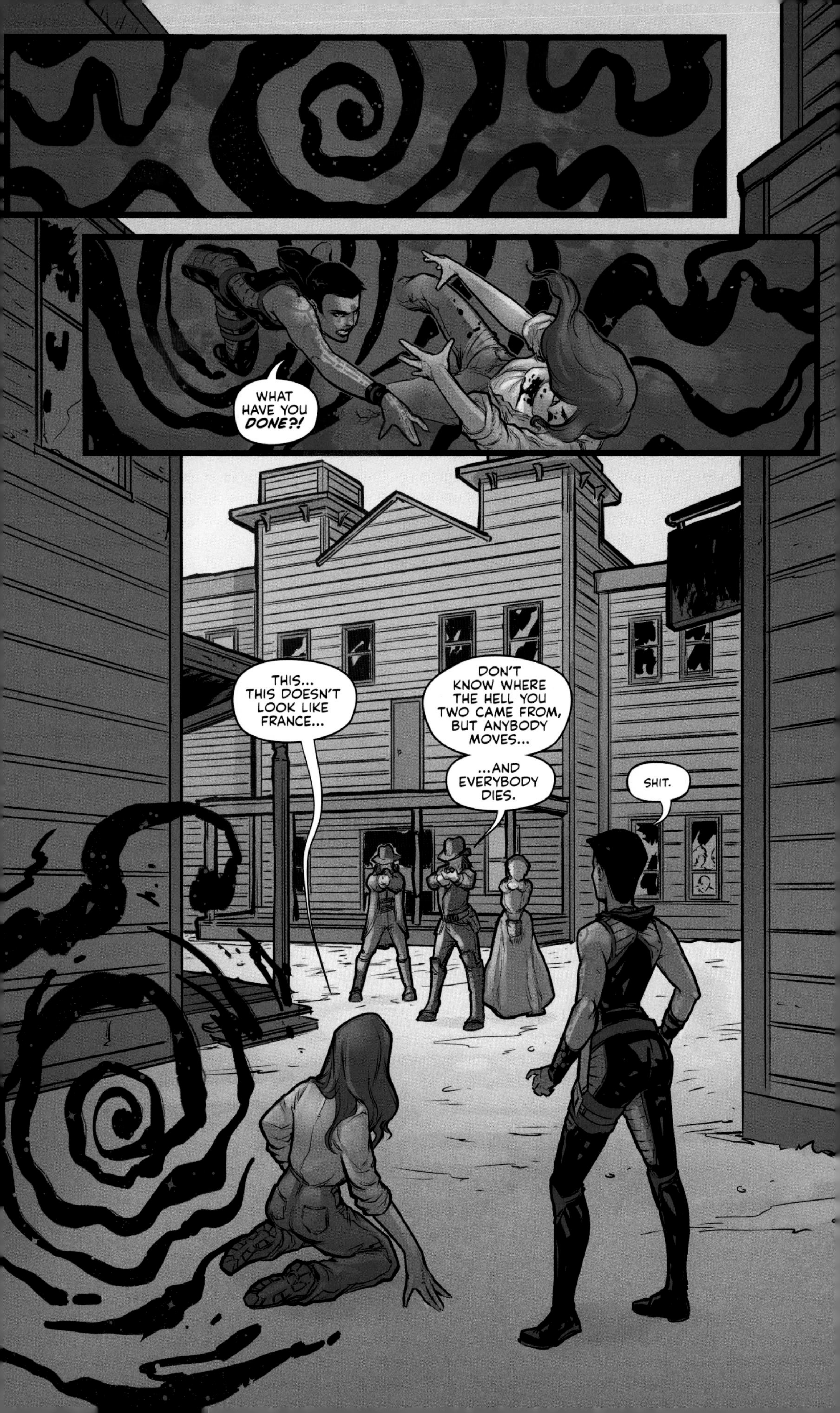
WHAT HAVE YOU *DONE?!*
THIS... THIS DOESN'T LOOK LIKE FRANCE...
DON'T KNOW WHERE THE HELL YOU TWO CAME FROM, BUT ANYBODY MOVES...
...AND EVERYBODY DIES.
SHIT.

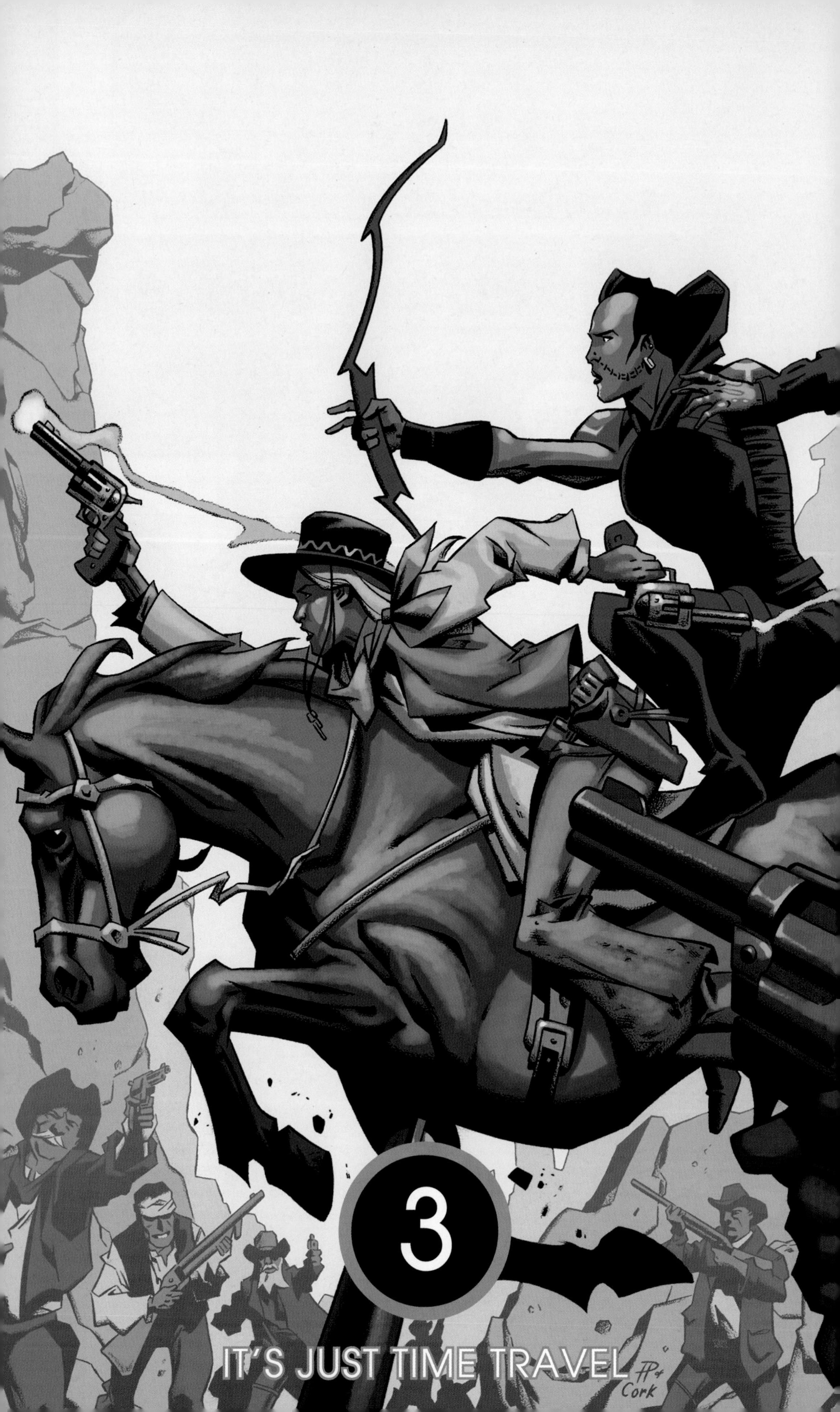
3
IT'S JUST TIME TRAVEL
JP & Cork

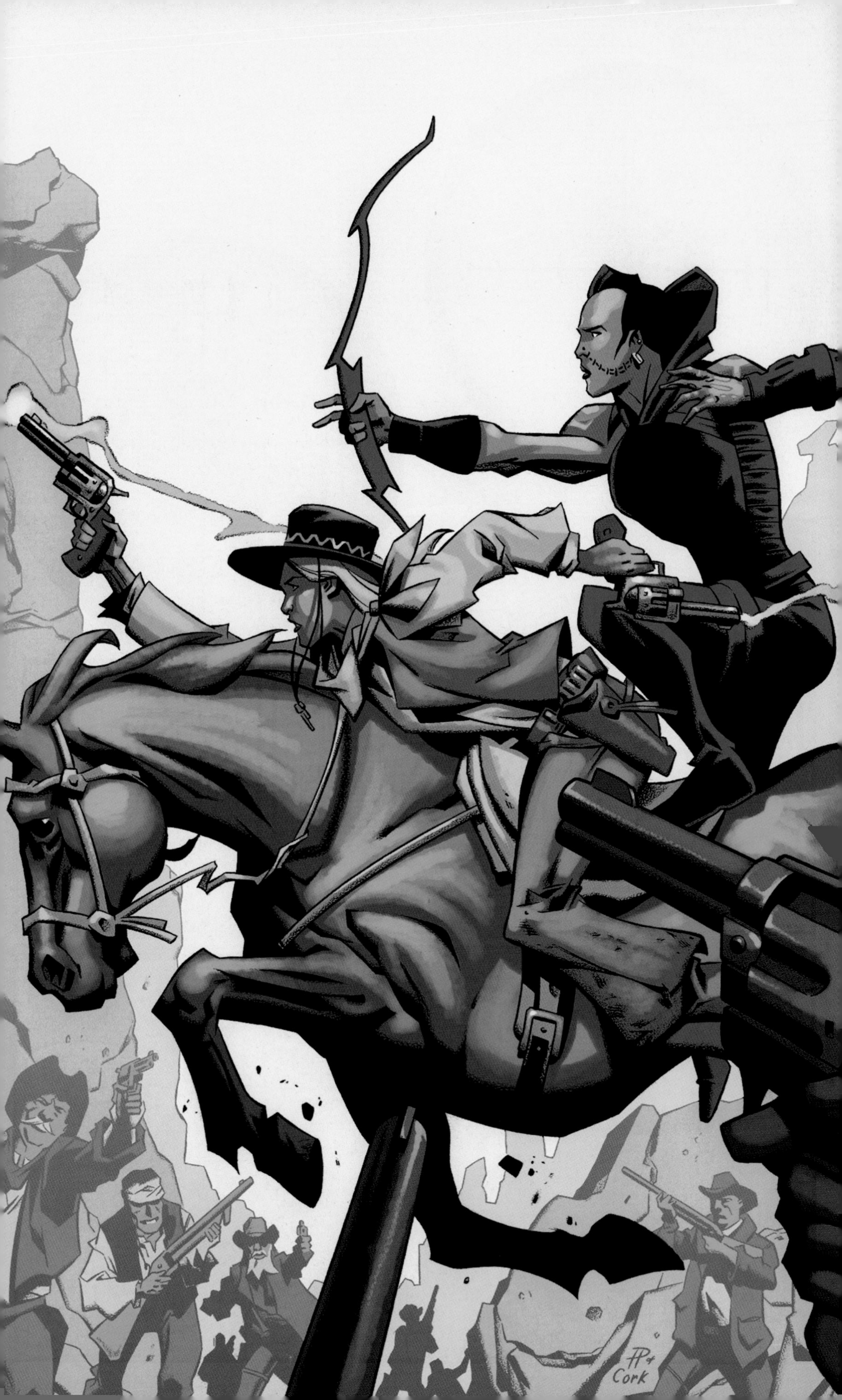
Cork

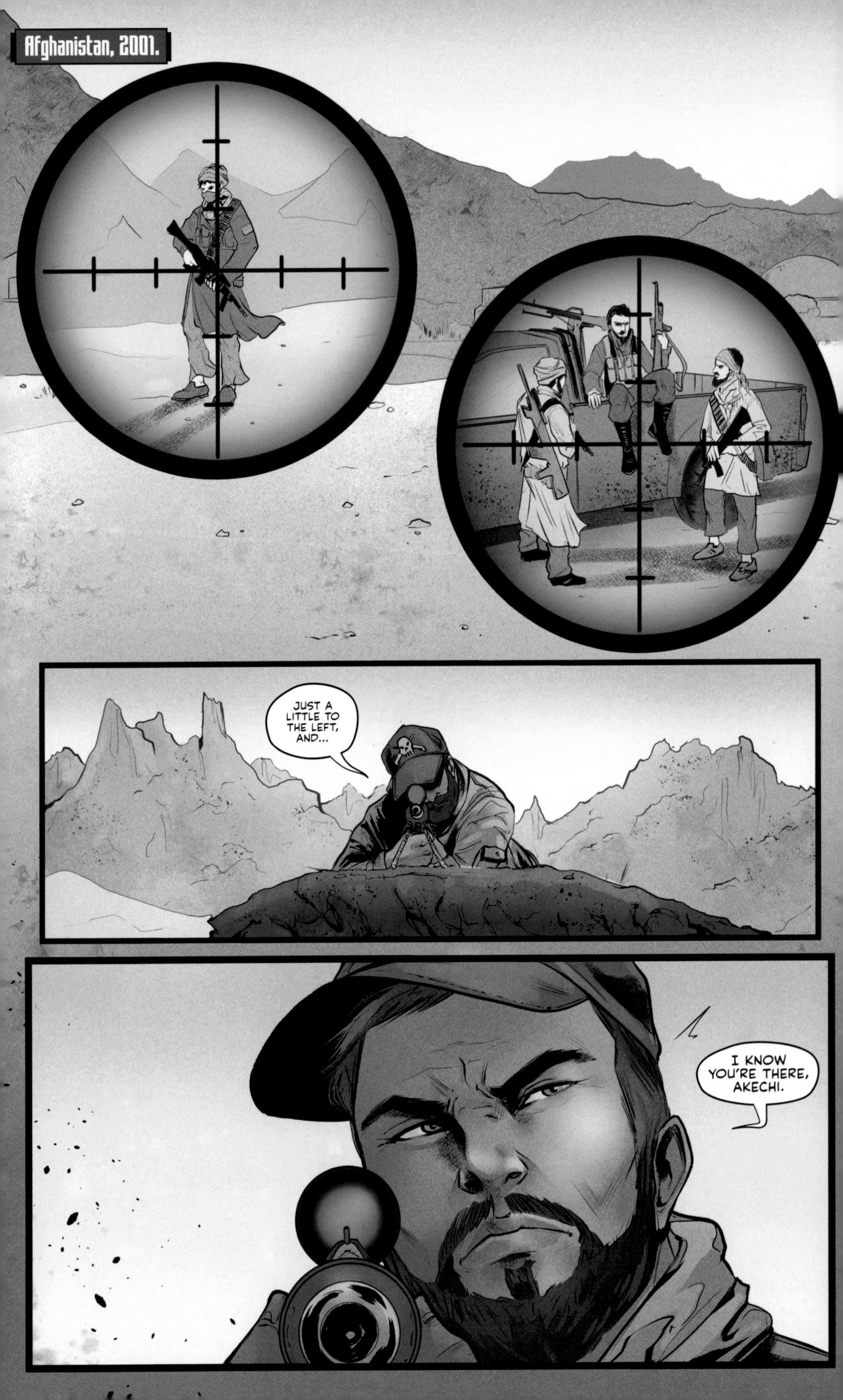
Afghanistan, 2001.
JUST A LITTLE TO THE LEFT, AND...
I KNOW YOU'RE THERE, AKECHI.

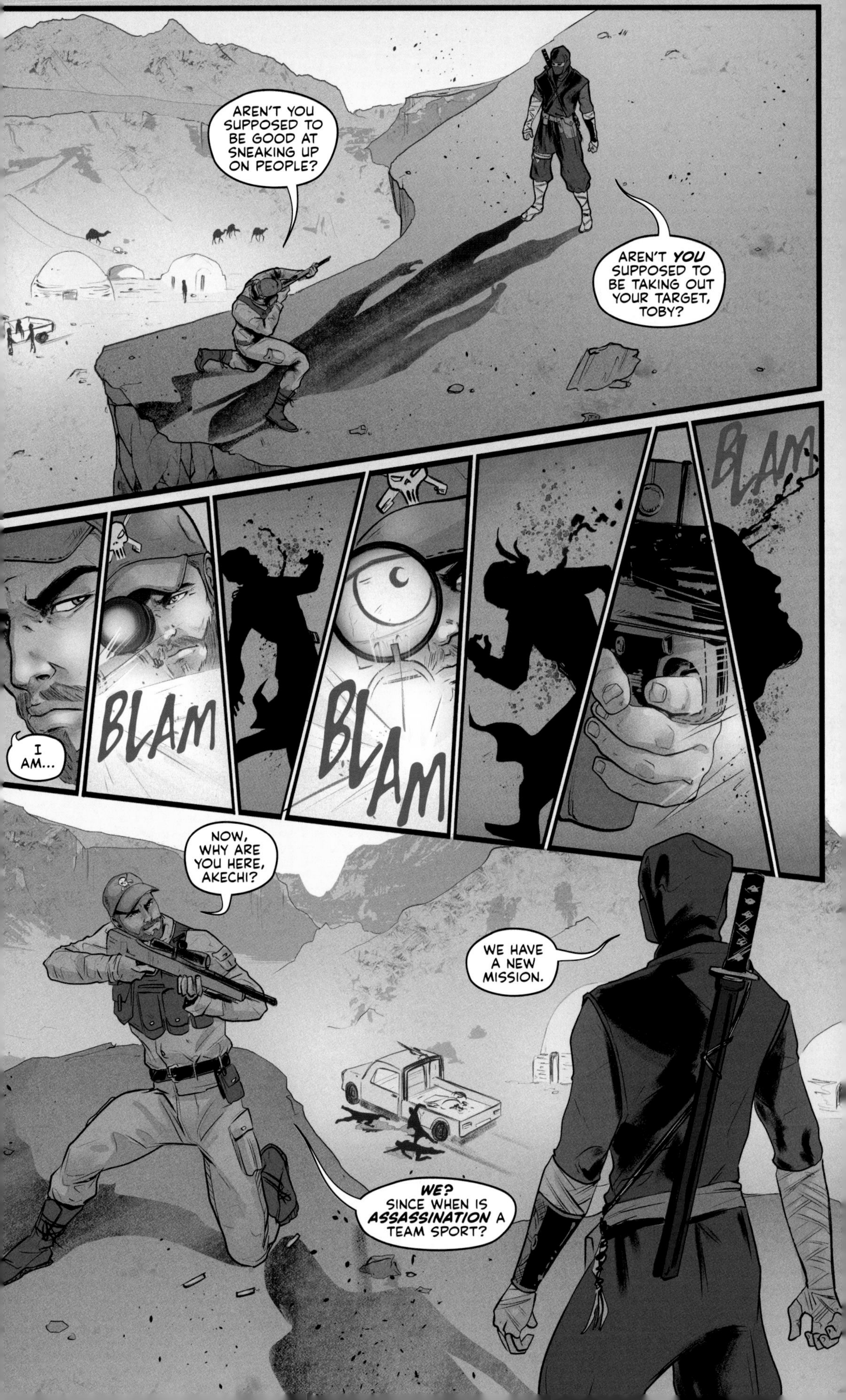

AREN'T YOU SUPPOSED TO BE GOOD AT SNEAKING UP ON PEOPLE?
AREN'T YOU SUPPOSED TO BE TAKING OUT YOUR TARGET, TOBY?
BLAM
I AM...
BLAM
BLAM
NOW, WHY ARE YOU HERE, AKECHI?
WE HAVE A NEW MISSION.
WE? SINCE WHEN IS ASSASSINATION A TEAM SPORT?

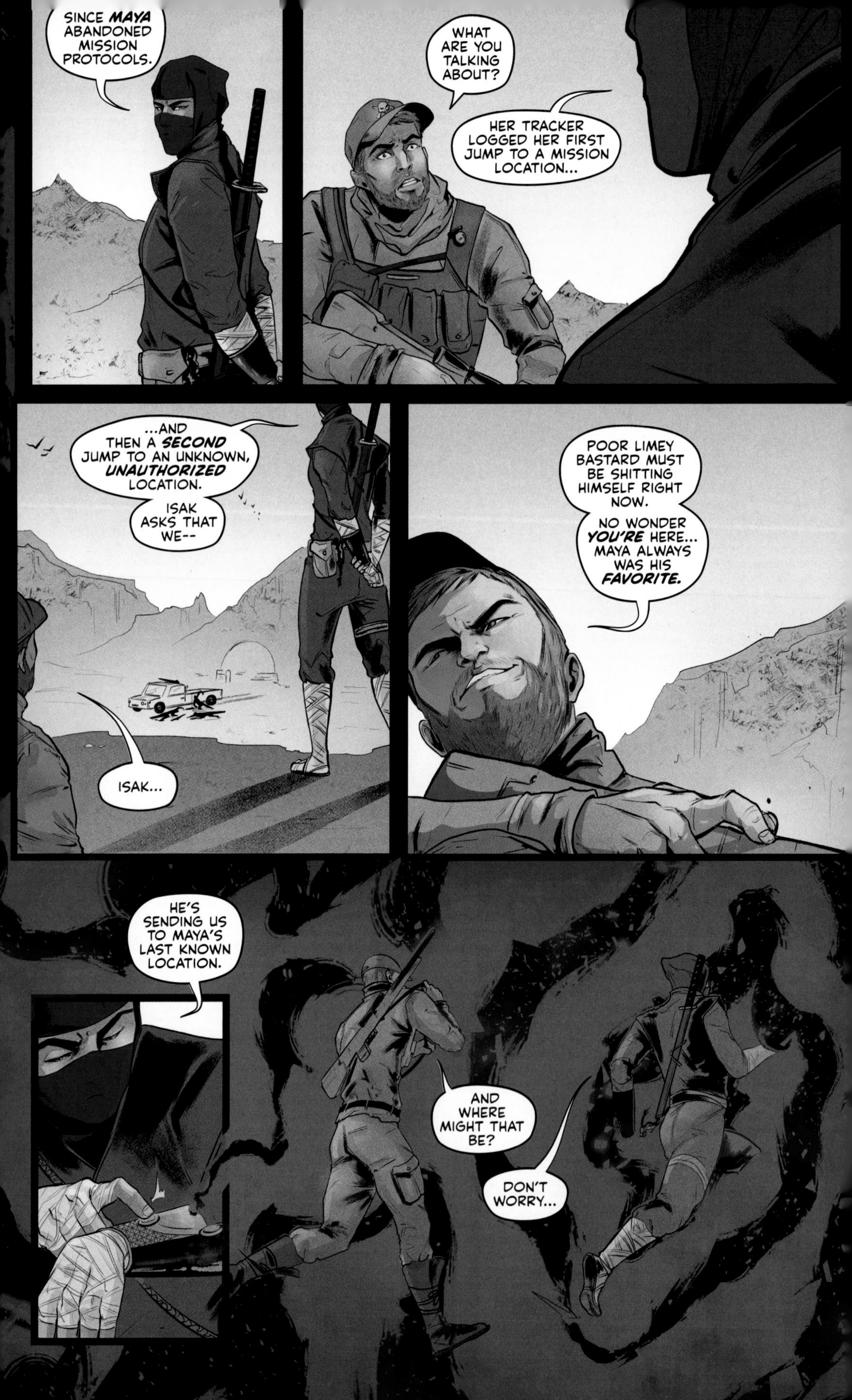
SINCE *MAYA* ABANDONED MISSION PROTOCOLS.
WHAT ARE YOU TALKING ABOUT?
HER TRACKER LOGGED HER FIRST JUMP TO A MISSION LOCATION...
...AND THEN A *SECOND* JUMP TO AN UNKNOWN, *UNAUTHORIZED* LOCATION.
ISAK ASKS THAT WE--
ISAK...
POOR LIMEY BASTARD MUST BE SHITTING HIMSELF RIGHT NOW.
NO WONDER *YOU'RE* HERE... MAYA ALWAYS WAS HIS *FAVORITE.*
HE'S SENDING US TO MAYA'S LAST KNOWN LOCATION.
AND WHERE MIGHT THAT BE?
DON'T WORRY...

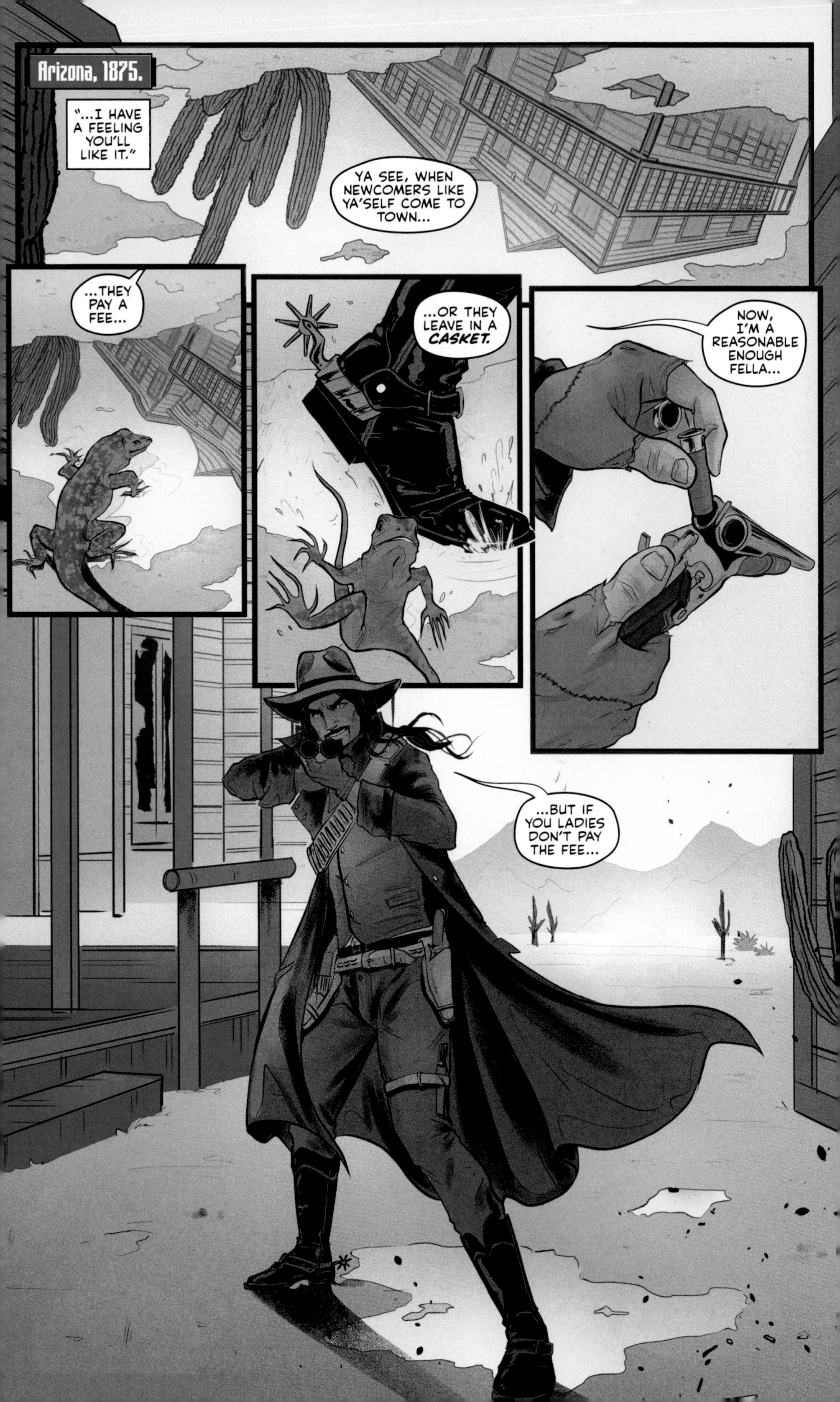

Arizona, 1875.
"...I HAVE A FEELING YOU'LL LIKE IT."
YA SEE, WHEN NEWCOMERS LIKE YA'SELF COME TO TOWN...
...THEY PAY A FEE...
...OR THEY LEAVE IN A *CASKET.*
NOW, I'M A REASONABLE ENOUGH FELLA...
...BUT IF YOU LADIES DON'T PAY THE FEE...

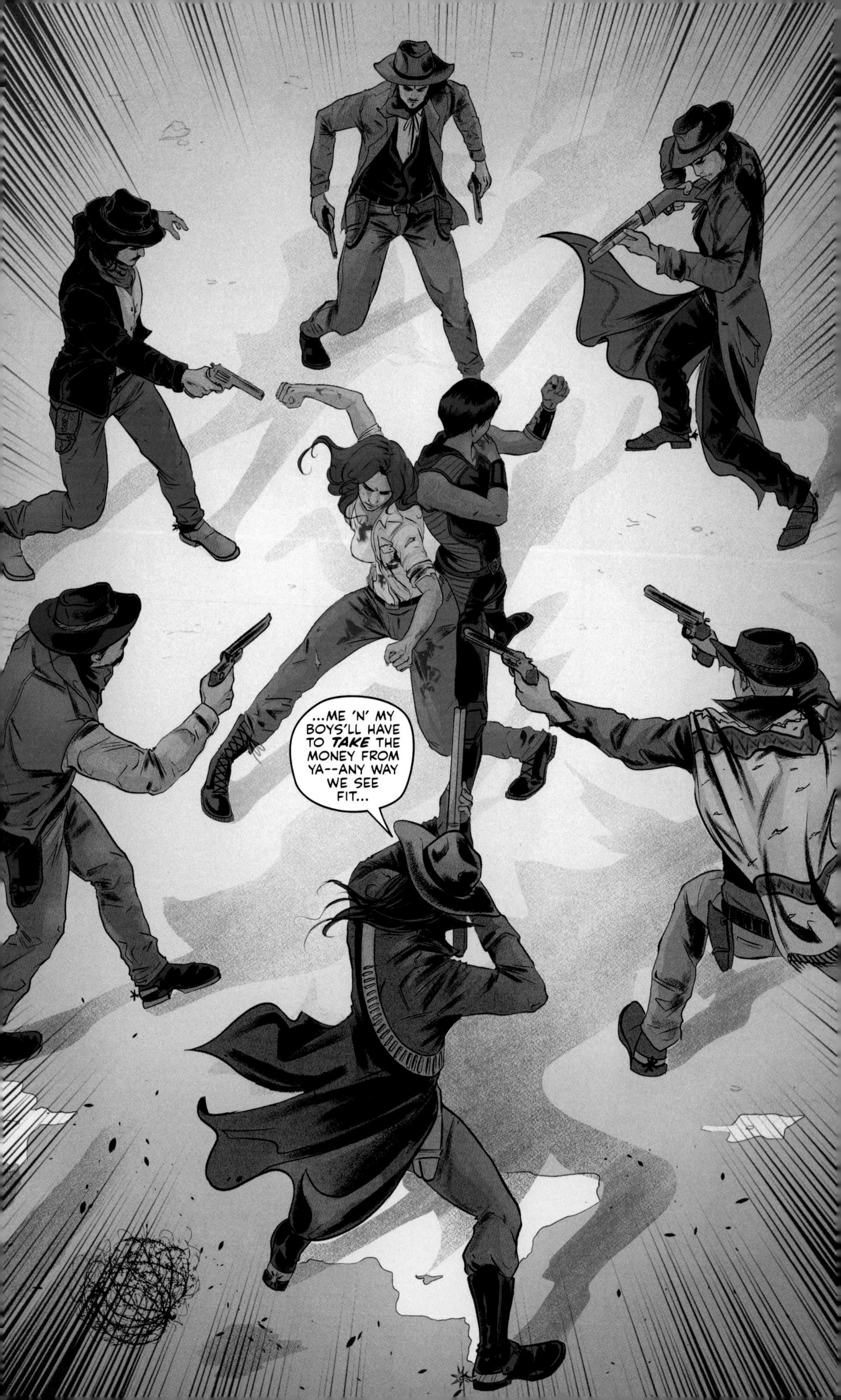
...ME 'N' MY BOYS'LL HAVE TO *TAKE* THE MONEY FROM YA--ANY WAY WE SEE FIT...

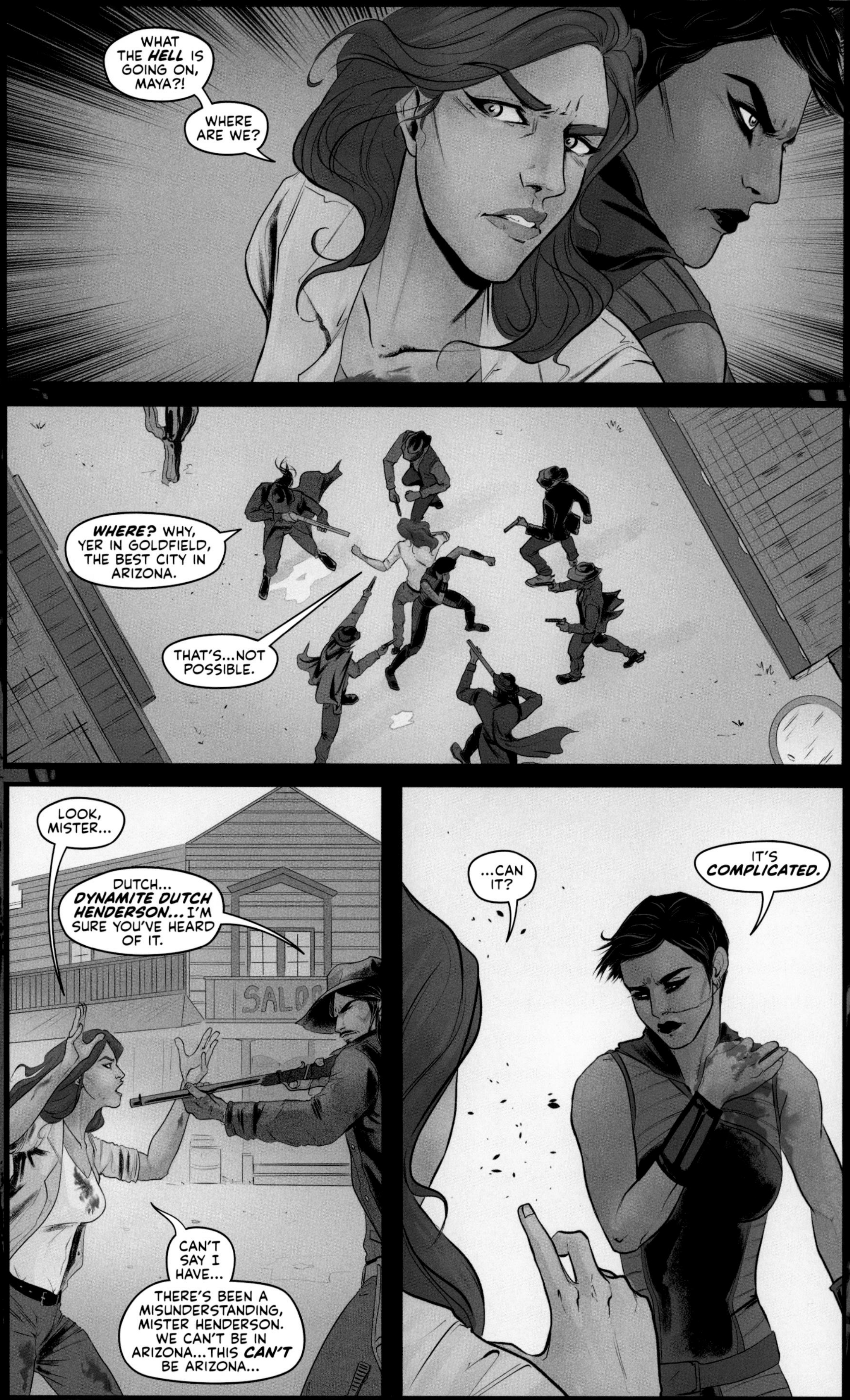
WHAT THE HELL IS GOING ON, MAYA?!
WHERE ARE WE?
WHERE? WHY, YER IN GOLDFIELD, THE BEST CITY IN ARIZONA.
THAT'S...NOT POSSIBLE.
LOOK, MISTER...
DUTCH... DYNAMITE DUTCH HENDERSON... I'M SURE YOU'VE HEARD OF IT.
SALO
CAN'T SAY I HAVE...
THERE'S BEEN A MISUNDERSTANDING, MISTER HENDERSON. WE CAN'T BE IN ARIZONA...THIS CAN'T BE ARIZONA...
...CAN IT?
IT'S COMPLICATED.

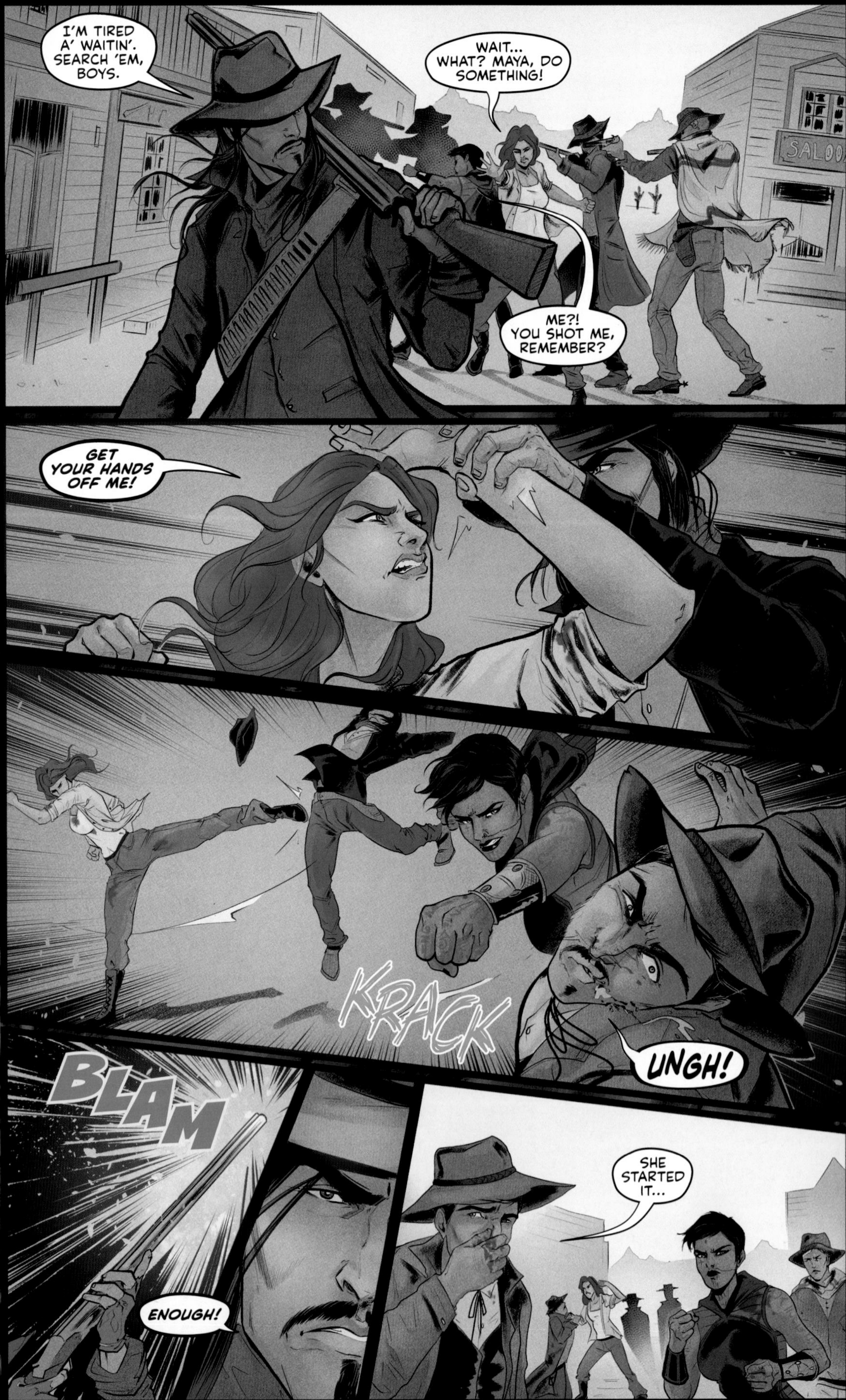
I'M TIRED A' WAITIN'. SEARCH 'EM, BOYS.
WAIT... WHAT? MAYA, DO SOMETHING!
ME?! YOU SHOT ME, REMEMBER?
SALOO
GET YOUR HANDS OFF ME!
KRACK
UNGH!
BLAM
ENOUGH!
SHE STARTED IT...

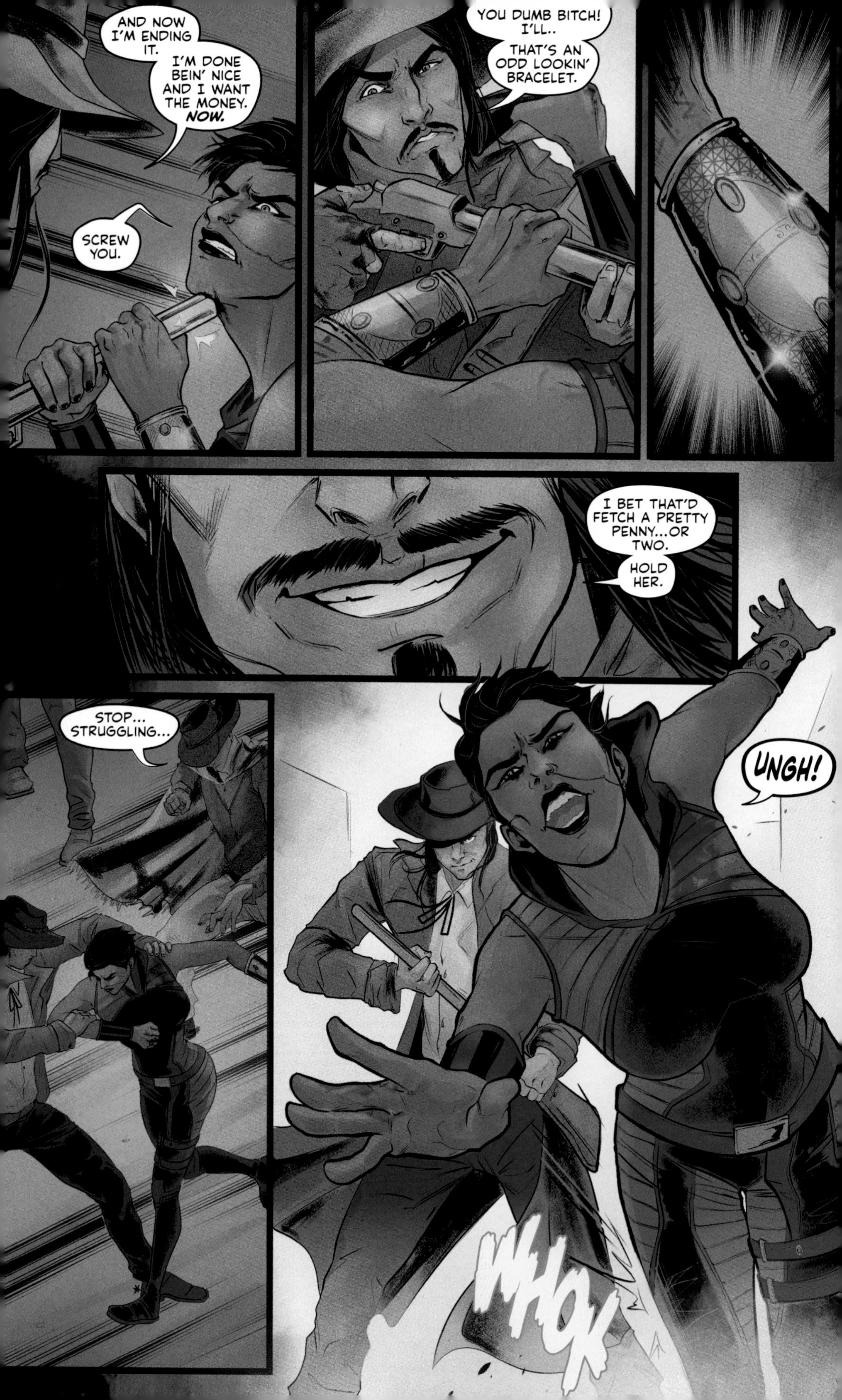
AND NOW I'M ENDING IT.
I'M DONE BEIN' NICE AND I WANT THE MONEY. ***NOW.***
SCREW YOU.
YOU DUMB BITCH! I'LL..
THAT'S AN ODD LOOKIN' BRACELET.
I BET THAT'D FETCH A PRETTY PENNY...OR TWO.
HOLD HER.
STOP... STRUGGLING...
UNGH!
WHOK

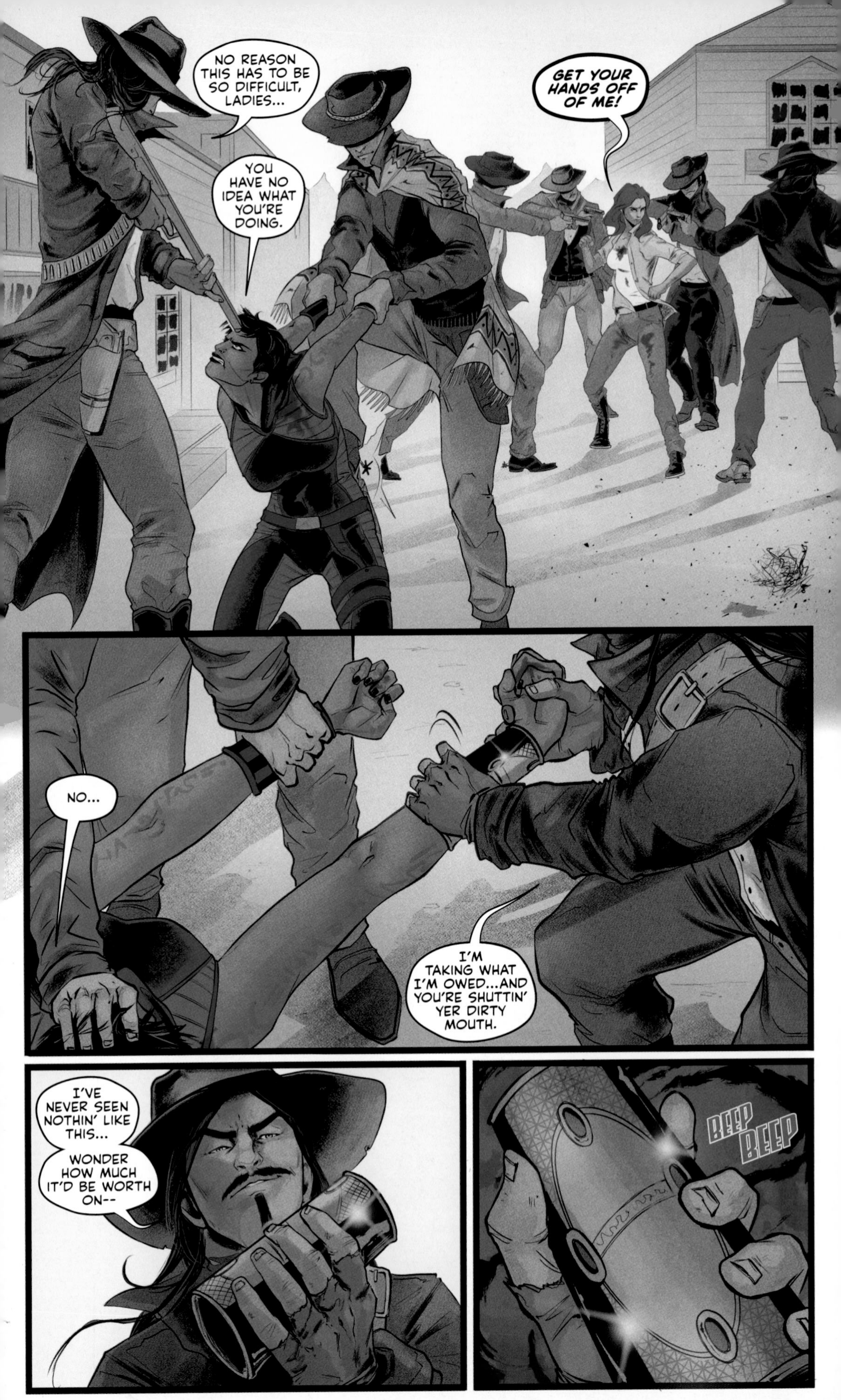
NO REASON THIS HAS TO BE SO DIFFICULT, LADIES...
YOU HAVE NO IDEA WHAT YOU'RE DOING.
GET YOUR HANDS OFF OF ME!
NO...
I'M TAKING WHAT I'M OWED...AND YOU'RE SHUTTIN' YER DIRTY MOUTH.
I'VE NEVER SEEN NOTHIN' LIKE THIS...
WONDER HOW MUCH IT'D BE WORTH ON--
BEEP BEEP

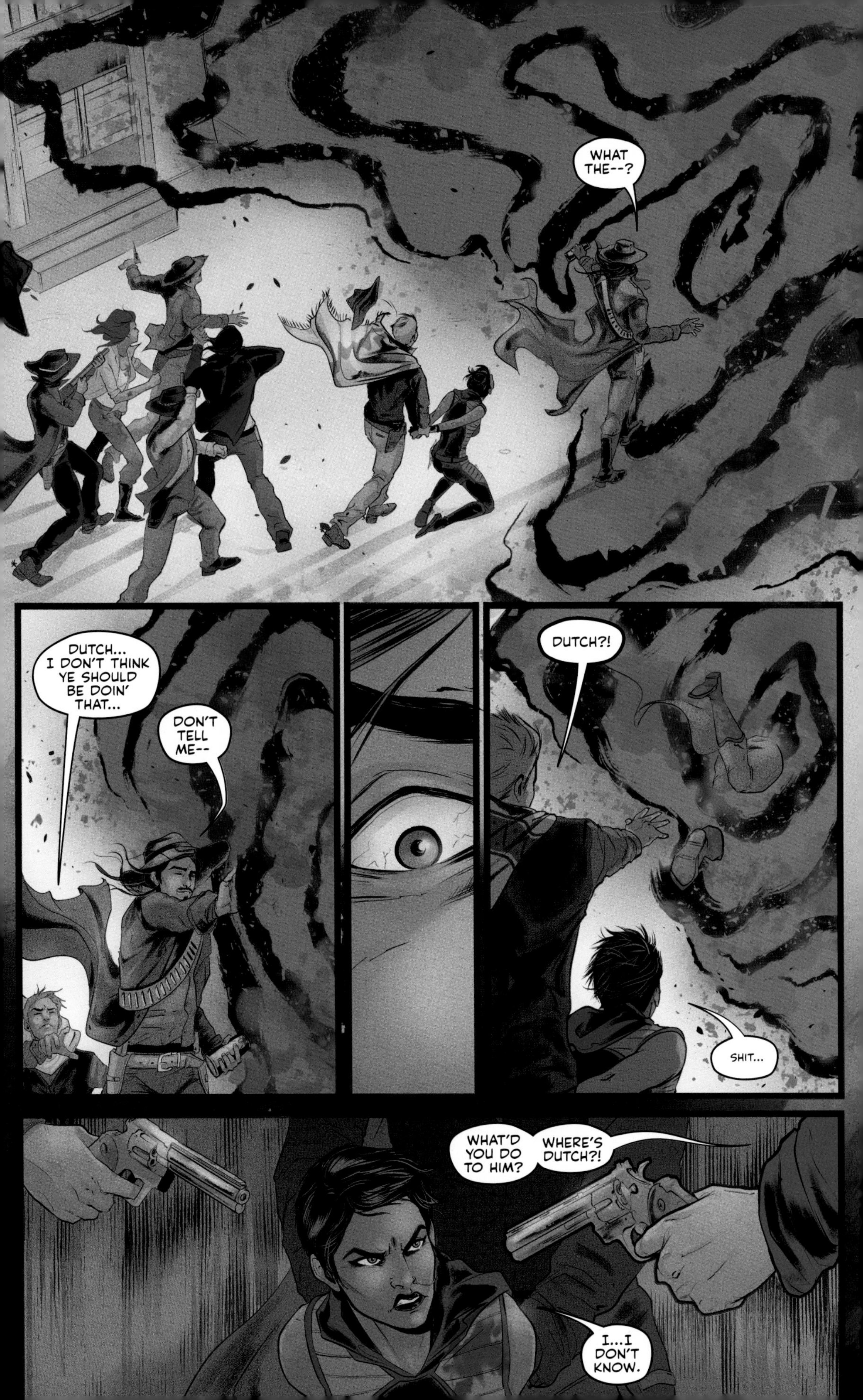
WHAT THE--?
DUTCH... I DON'T THINK YE SHOULD BE DOIN' THAT...
DON'T TELL ME--
DUTCH?!
SHIT...
WHERE'S DUTCH?!
WHAT'D YOU DO TO HIM?
I...I DON'T KNOW.

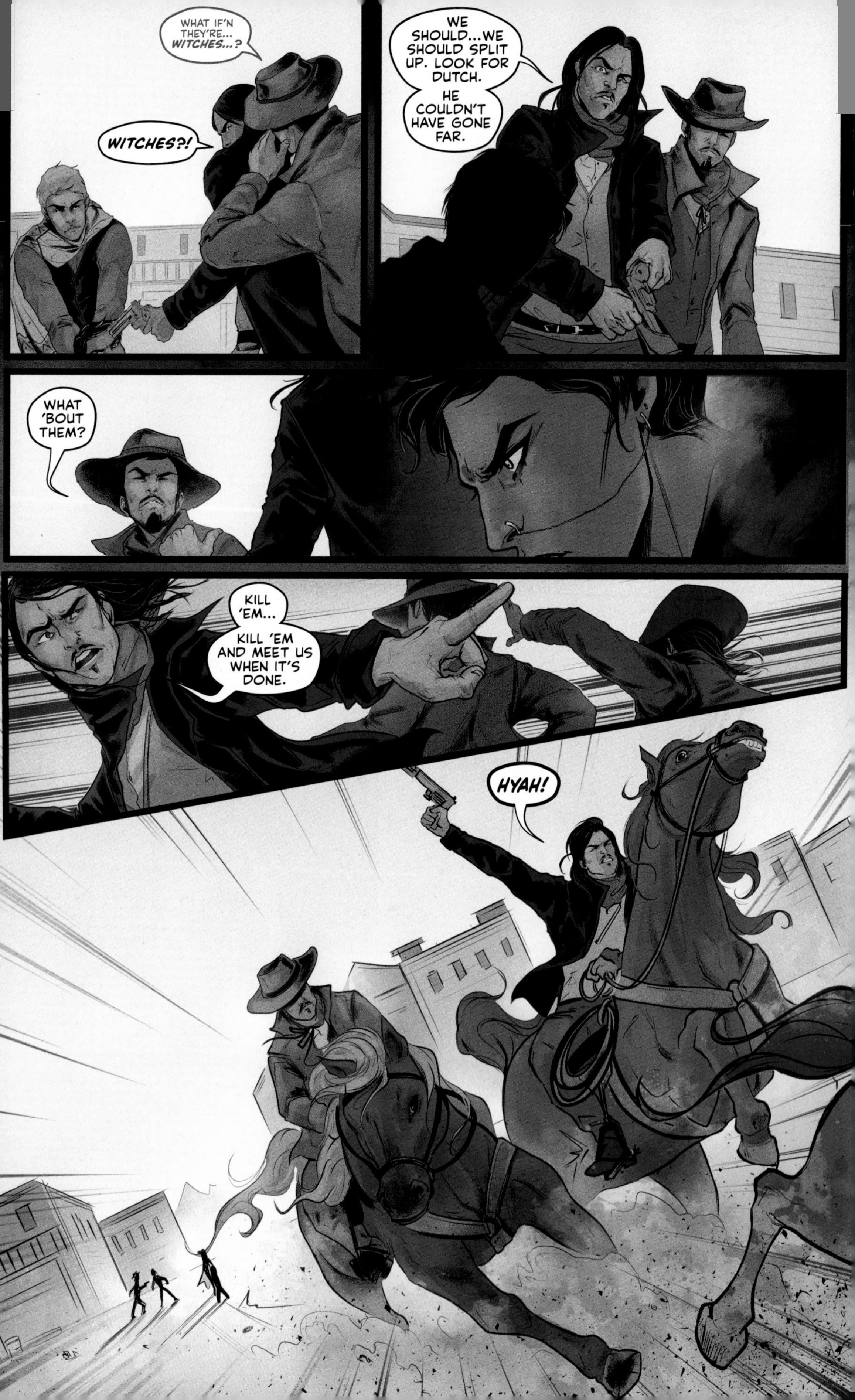
WHAT IF'N THEY'RE... *WITCHES...?*
WITCHES?!
WE SHOULD...WE SHOULD SPLIT UP. LOOK FOR DUTCH.
HE COULDN'T HAVE GONE FAR.
WHAT 'BOUT THEM?
KILL 'EM...
KILL 'EM AND MEET US WHEN IT'S DONE.
HYAH!

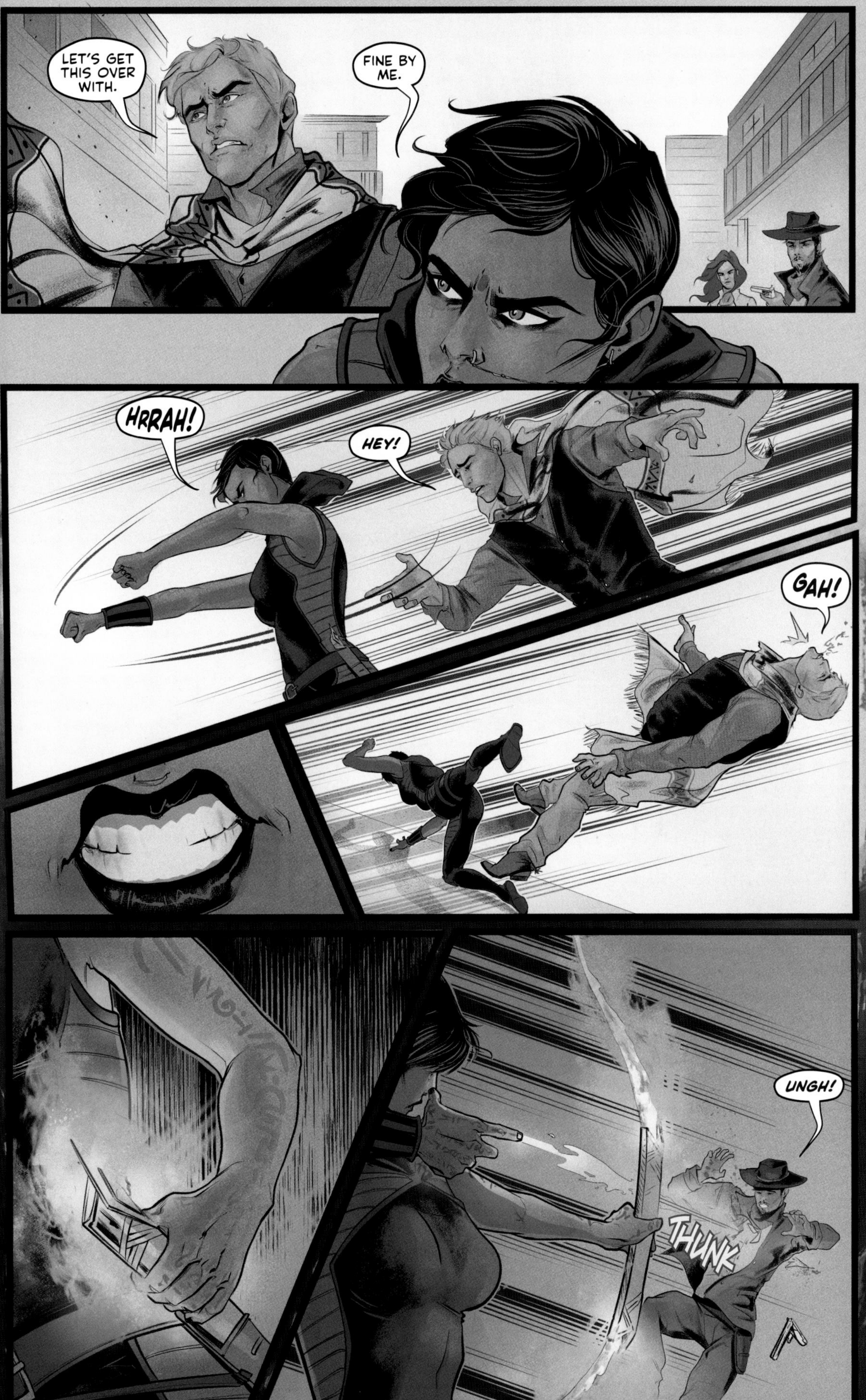
LET'S GET THIS OVER WITH.
FINE BY ME.
HRRAH!
HEY!
GAH!
UNGH!
THUNK

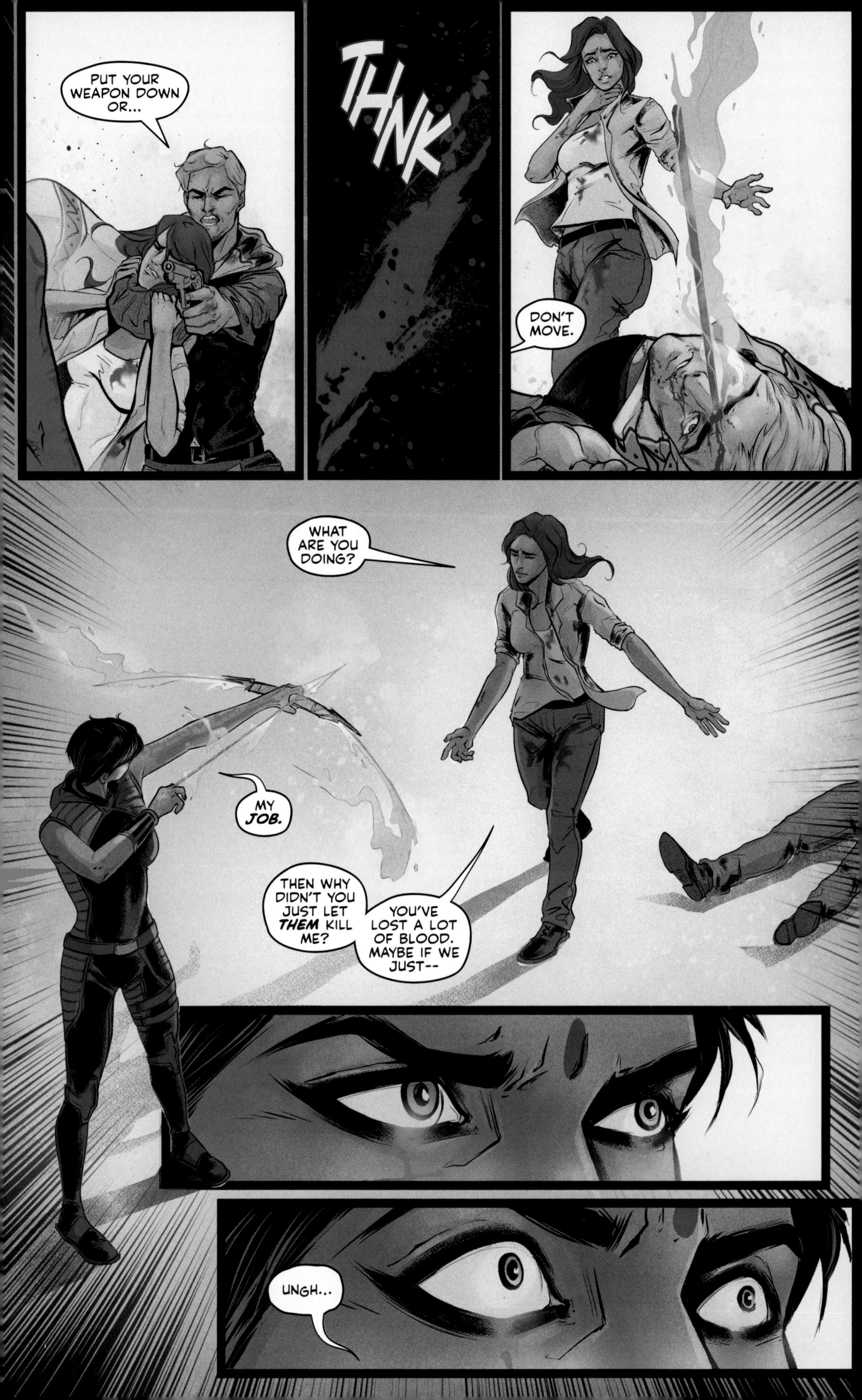
PUT YOUR WEAPON DOWN OR...
THNK
DON'T MOVE.
WHAT ARE YOU DOING?
MY *JOB.*
YOU'VE LOST A LOT OF BLOOD. MAYBE IF WE JUST--
THEN WHY DIDN'T YOU JUST LET *THEM* KILL ME?
UNGH...

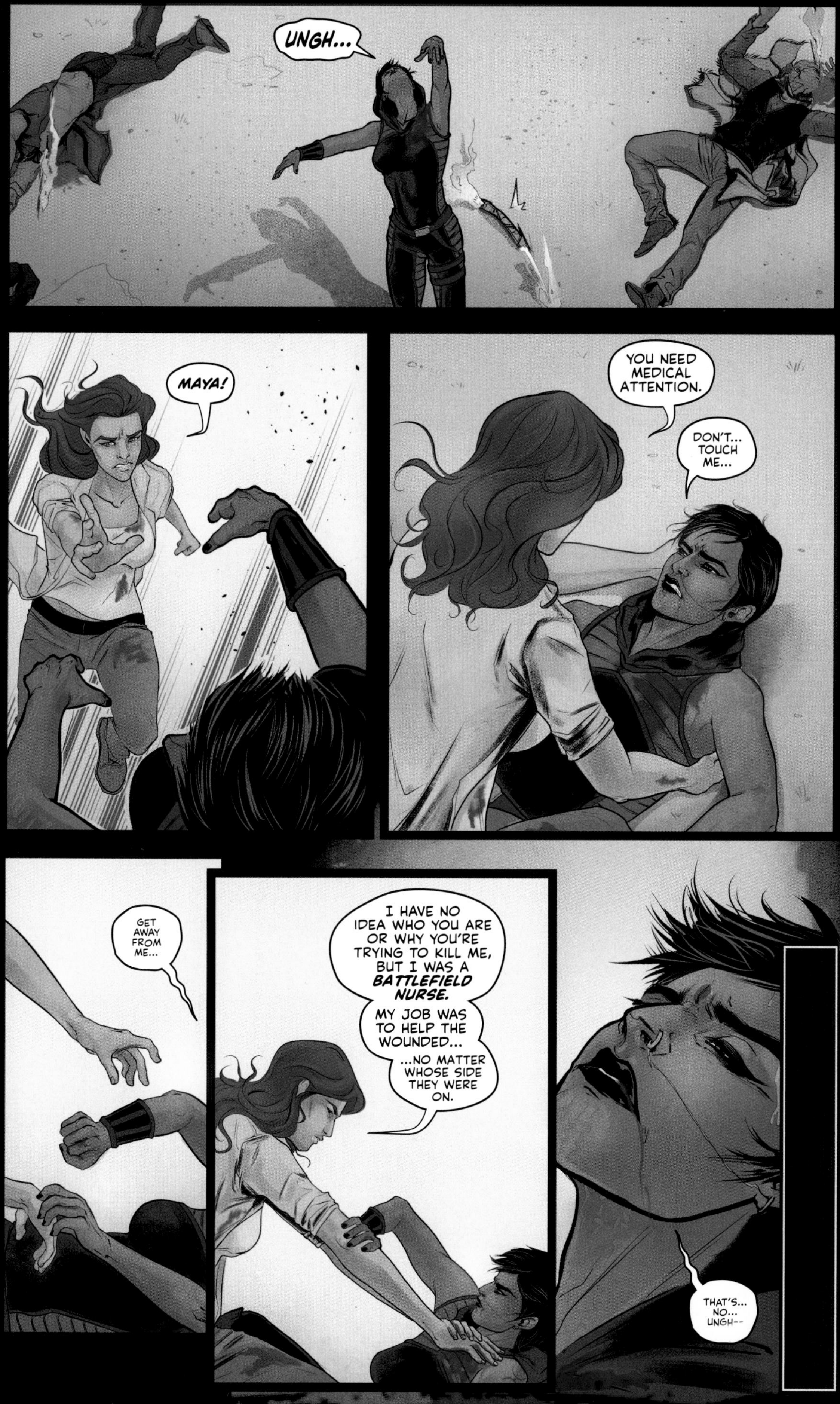
UNGH...
MAYA!
YOU NEED MEDICAL ATTENTION.
DON'T... TOUCH ME...
GET AWAY FROM ME...
I HAVE NO IDEA WHO YOU ARE OR WHY YOU'RE TRYING TO KILL ME, BUT I WAS A BATTLEFIELD NURSE.
MY JOB WAS TO HELP THE WOUNDED...
...NO MATTER WHOSE SIDE THEY WERE ON.
THAT'S... NO... UNGH--

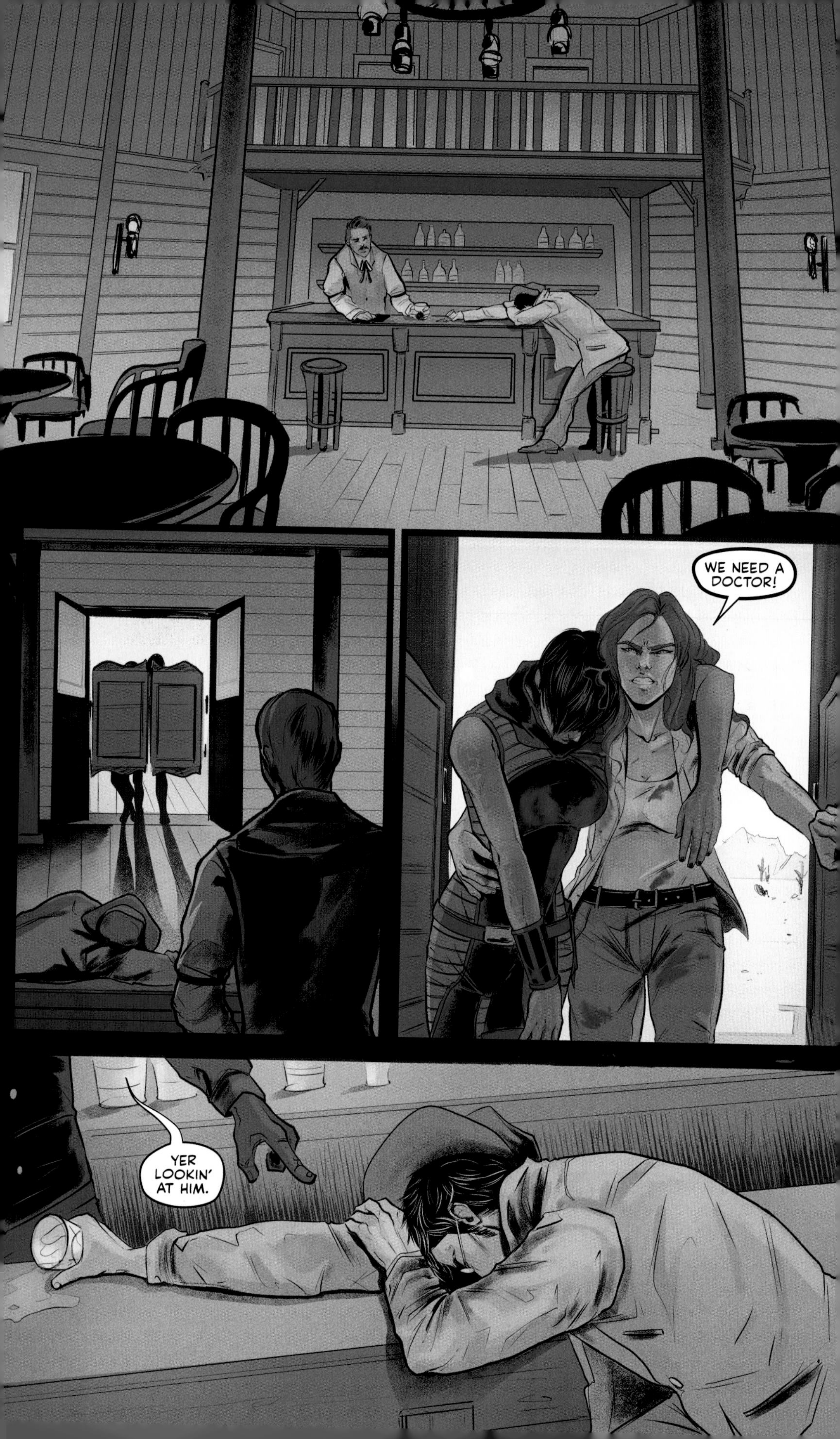
WE NEED A DOCTOR!
YER LOOKIN' AT HIM.

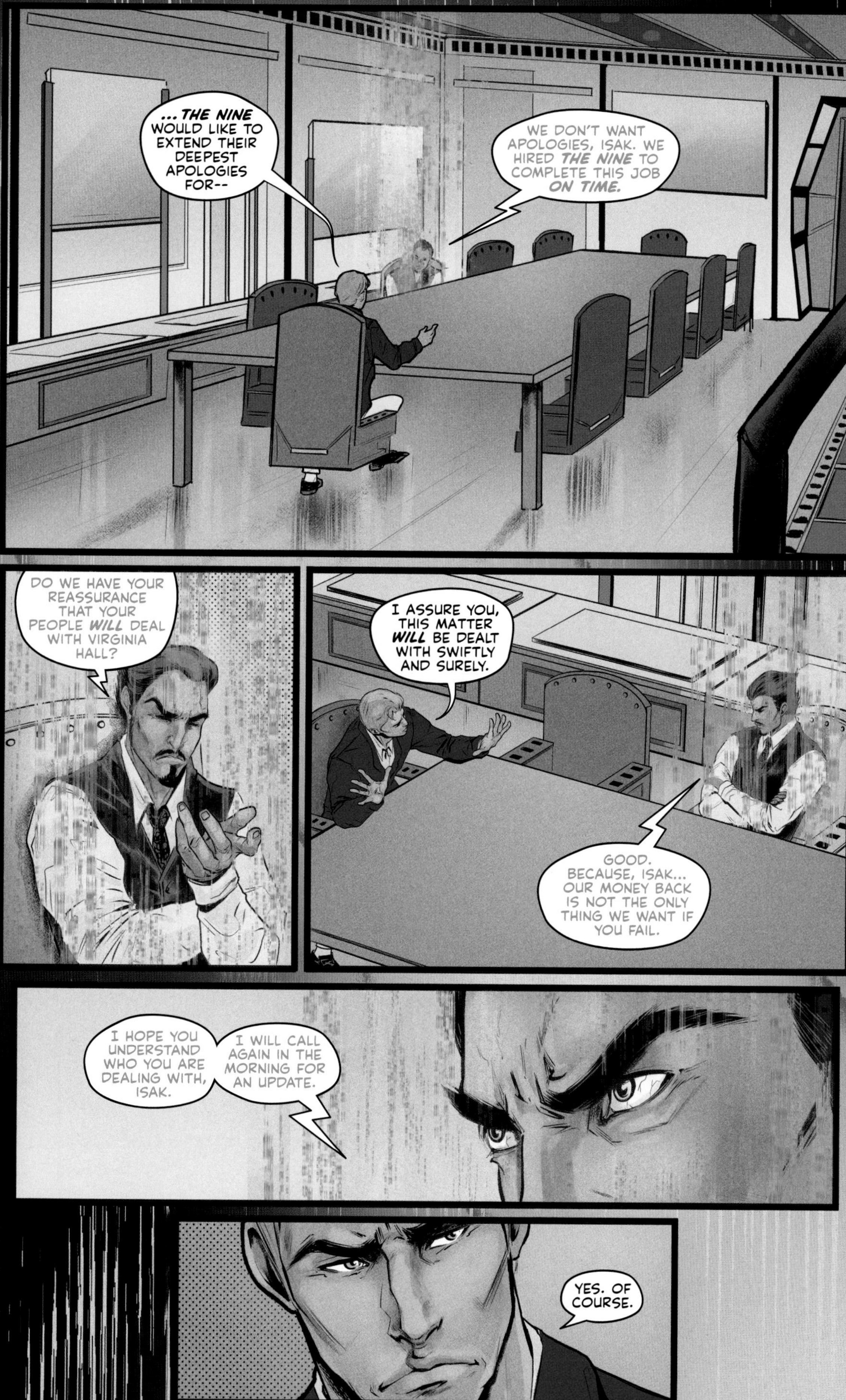
...THE NINE WOULD LIKE TO EXTEND THEIR DEEPEST APOLOGIES FOR--
WE DON'T WANT APOLOGIES, ISAK. WE HIRED THE NINE TO COMPLETE THIS JOB ON TIME.
DO WE HAVE YOUR REASSURANCE THAT YOUR PEOPLE WILL DEAL WITH VIRGINIA HALL?
I ASSURE YOU, THIS MATTER WILL BE DEALT WITH SWIFTLY AND SURELY.
GOOD. BECAUSE, ISAK... OUR MONEY BACK IS NOT THE ONLY THING WE WANT IF YOU FAIL.
I HOPE YOU UNDERSTAND WHO YOU ARE DEALING WITH, ISAK.
I WILL CALL AGAIN IN THE MORNING FOR AN UPDATE.
YES. OF COURSE.

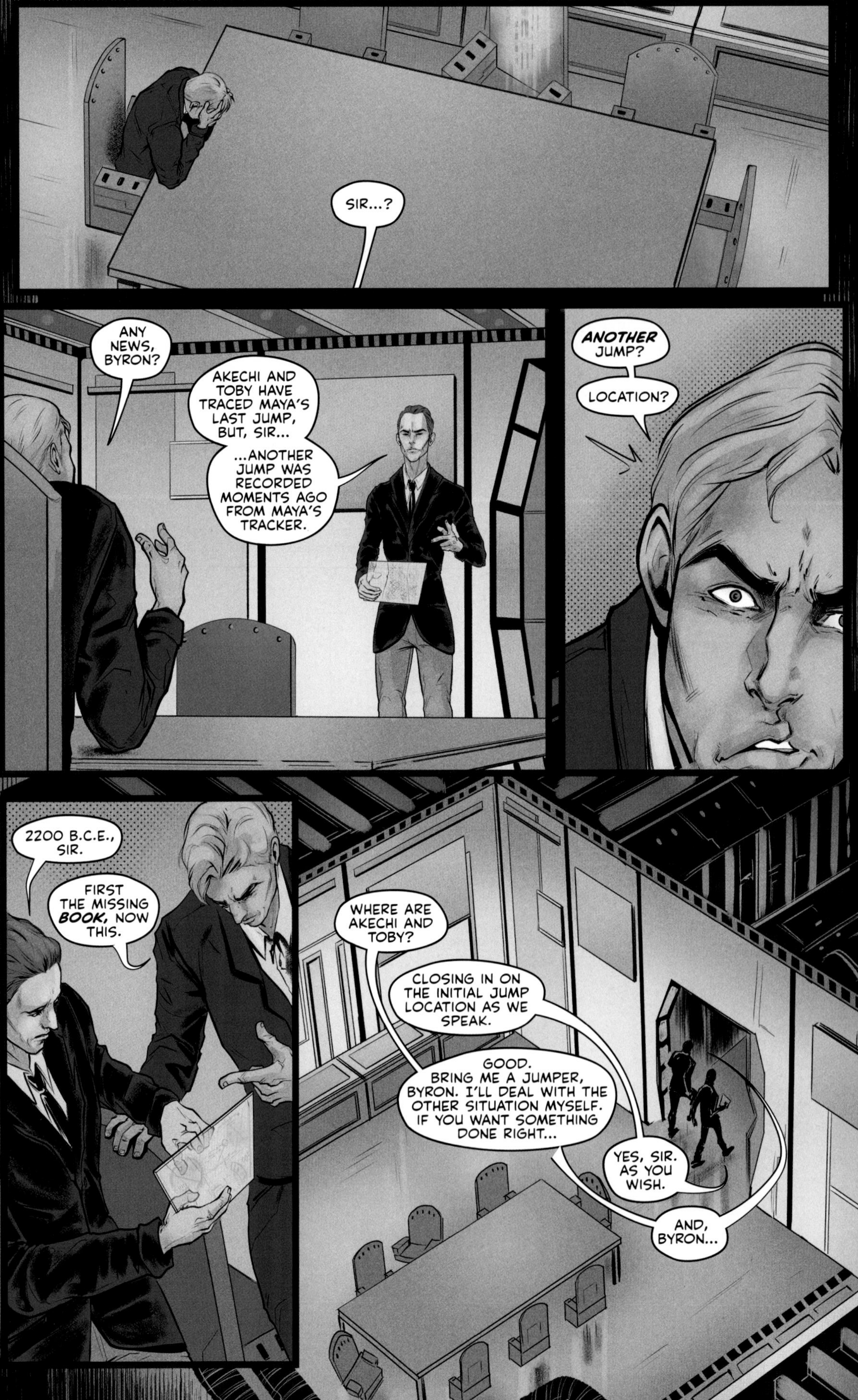
SIR...?
ANY NEWS, BYRON?
AKECHI AND TOBY HAVE TRACED MAYA'S LAST JUMP, BUT, SIR...
...ANOTHER JUMP WAS RECORDED MOMENTS AGO FROM MAYA'S TRACKER.
ANOTHER JUMP?
LOCATION?
2200 B.C.E., SIR.
FIRST THE MISSING *BOOK,* NOW THIS.
WHERE ARE AKECHI AND TOBY?
CLOSING IN ON THE INITIAL JUMP LOCATION AS WE SPEAK.
GOOD. BRING ME A JUMPER, BYRON. I'LL DEAL WITH THE OTHER SITUATION MYSELF. IF YOU WANT SOMETHING DONE RIGHT...
YES, SIR. AS YOU WISH.
AND, BYRON...

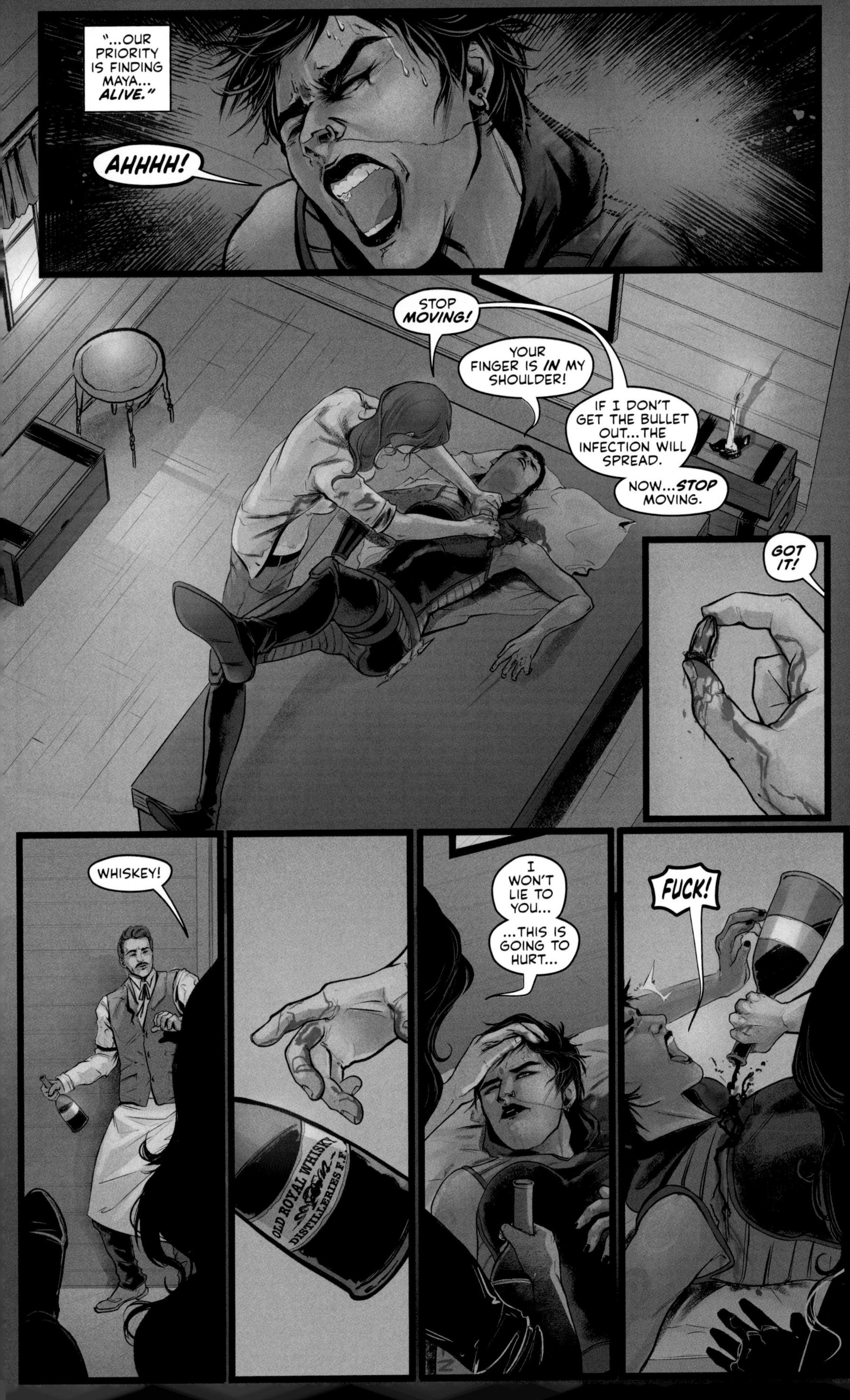
"...OUR PRIORITY IS FINDING MAYA... ALIVE."
AHHHH!
STOP MOVING!
YOUR FINGER IS IN MY SHOULDER!
IF I DON'T GET THE BULLET OUT...THE INFECTION WILL SPREAD.
NOW...STOP MOVING.
GOT IT!
WHISKEY!
OLD ROYAL WHISKY
DISTILLERIES F.F.
I WON'T LIE TO YOU...
...THIS IS GOING TO HURT...
FUCK!

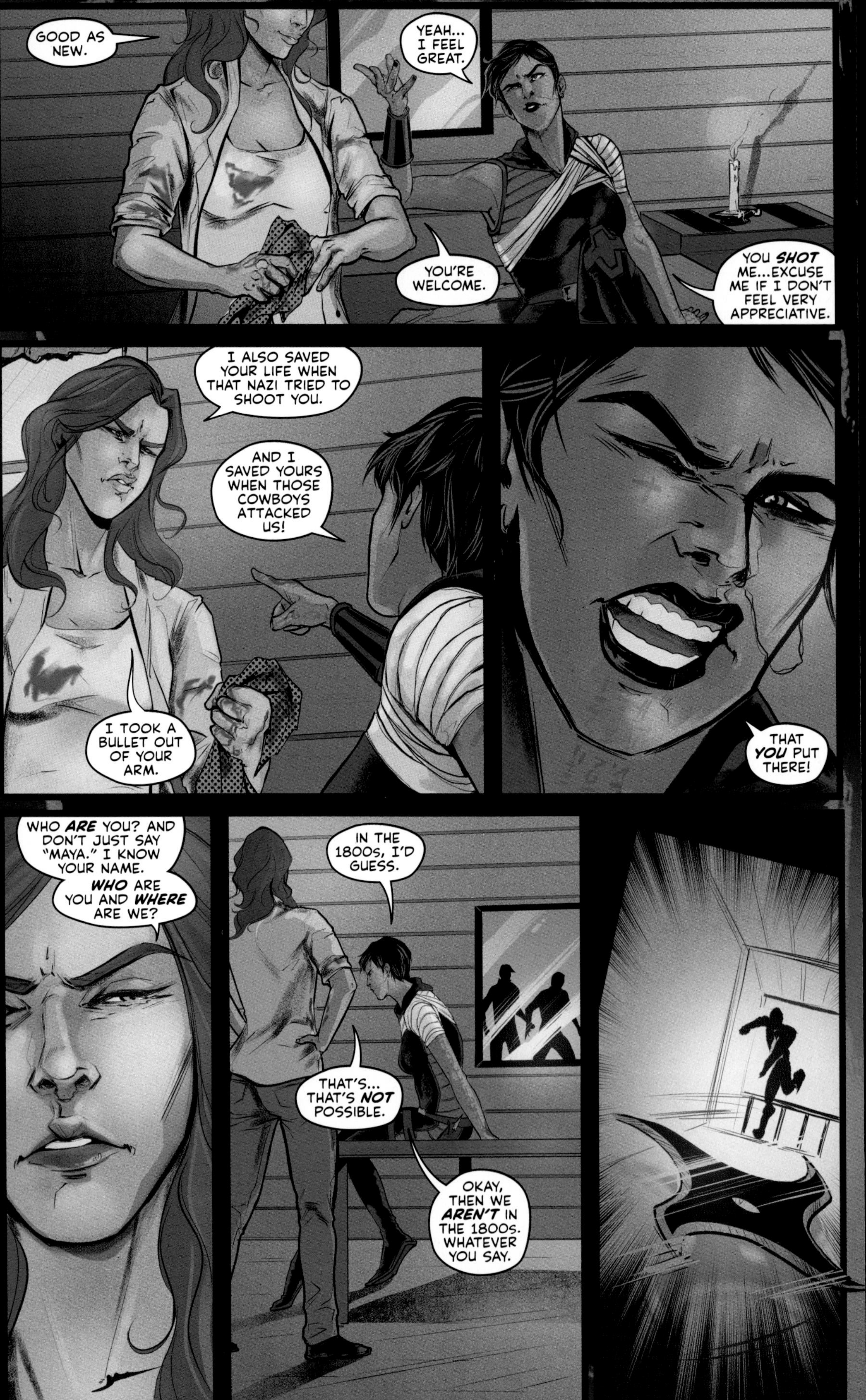
GOOD AS NEW.
YEAH... I FEEL GREAT.
YOU'RE WELCOME.
YOU **SHOT** ME...EXCUSE ME IF I DON'T FEEL VERY APPRECIATIVE.
I ALSO SAVED YOUR LIFE WHEN THAT NAZI TRIED TO SHOOT YOU.
AND I SAVED YOURS WHEN THOSE COWBOYS ATTACKED US!
I TOOK A BULLET OUT OF YOUR ARM.
THAT **YOU** PUT THERE!
WHO **ARE** YOU? AND DON'T JUST SAY "MAYA." I KNOW YOUR NAME. **WHO** ARE YOU AND **WHERE** ARE WE?
IN THE 1800S, I'D GUESS.
THAT'S... THAT'S **NOT** POSSIBLE.
OKAY, THEN WE **AREN'T** IN THE 1800S. WHATEVER YOU SAY.

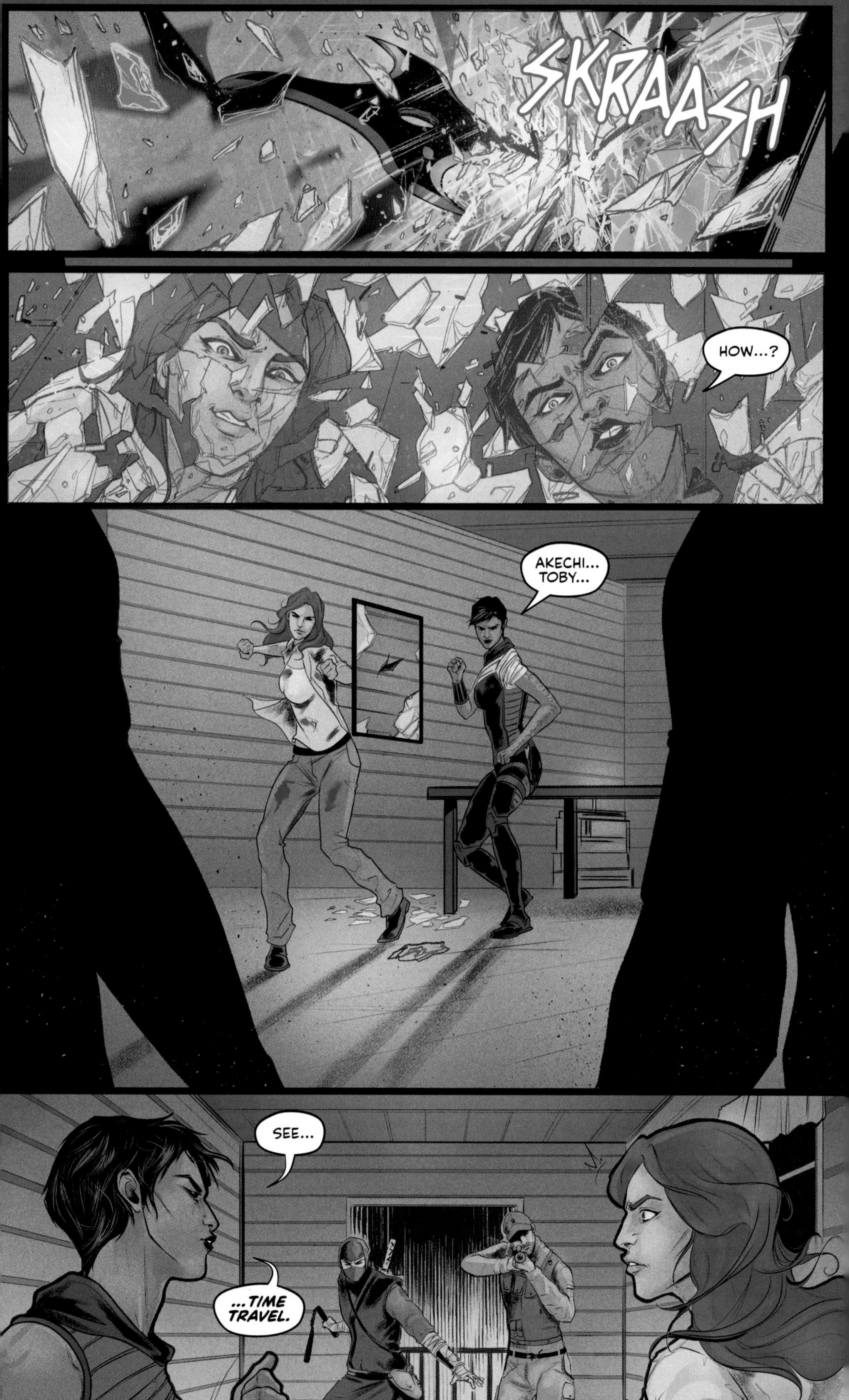
SKRAASH
HOW...?
AKECHI... TOBY...
SEE...
...TIME TRAVEL.

4

WE DON'T ASK WHY

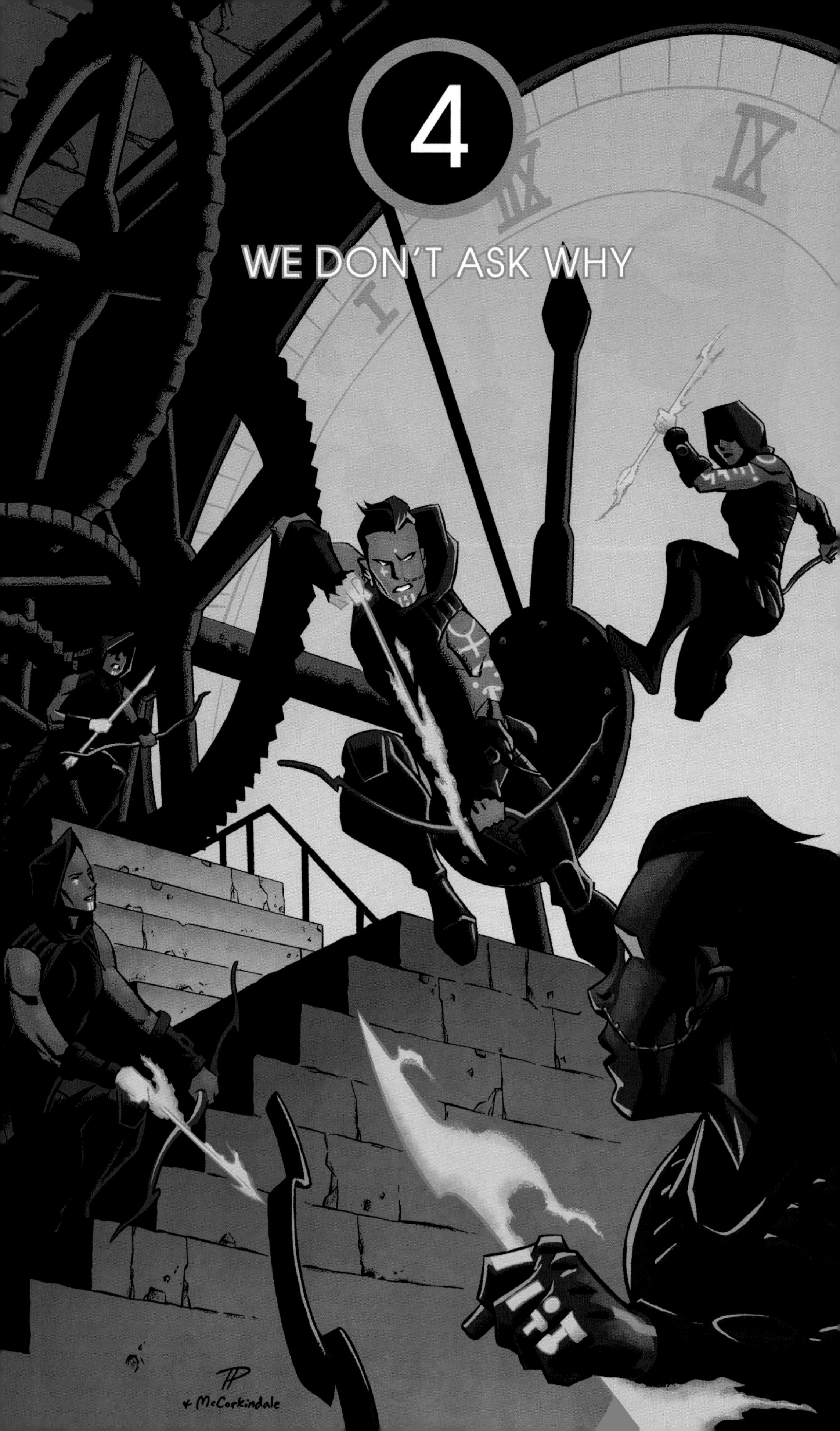
+ McCorkindale

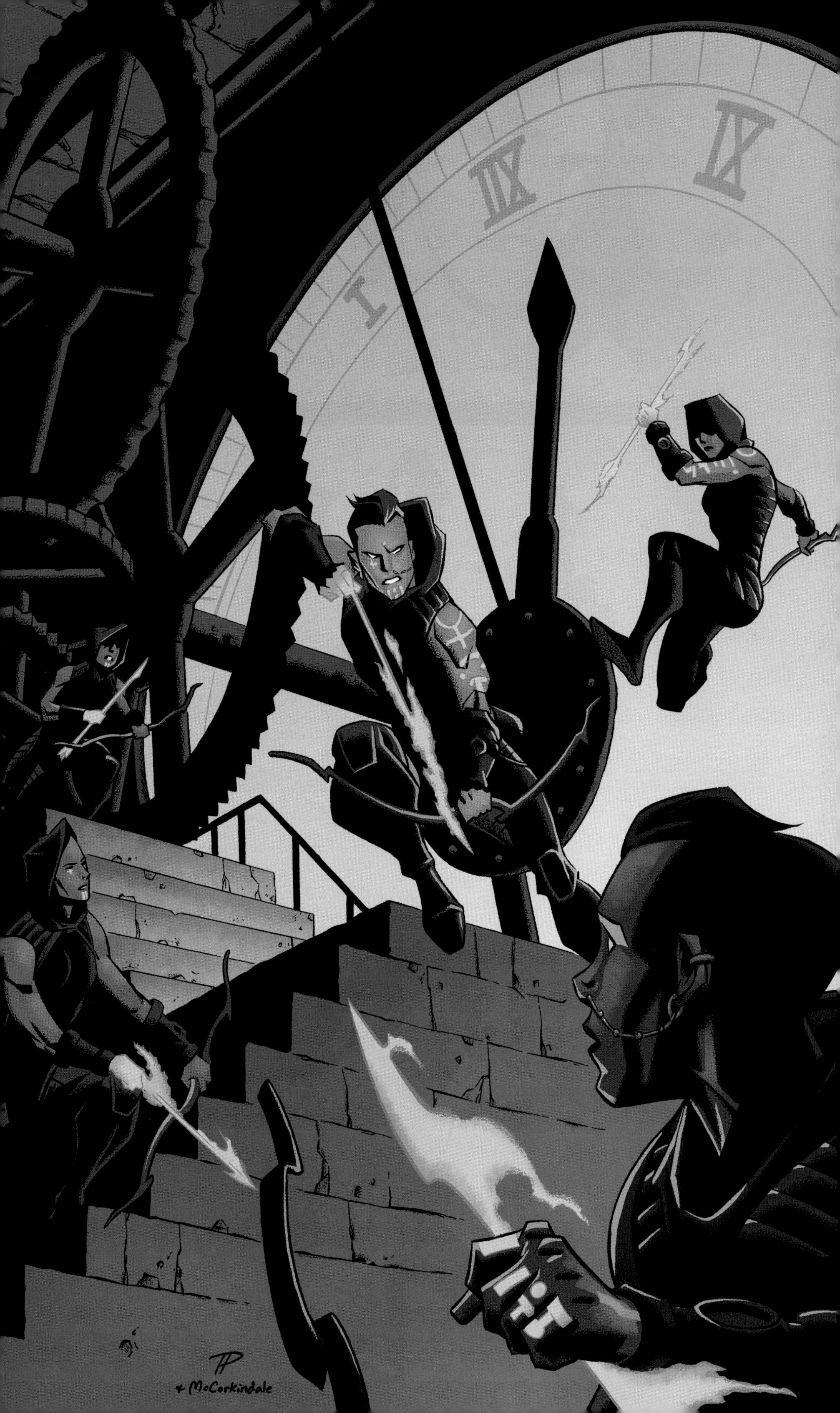
TP
& McCorkindale

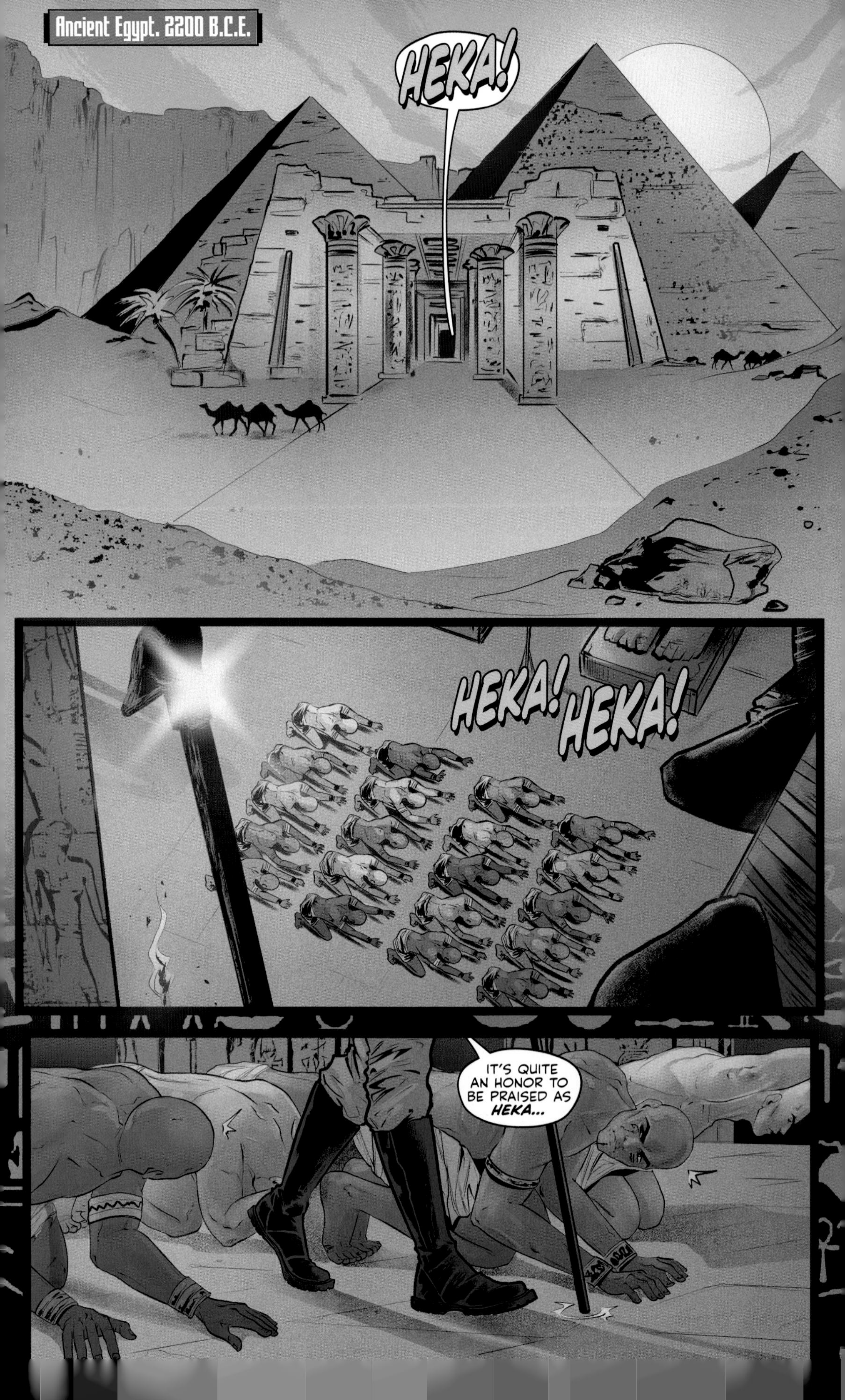
Ancient Egypt. 2200 B.C.E.
HEKA!
HEKA! HEKA!
IT'S QUITE AN HONOR TO BE PRAISED AS HEKA...

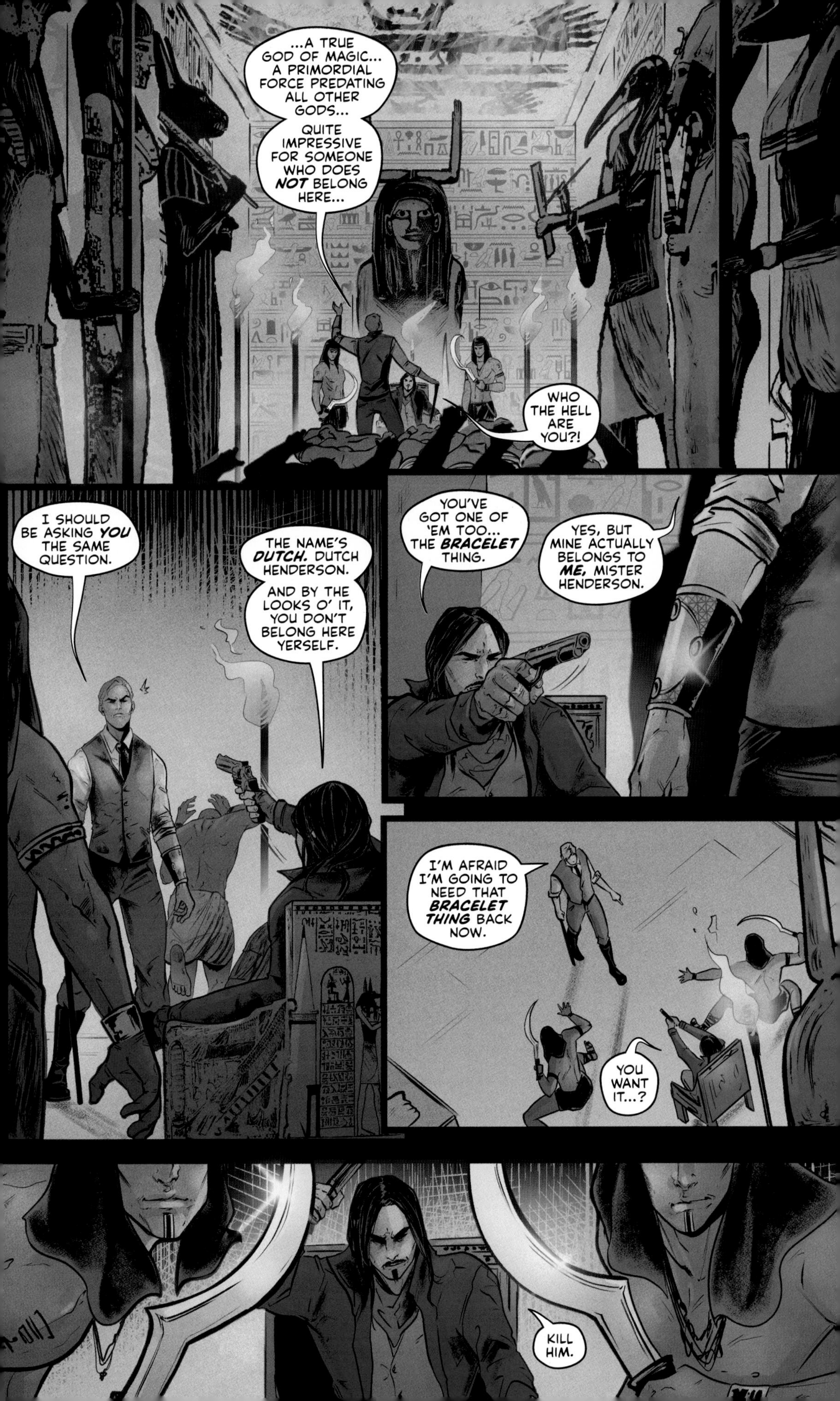
...A TRUE GOD OF MAGIC... A PRIMORDIAL FORCE PREDATING ALL OTHER GODS...
QUITE IMPRESSIVE FOR SOMEONE WHO DOES NOT BELONG HERE...
WHO THE HELL ARE YOU?!
I SHOULD BE ASKING YOU THE SAME QUESTION.
THE NAME'S DUTCH. DUTCH HENDERSON.
AND BY THE LOOKS O' IT, YOU DON'T BELONG HERE YERSELF.
YOU'VE GOT ONE OF 'EM TOO... THE BRACELET THING.
YES, BUT MINE ACTUALLY BELONGS TO ME, MISTER HENDERSON.
I'M AFRAID I'M GOING TO NEED THAT BRACELET THING BACK NOW.
YOU WANT IT...?
KILL HIM.

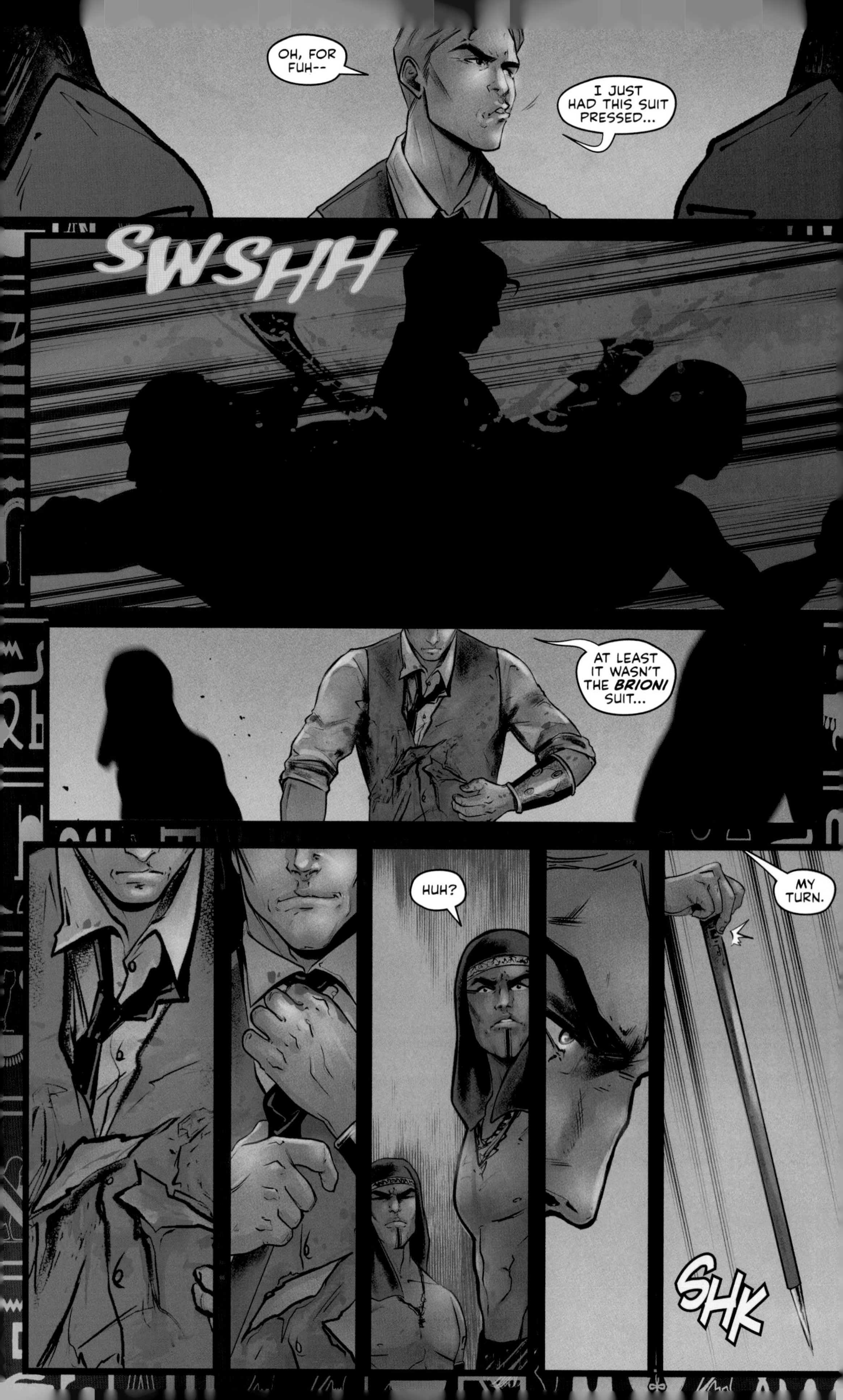
OH, FOR FUH--
I JUST HAD THIS SUIT PRESSED...
SWSHH
AT LEAST IT WASN'T THE BRIONI SUIT...
HUH?
MY TURN.
SHK

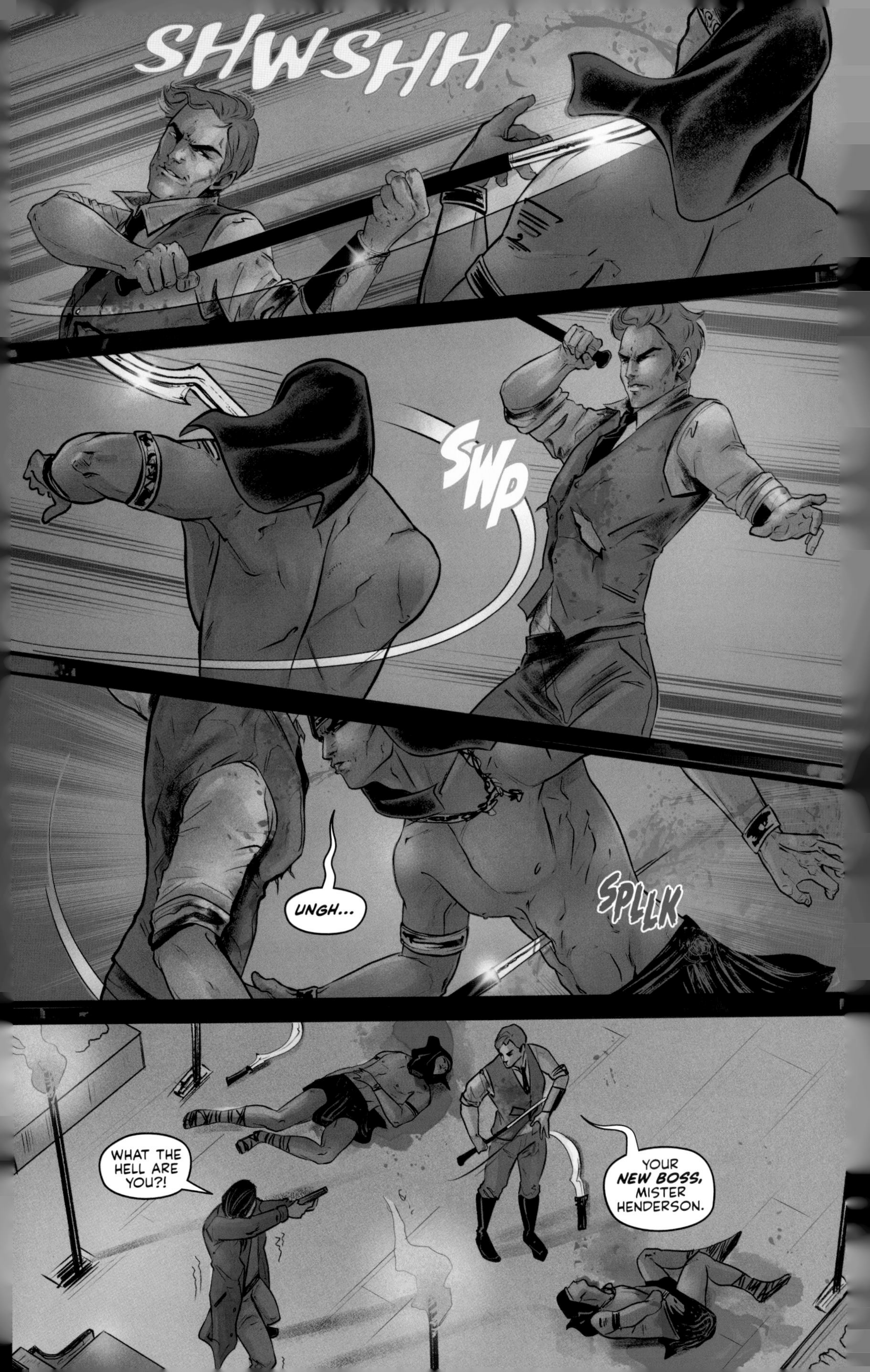
SHWSHH
SWP
UNGH...
SPLLK
WHAT THE HELL ARE YOU?!
YOUR NEW BOSS, MISTER HENDERSON.

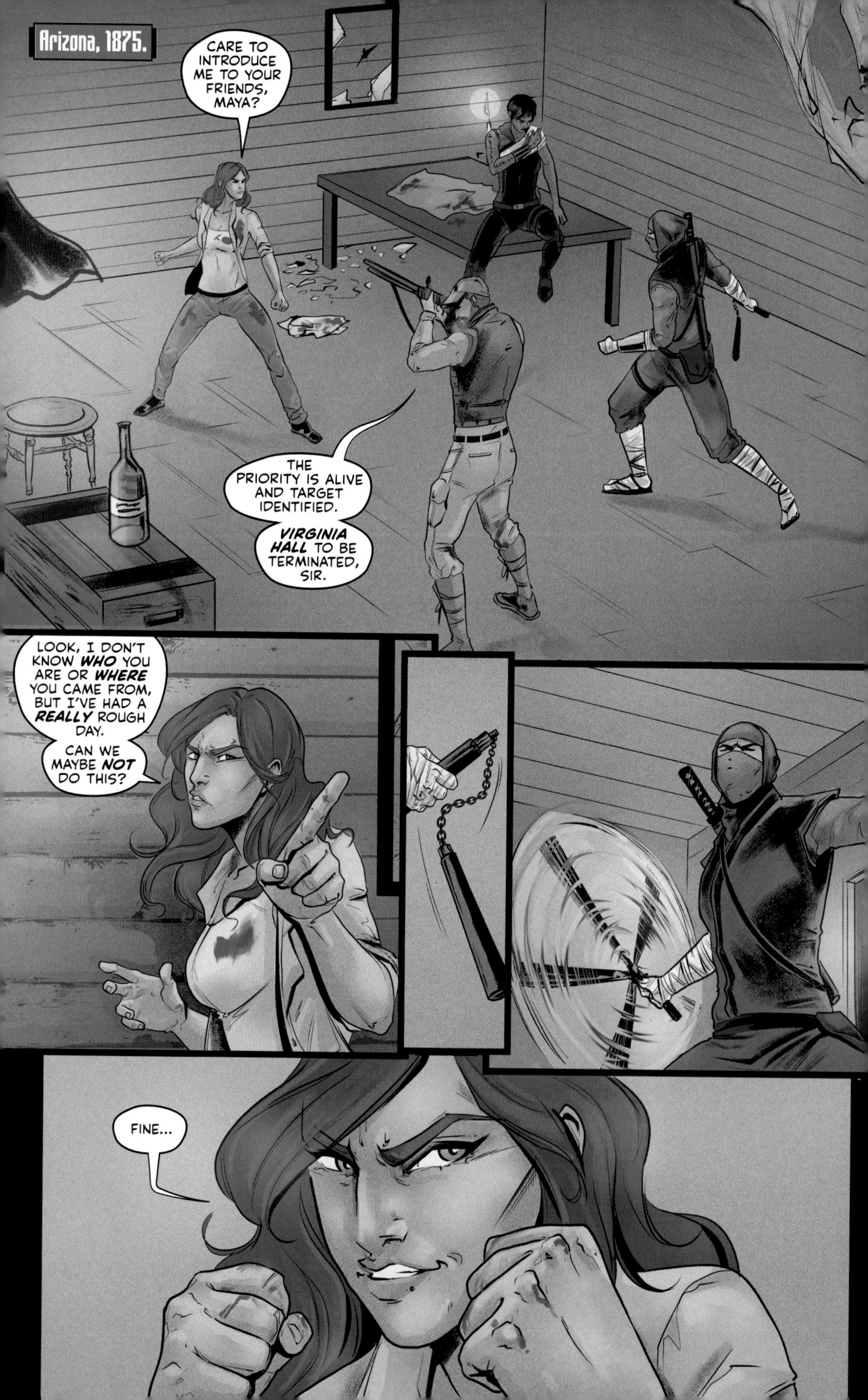

Arizona, 1875.
CARE TO INTRODUCE ME TO YOUR FRIENDS, MAYA?
THE PRIORITY IS ALIVE AND TARGET IDENTIFIED.
VIRGINIA HALL TO BE TERMINATED, SIR.
LOOK, I DON'T KNOW WHO YOU ARE OR WHERE YOU CAME FROM, BUT I'VE HAD A REALLY ROUGH DAY.
CAN WE MAYBE NOT DO THIS?
FINE...

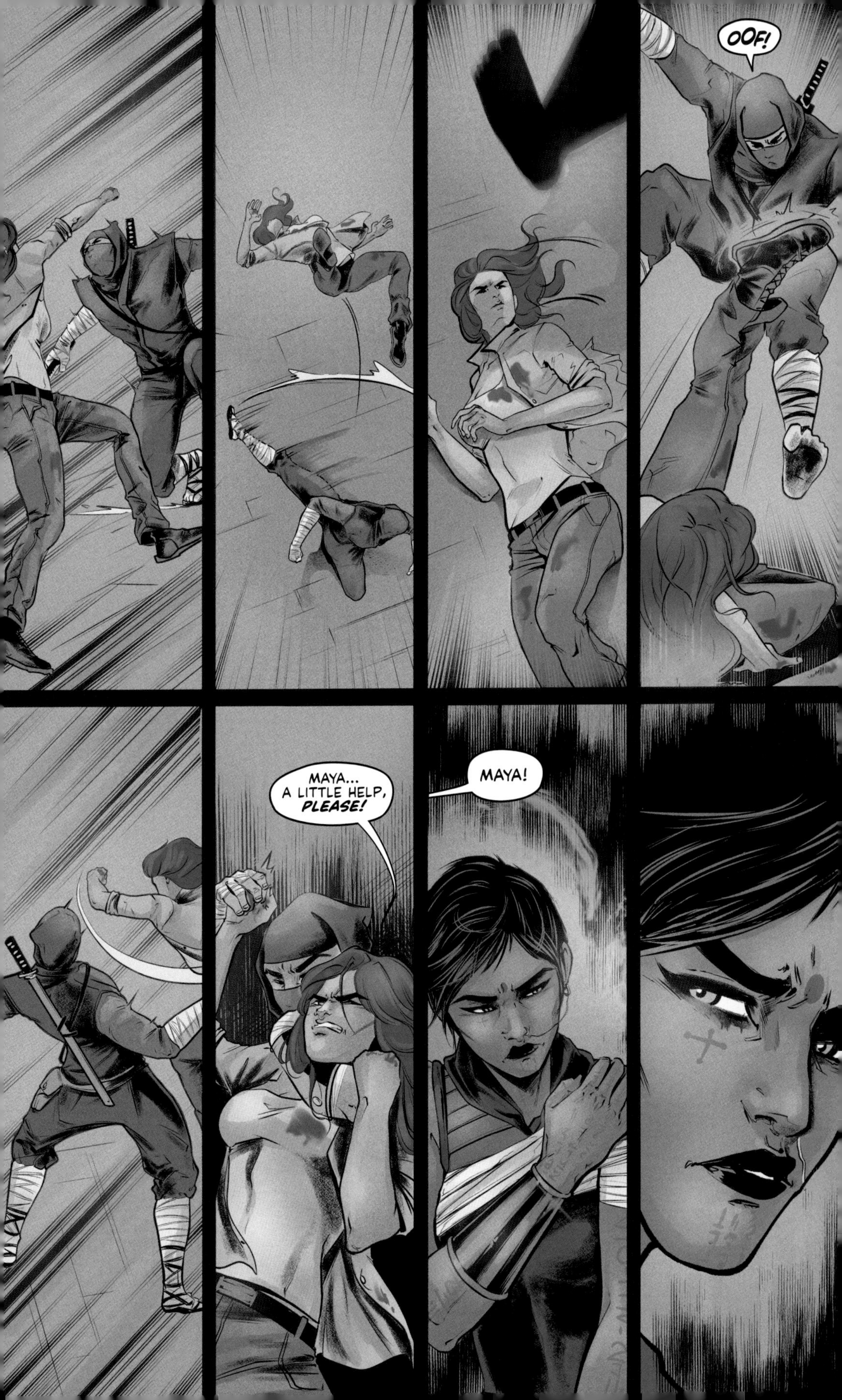

OOF!
MAYA... A LITTLE HELP, PLEASE!
MAYA!

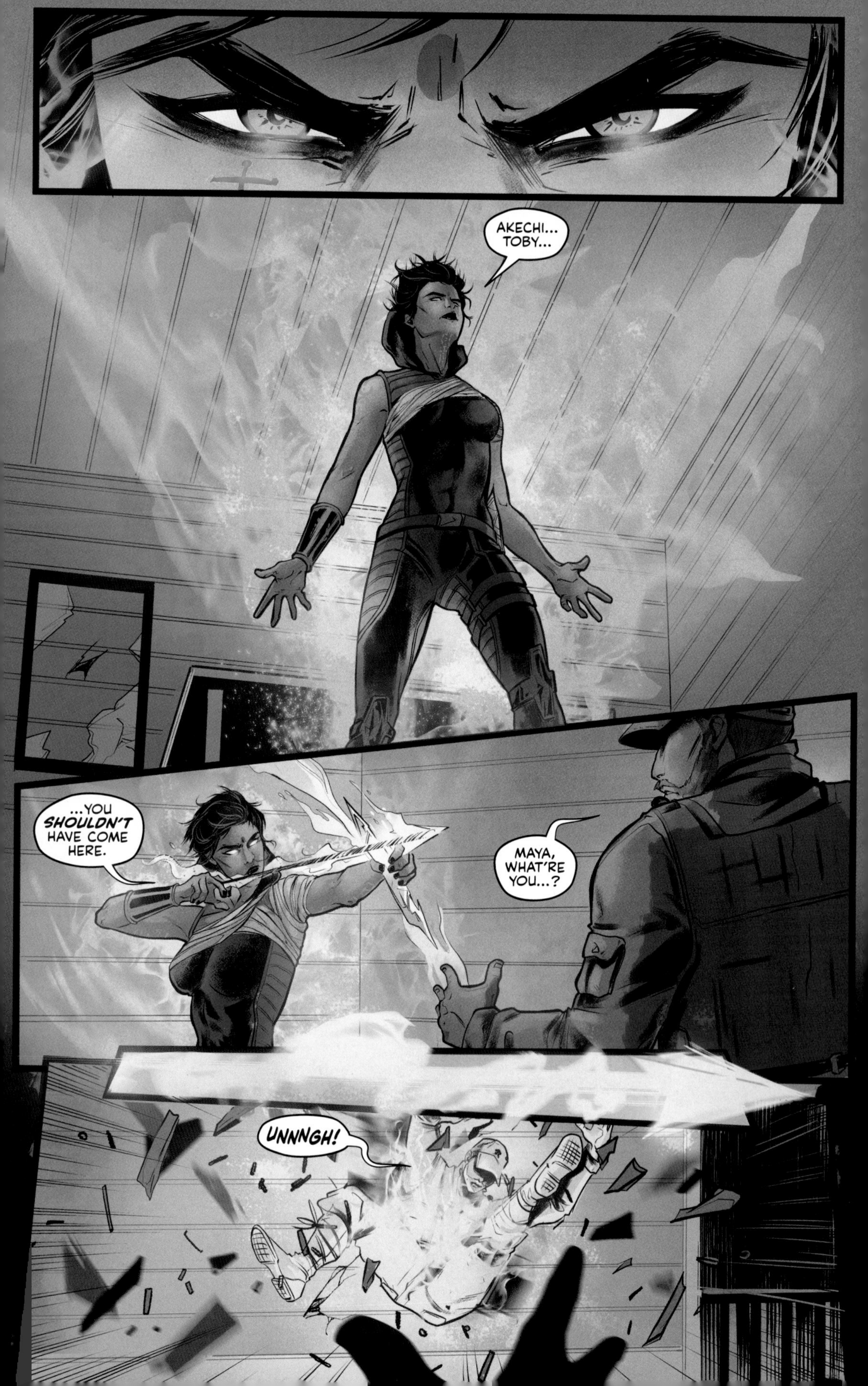
AKECHI... TOBY...
...YOU SHOULDN'T HAVE COME HERE.
MAYA, WHAT'RE YOU...?
UNNNGH!

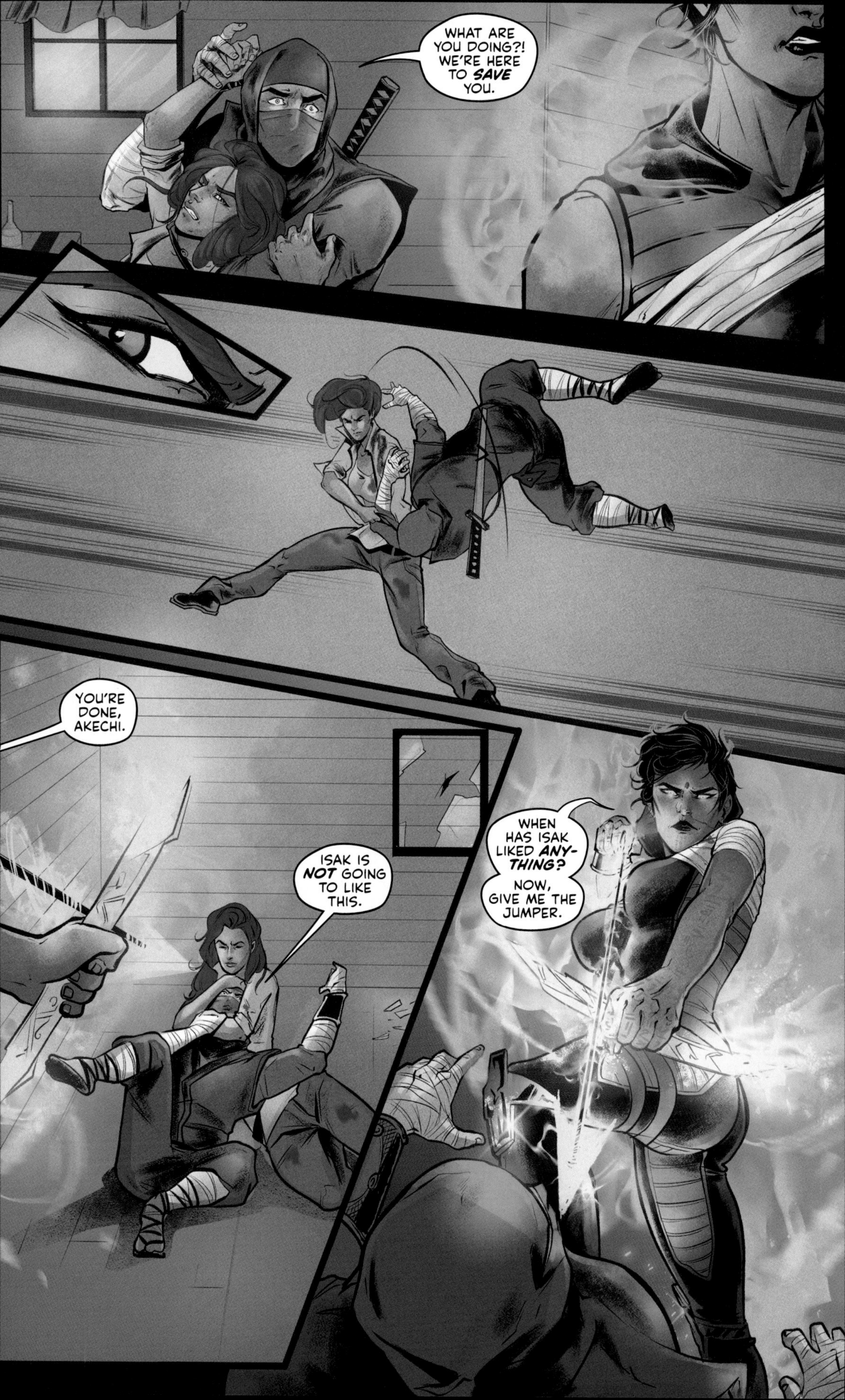
WHAT ARE YOU DOING?! WE'RE HERE TO *SAVE* YOU.
YOU'RE DONE, AKECHI.
ISAK IS *NOT* GOING TO LIKE THIS.
WHEN HAS ISAK LIKED *ANY-THING?*
NOW, GIVE ME THE JUMPER.

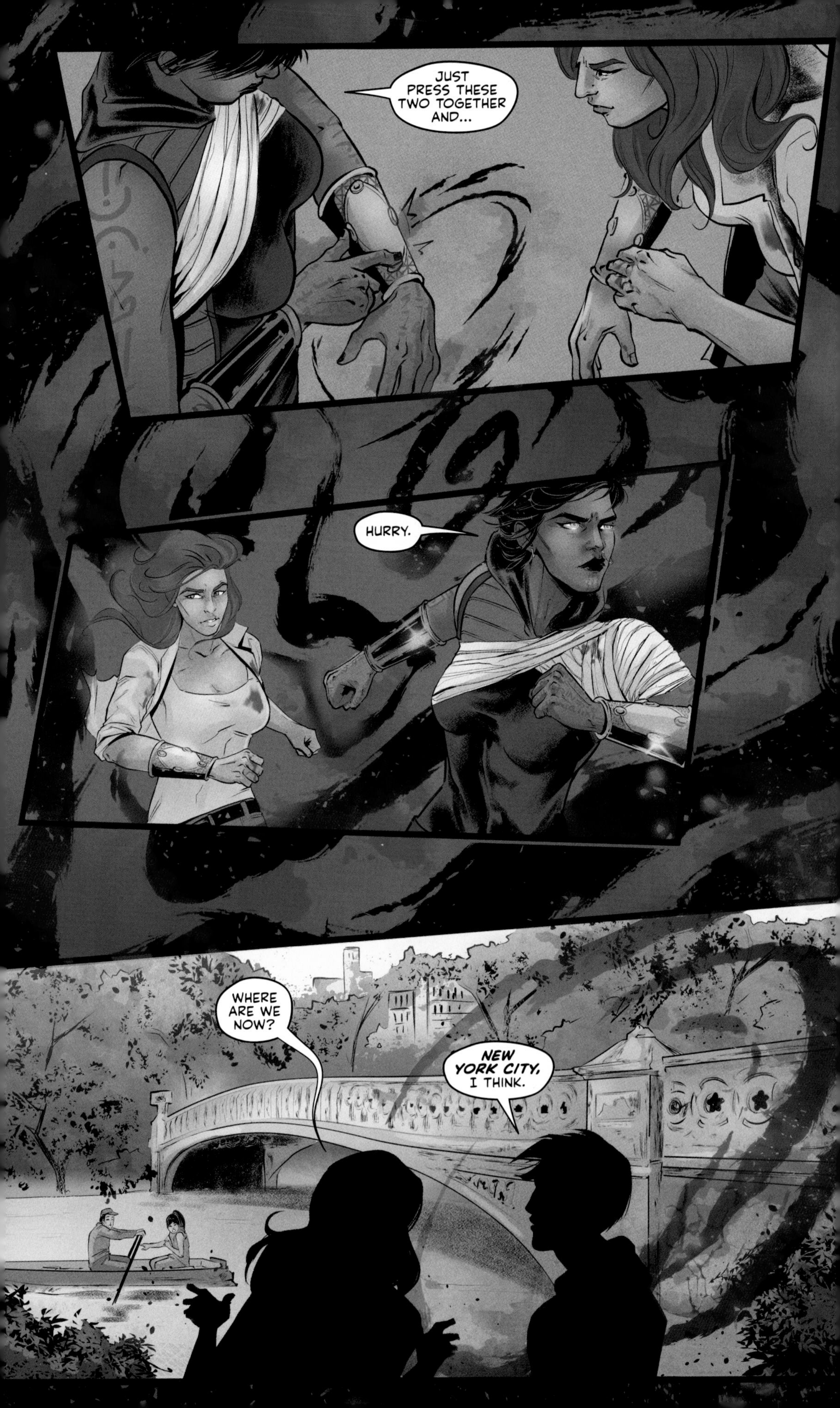
JUST PRESS THESE TWO TOGETHER AND...
HURRY.
WHERE ARE WE NOW?
NEW YORK CITY, I THINK.

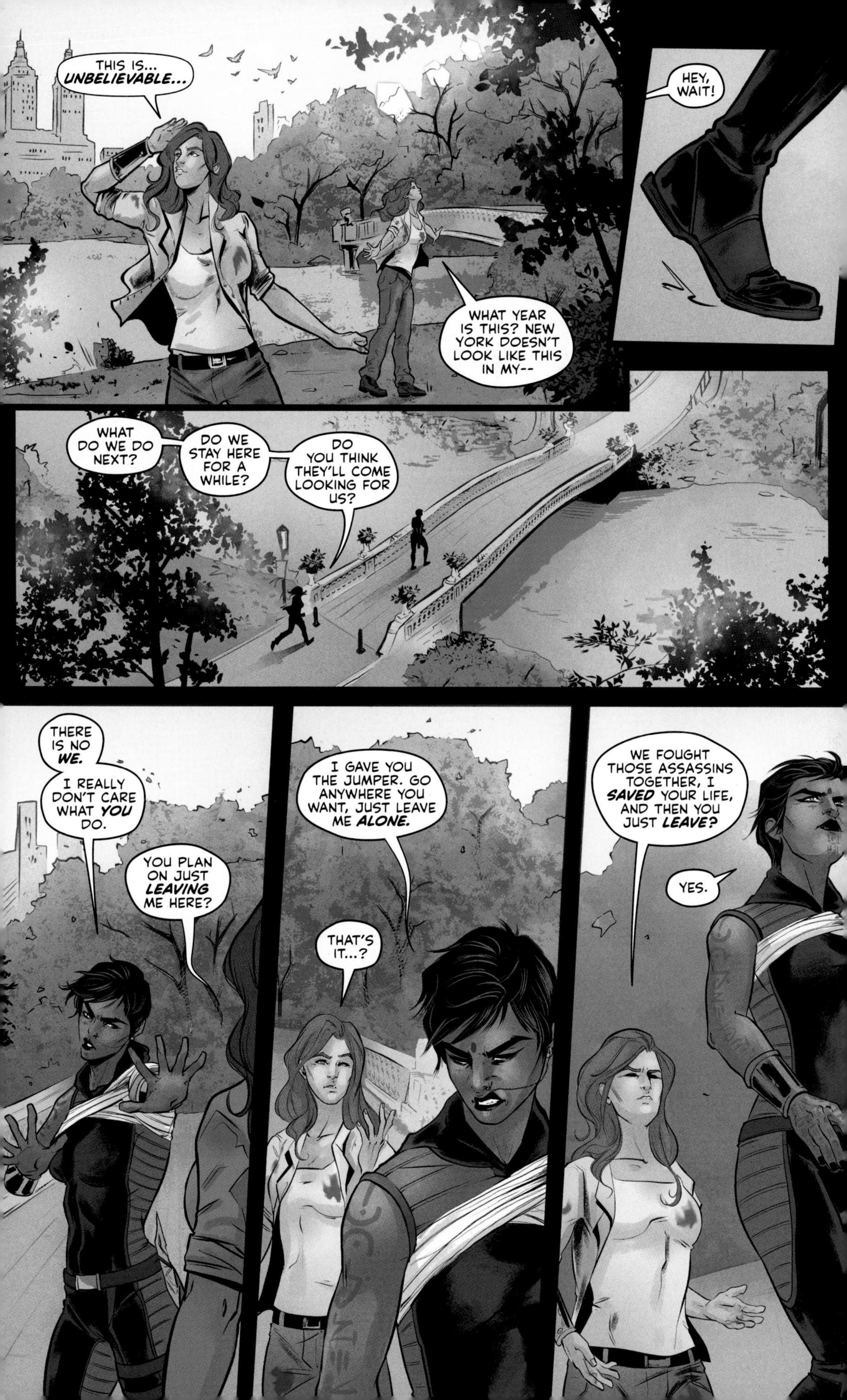
THIS IS... **UNBELIEVABLE...**
WHAT YEAR IS THIS? NEW YORK DOESN'T LOOK LIKE THIS IN MY--
HEY, WAIT!
WHAT DO WE DO NEXT?
DO WE STAY HERE FOR A WHILE?
DO YOU THINK THEY'LL COME LOOKING FOR US?
THERE IS NO **WE.**
I REALLY DON'T CARE WHAT **YOU** DO.
YOU PLAN ON JUST **LEAVING** ME HERE?
I GAVE YOU THE JUMPER. GO ANYWHERE YOU WANT, JUST LEAVE ME **ALONE.**
THAT'S IT...?
WE FOUGHT THOSE ASSASSINS TOGETHER, I **SAVED** YOUR LIFE, AND THEN YOU JUST **LEAVE?**
YES.

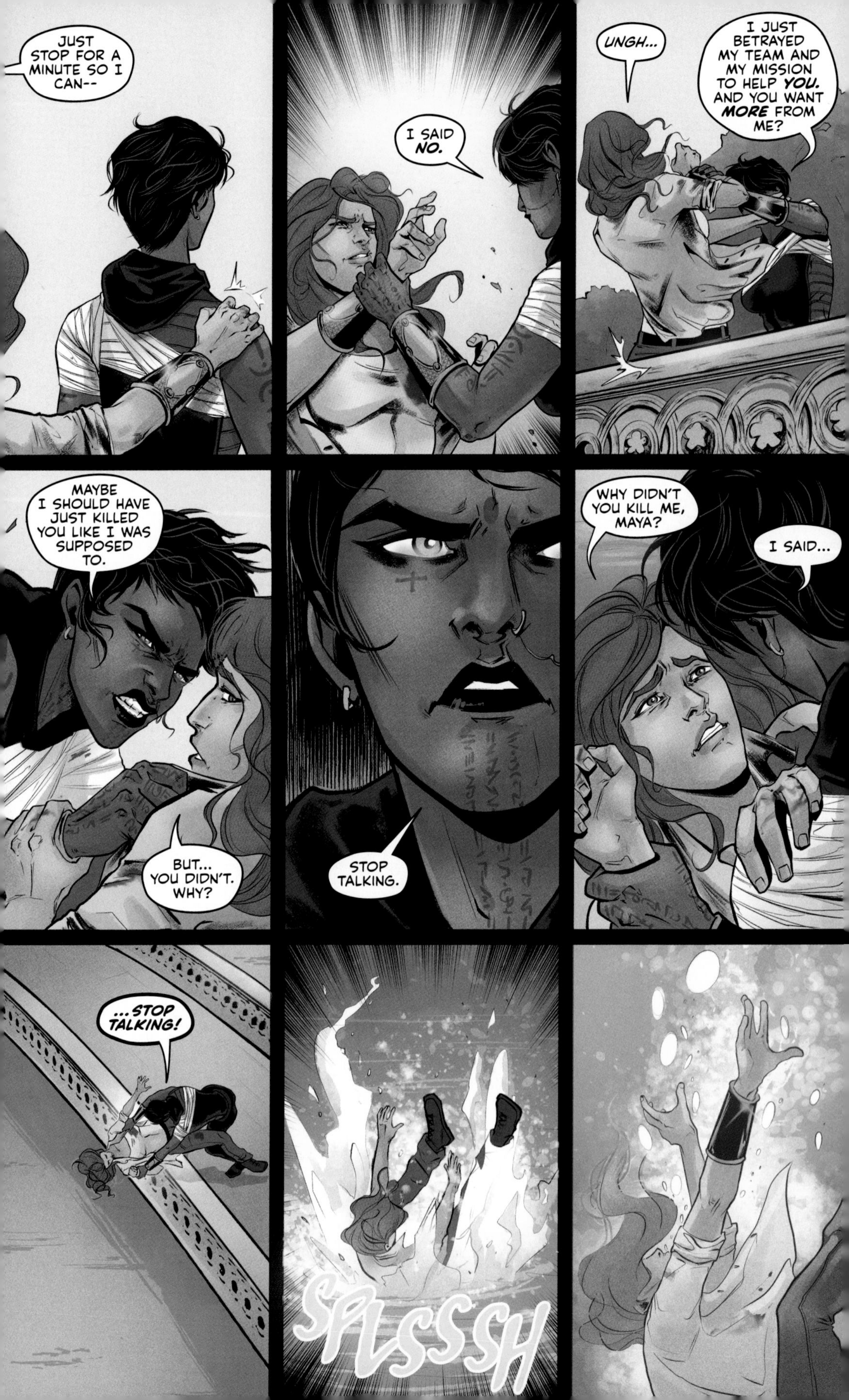
JUST STOP FOR A MINUTE SO I CAN--
I SAID NO.
UNGH...
I JUST BETRAYED MY TEAM AND MY MISSION TO HELP YOU. AND YOU WANT MORE FROM ME?
MAYBE I SHOULD HAVE JUST KILLED YOU LIKE I WAS SUPPOSED TO.
BUT... YOU DIDN'T. WHY?
STOP TALKING.
WHY DIDN'T YOU KILL ME, MAYA?
I SAID...
...STOP TALKING!
SPLSSSH

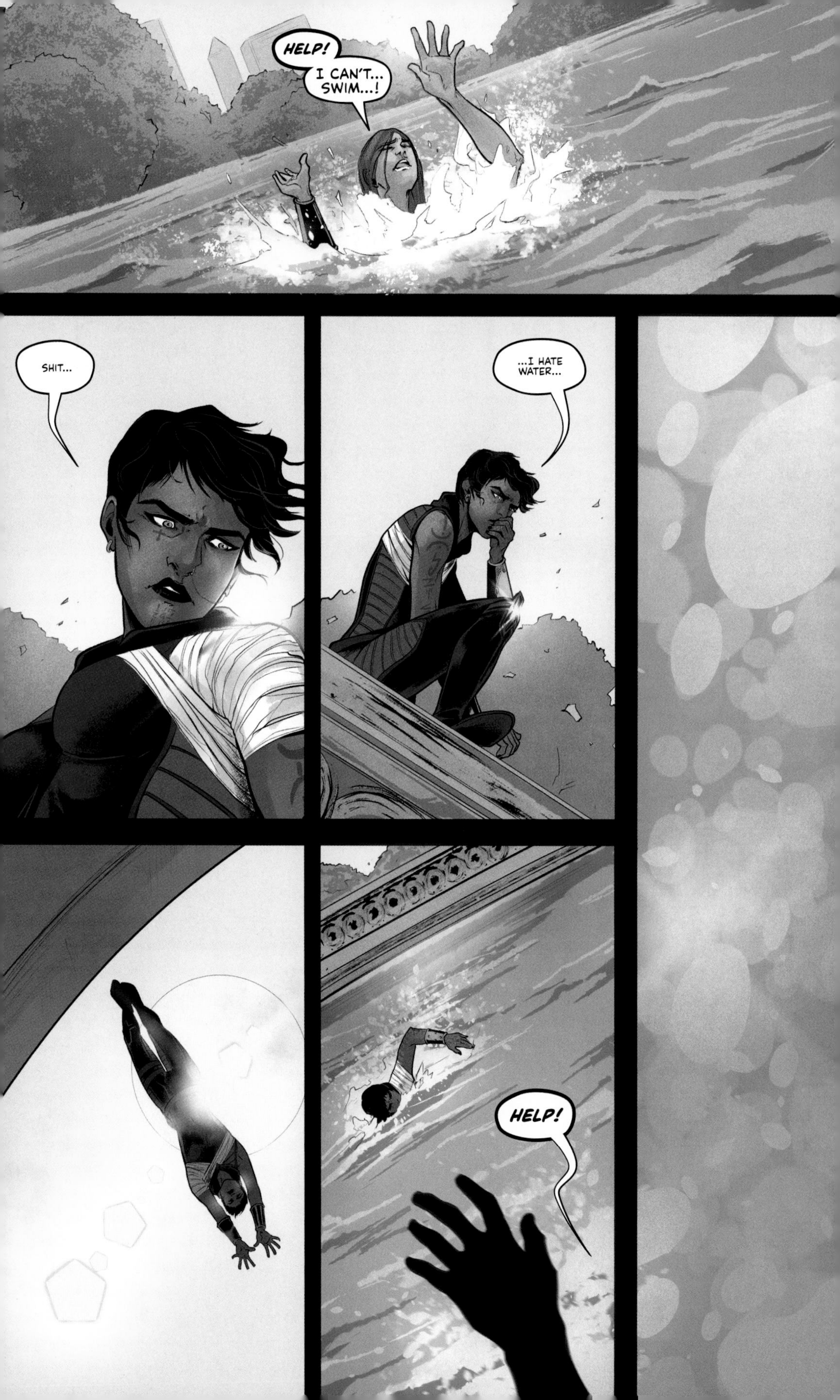
HELP!
I CAN'T... SWIM...!
SHIT...
...I HATE WATER...
HELP!

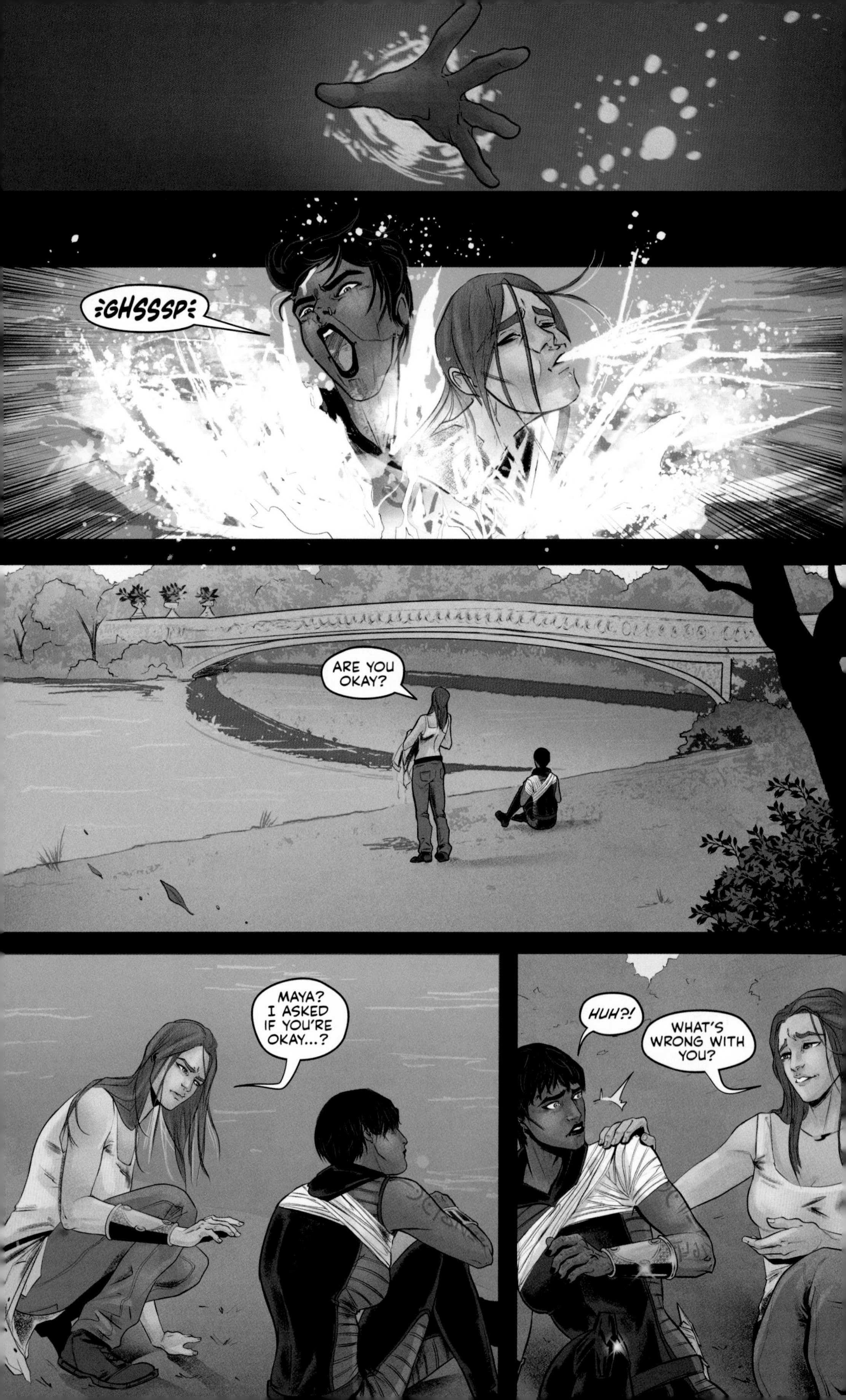
GHSSSP
ARE YOU OKAY?
MAYA? I ASKED IF YOU'RE OKAY...?
HUH?!
WHAT'S WRONG WITH YOU?

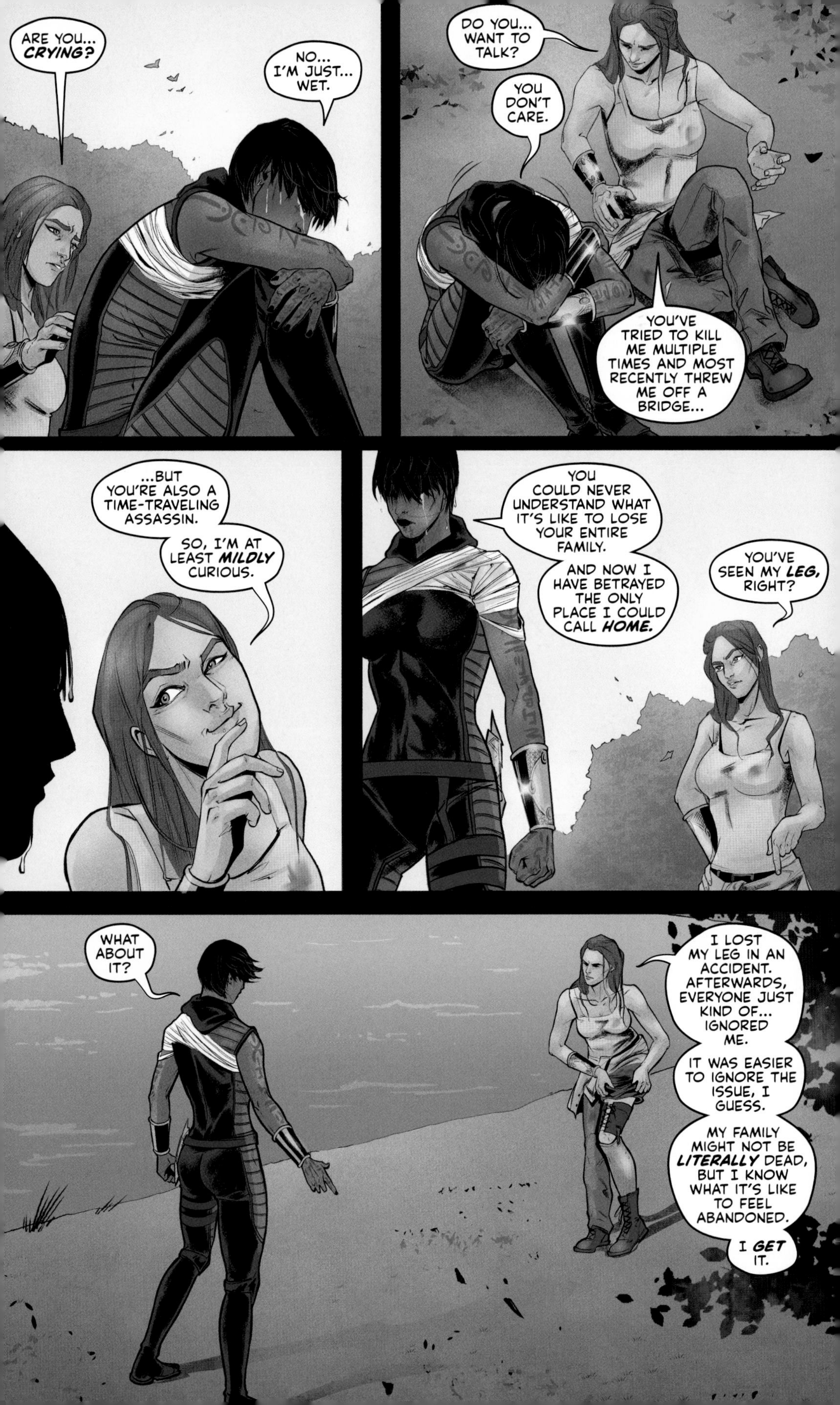
ARE YOU... CRYING?
NO... I'M JUST... WET.
DO YOU... WANT TO TALK?
YOU DON'T CARE.
YOU'VE TRIED TO KILL ME MULTIPLE TIMES AND MOST RECENTLY THREW ME OFF A BRIDGE...
...BUT YOU'RE ALSO A TIME-TRAVELING ASSASSIN.
SO, I'M AT LEAST MILDLY CURIOUS.
YOU COULD NEVER UNDERSTAND WHAT IT'S LIKE TO LOSE YOUR ENTIRE FAMILY.
AND NOW I HAVE BETRAYED THE ONLY PLACE I COULD CALL HOME.
YOU'VE SEEN MY LEG, RIGHT?
WHAT ABOUT IT?
I LOST MY LEG IN AN ACCIDENT. AFTERWARDS, EVERYONE JUST KIND OF... IGNORED ME.
IT WAS EASIER TO IGNORE THE ISSUE, I GUESS.
MY FAMILY MIGHT NOT BE LITERALLY DEAD, BUT I KNOW WHAT IT'S LIKE TO FEEL ABANDONED.
I GET IT.

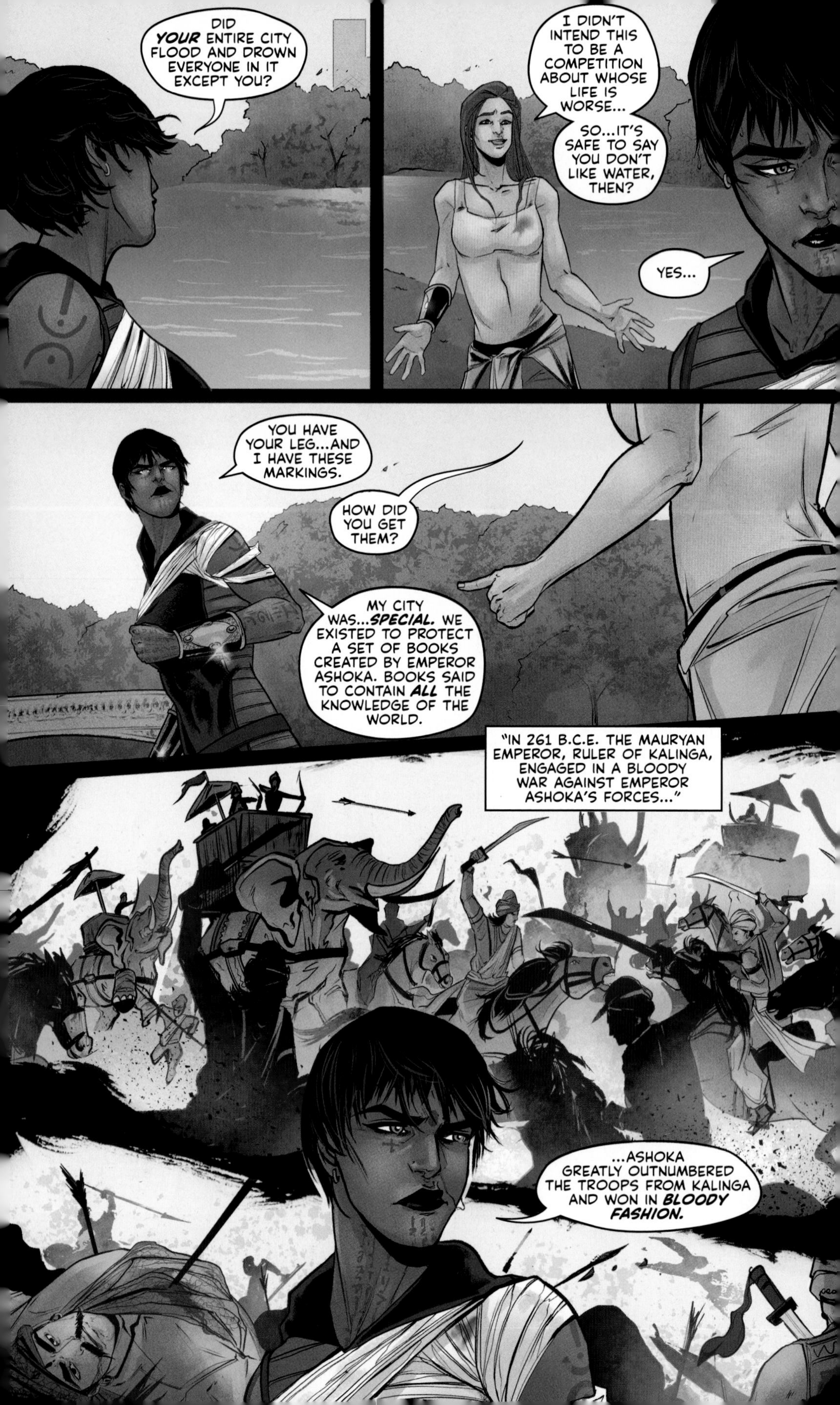
DID *YOUR* ENTIRE CITY FLOOD AND DROWN EVERYONE IN IT EXCEPT YOU?
I DIDN'T INTEND THIS TO BE A COMPETITION ABOUT WHOSE LIFE IS WORSE...
SO...IT'S SAFE TO SAY YOU DON'T LIKE WATER, THEN?
YES...
YOU HAVE YOUR LEG...AND I HAVE THESE MARKINGS.
HOW DID YOU GET THEM?
MY CITY WAS...*SPECIAL.* WE EXISTED TO PROTECT A SET OF BOOKS CREATED BY EMPEROR ASHOKA. BOOKS SAID TO CONTAIN *ALL* THE KNOWLEDGE OF THE WORLD.
"IN 261 B.C.E. THE MAURYAN EMPEROR, RULER OF KALINGA, ENGAGED IN A BLOODY WAR AGAINST EMPEROR ASHOKA'S FORCES..."
...ASHOKA GREATLY OUTNUMBERED THE TROOPS FROM KALINGA AND WON IN *BLOODY FASHION.*

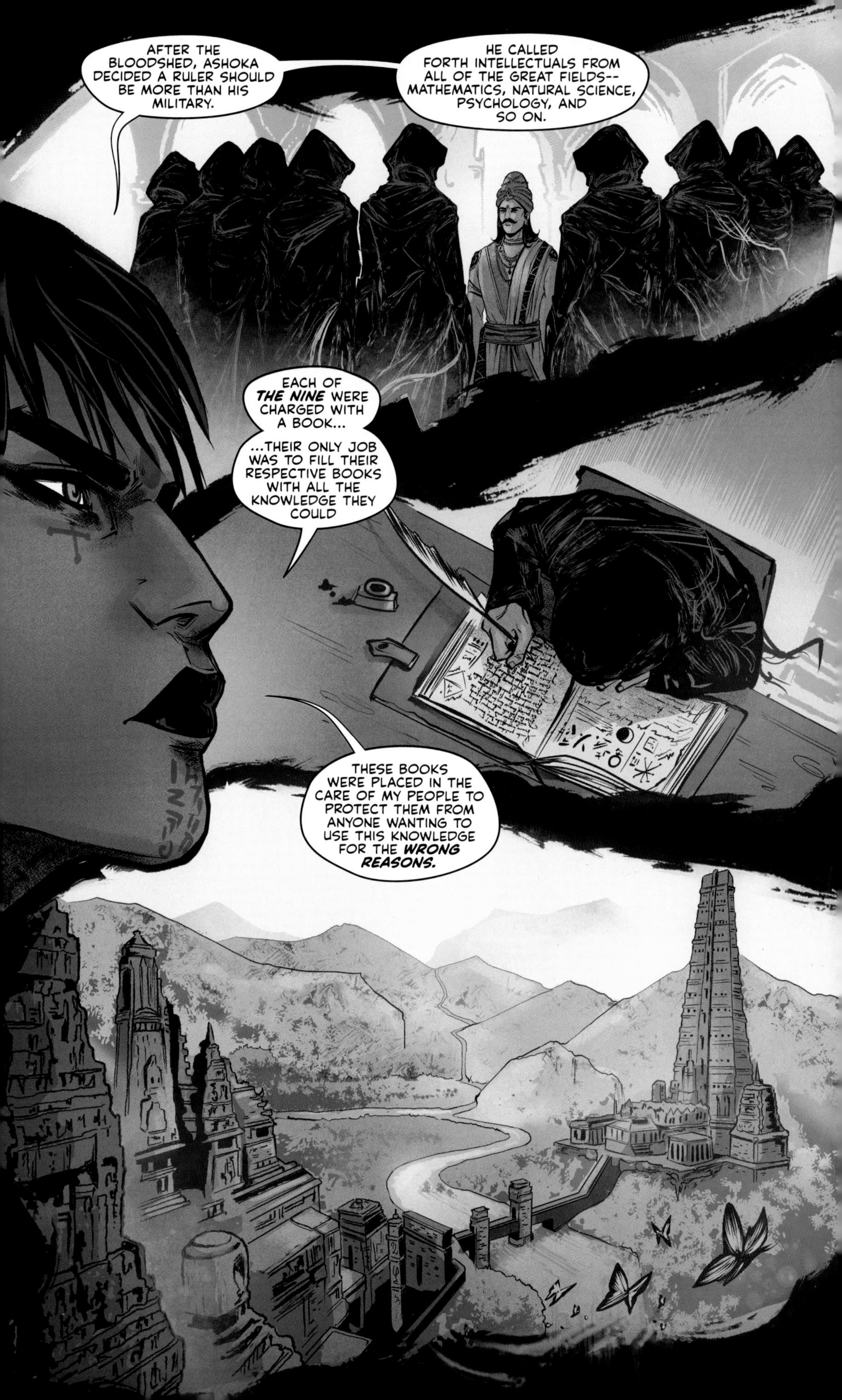

AFTER THE BLOODSHED, ASHOKA DECIDED A RULER SHOULD BE MORE THAN HIS MILITARY.
HE CALLED FORTH INTELLECTUALS FROM ALL OF THE GREAT FIELDS-- MATHEMATICS, NATURAL SCIENCE, PSYCHOLOGY, AND SO ON.
EACH OF ***THE NINE*** WERE CHARGED WITH A BOOK...
...THEIR ONLY JOB WAS TO FILL THEIR RESPECTIVE BOOKS WITH ALL THE KNOWLEDGE THEY COULD
THESE BOOKS WERE PLACED IN THE CARE OF MY PEOPLE TO PROTECT THEM FROM ANYONE WANTING TO USE THIS KNOWLEDGE FOR THE ***WRONG REASONS.***

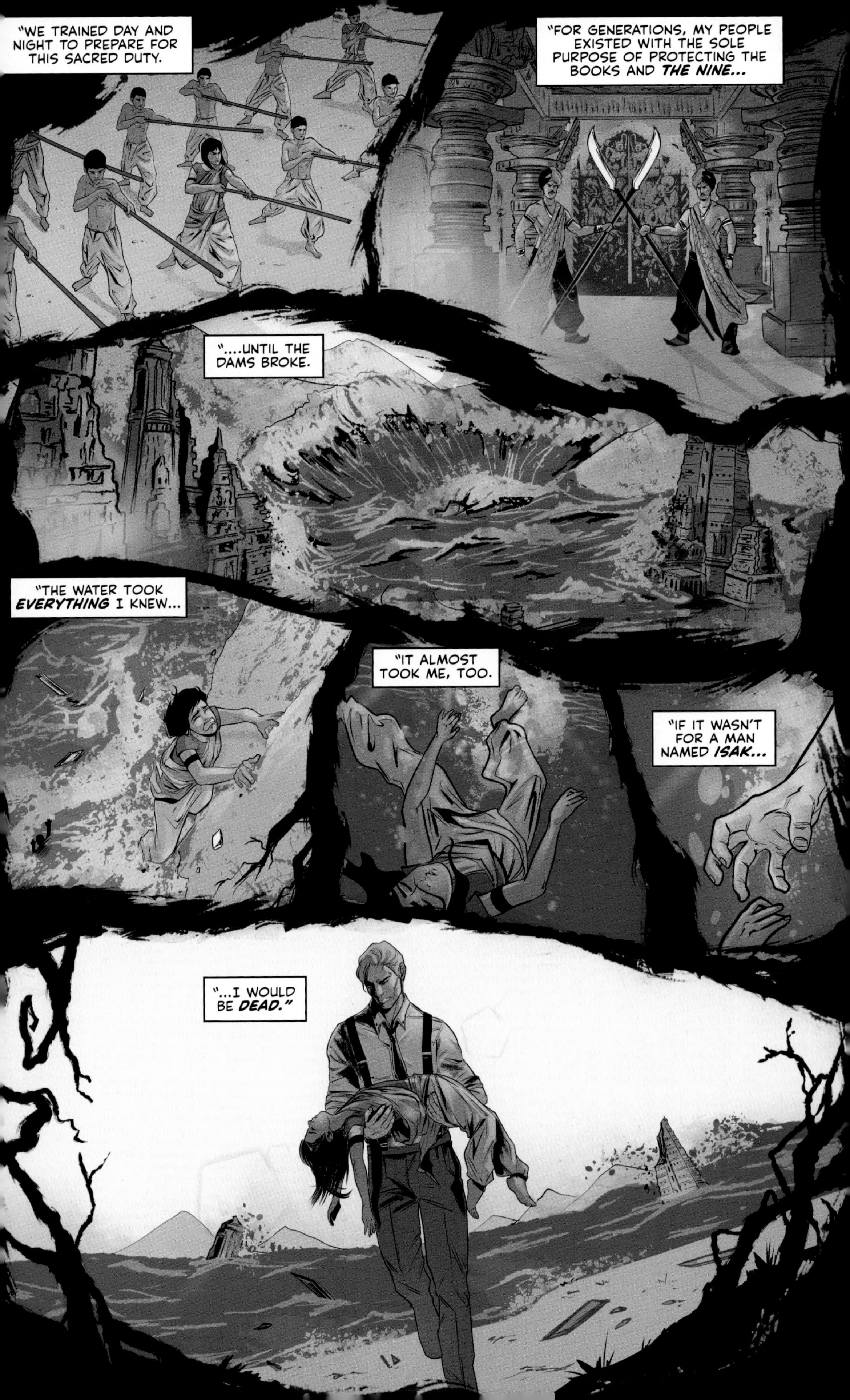
"WE TRAINED DAY AND NIGHT TO PREPARE FOR THIS SACRED DUTY.
"FOR GENERATIONS, MY PEOPLE EXISTED WITH THE SOLE PURPOSE OF PROTECTING THE BOOKS AND ***THE NINE...***
"....UNTIL THE DAMS BROKE.
"THE WATER TOOK ***EVERYTHING*** I KNEW...
"IT ALMOST TOOK ME, TOO.
"IF IT WASN'T FOR A MAN NAMED ***ISAK...***
"...I WOULD BE ***DEAD.***"

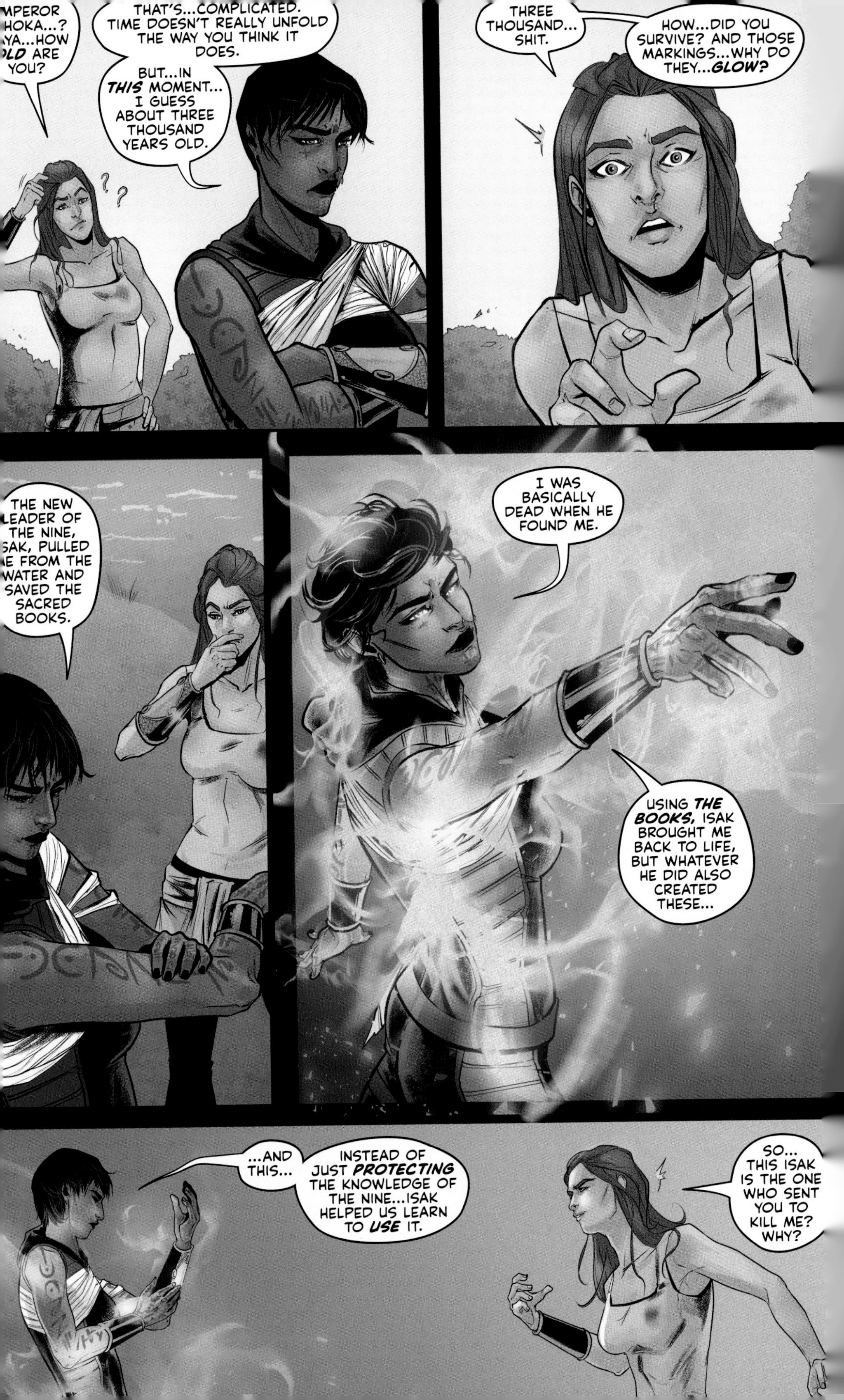

MPEROR HOKA...? YA...HOW OLD ARE YOU?
THAT'S...COMPLICATED. TIME DOESN'T REALLY UNFOLD THE WAY YOU THINK IT DOES.
BUT...IN THIS MOMENT... I GUESS ABOUT THREE THOUSAND YEARS OLD.
THREE THOUSAND... SHIT.
HOW...DID YOU SURVIVE? AND THOSE MARKINGS...WHY DO THEY...GLOW?
THE NEW LEADER OF THE NINE, SAK, PULLED E FROM THE WATER AND SAVED THE SACRED BOOKS.
I WAS BASICALLY DEAD WHEN HE FOUND ME.
USING THE BOOKS, ISAK BROUGHT ME BACK TO LIFE, BUT WHATEVER HE DID ALSO CREATED THESE...
...AND THIS...
INSTEAD OF JUST PROTECTING THE KNOWLEDGE OF THE NINE...ISAK HELPED US LEARN TO USE IT.
SO... THIS ISAK IS THE ONE WHO SENT YOU TO KILL ME? WHY?

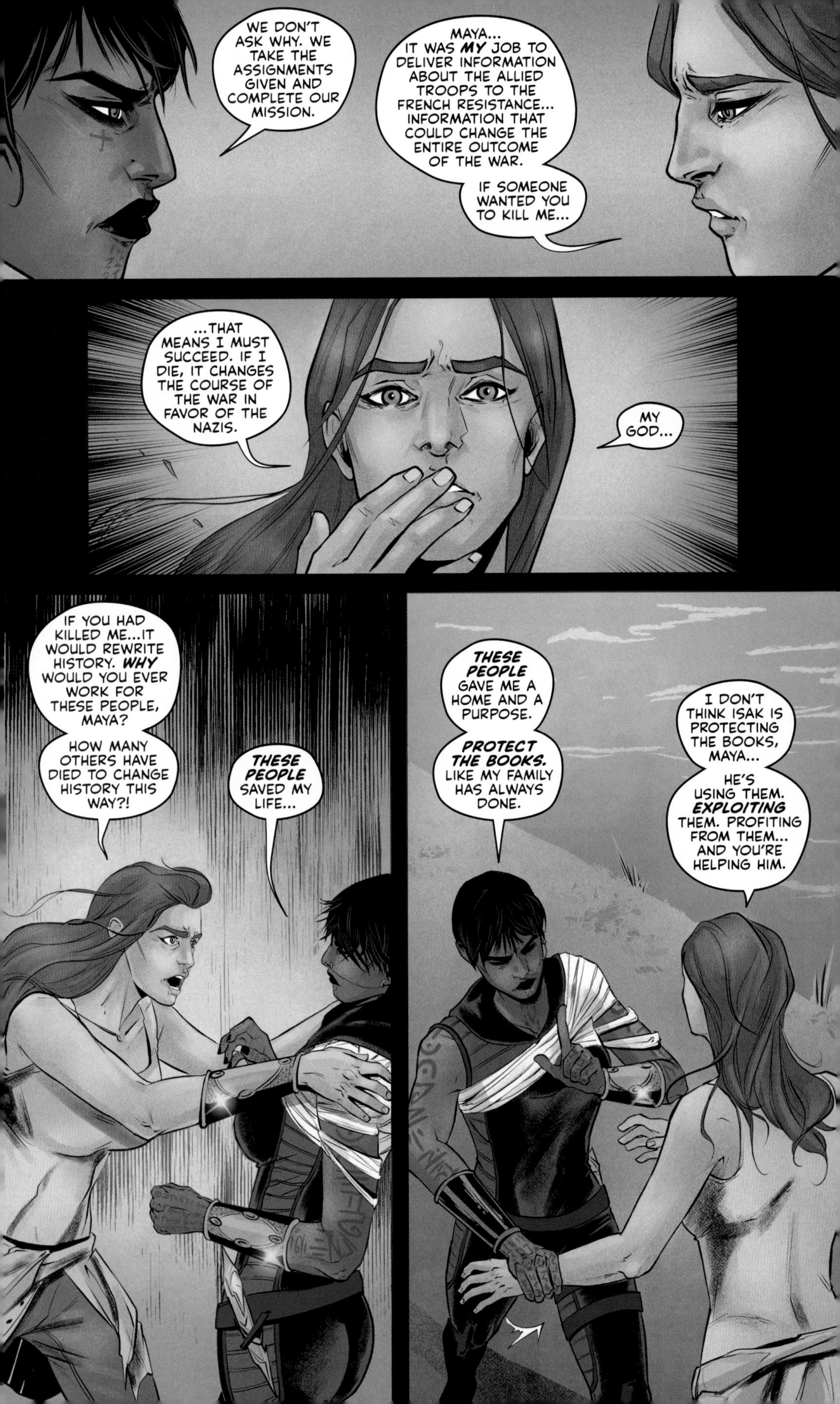
WE DON'T ASK WHY. WE TAKE THE ASSIGNMENTS GIVEN AND COMPLETE OUR MISSION.
MAYA... IT WAS ***MY*** JOB TO DELIVER INFORMATION ABOUT THE ALLIED TROOPS TO THE FRENCH RESISTANCE... INFORMATION THAT COULD CHANGE THE ENTIRE OUTCOME OF THE WAR.
IF SOMEONE WANTED YOU TO KILL ME...
...THAT MEANS I MUST SUCCEED. IF I DIE, IT CHANGES THE COURSE OF THE WAR IN FAVOR OF THE NAZIS.
MY GOD...
IF YOU HAD KILLED ME...IT WOULD REWRITE HISTORY. ***WHY*** WOULD YOU EVER WORK FOR THESE PEOPLE, MAYA?
HOW MANY OTHERS HAVE DIED TO CHANGE HISTORY THIS WAY?!
THESE PEOPLE SAVED MY LIFE...
THESE PEOPLE GAVE ME A HOME AND A PURPOSE.
PROTECT THE BOOKS. LIKE MY FAMILY HAS ALWAYS DONE.
I DON'T THINK ISAK IS PROTECTING THE BOOKS, MAYA...
HE'S USING THEM. ***EXPLOITING*** THEM. PROFITING FROM THEM... AND YOU'RE HELPING HIM.

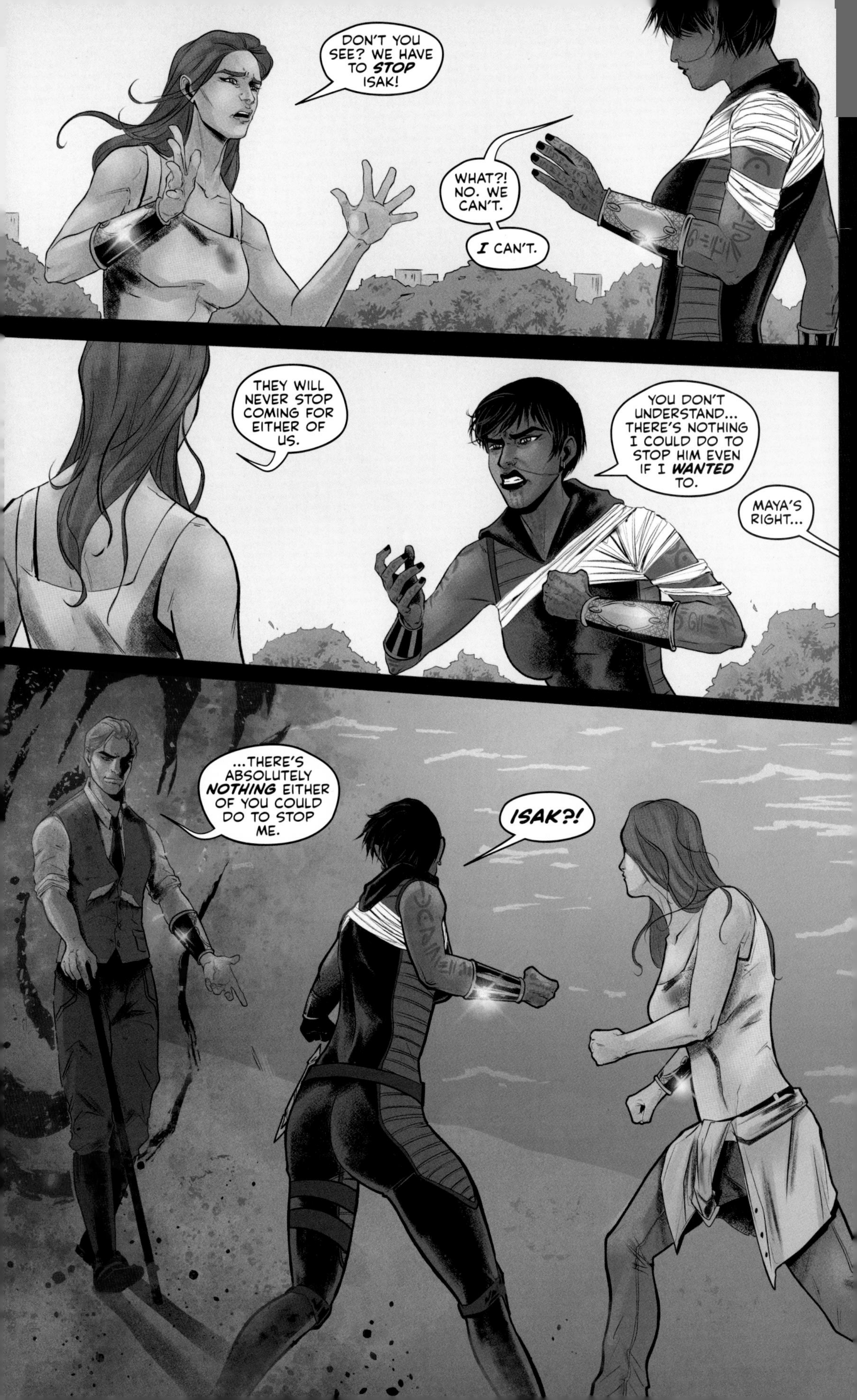
DON'T YOU SEE? WE HAVE TO STOP ISAK!
WHAT?! NO. WE CAN'T.
I CAN'T.
THEY WILL NEVER STOP COMING FOR EITHER OF US.
YOU DON'T UNDERSTAND... THERE'S NOTHING I COULD DO TO STOP HIM EVEN IF I WANTED TO.
MAYA'S RIGHT...
...THERE'S ABSOLUTELY NOTHING EITHER OF YOU COULD DO TO STOP ME.
ISAK?!

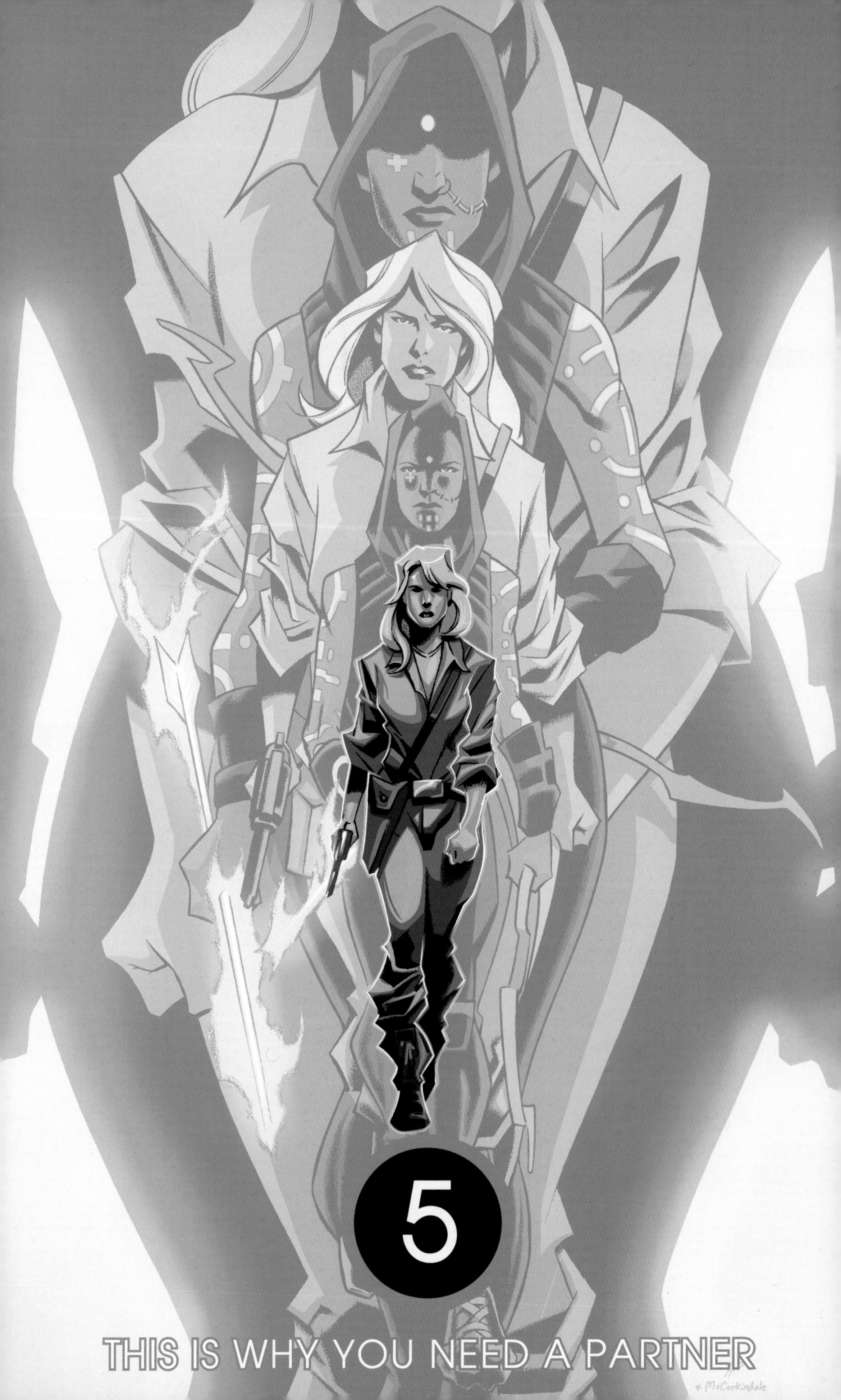

5

THIS IS WHY YOU NEED A PARTNER

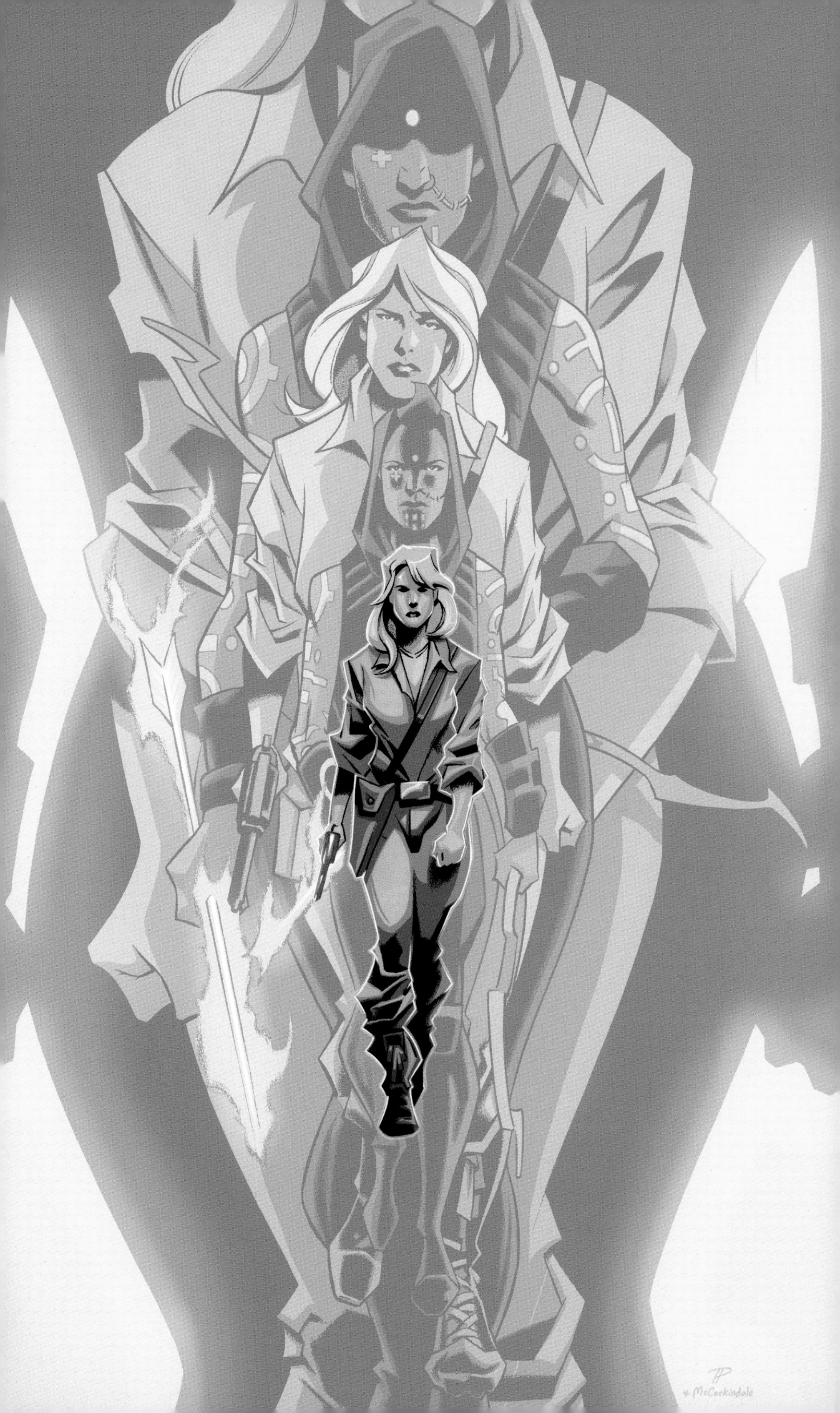
TP
& McCorkindale

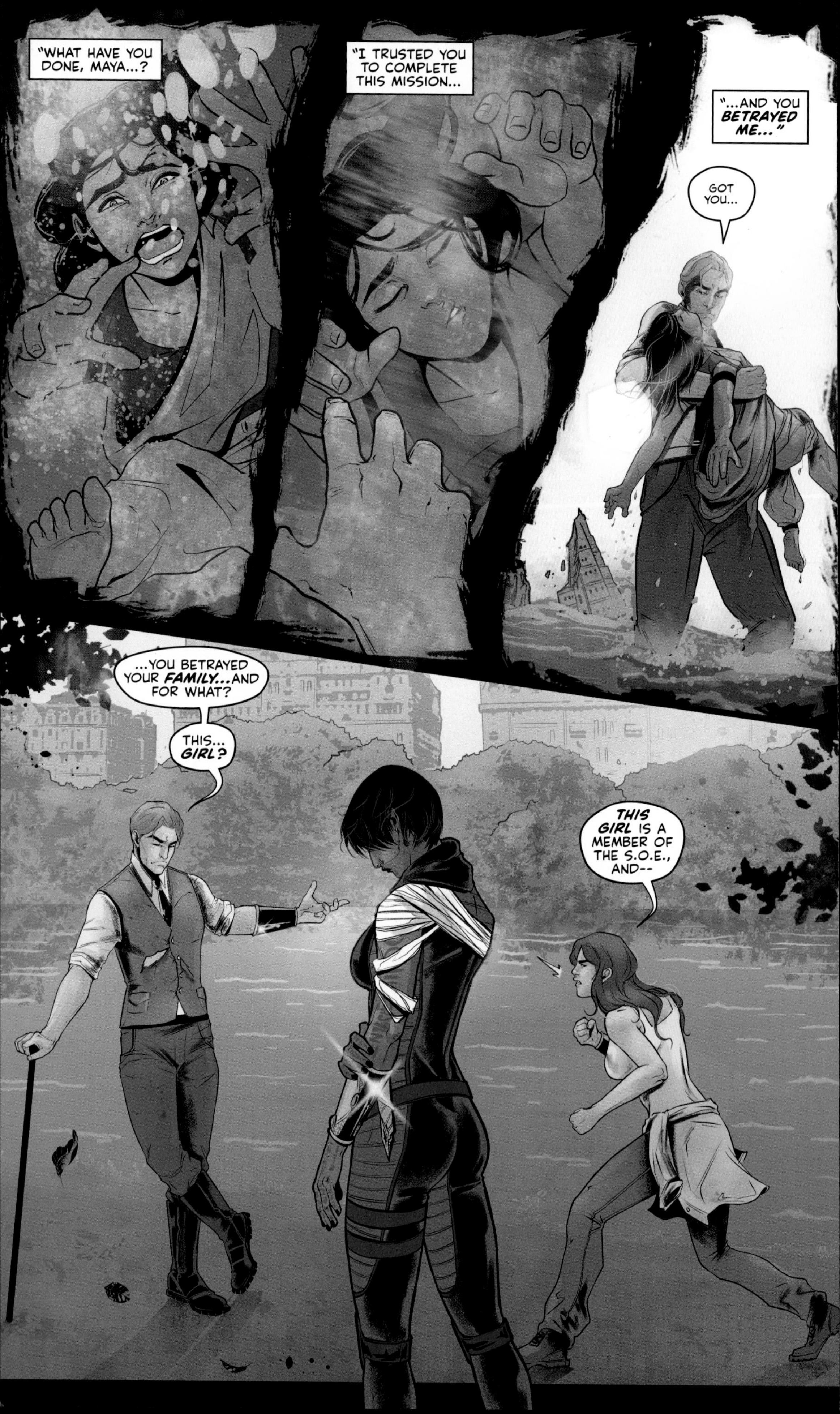
"WHAT HAVE YOU DONE, MAYA...?
"I TRUSTED YOU TO COMPLETE THIS MISSION...
"...AND YOU BETRAYED ME..."
GOT YOU...
...YOU BETRAYED YOUR FAMILY...AND FOR WHAT?
THIS... GIRL?
THIS GIRL IS A MEMBER OF THE S.O.E., AND--

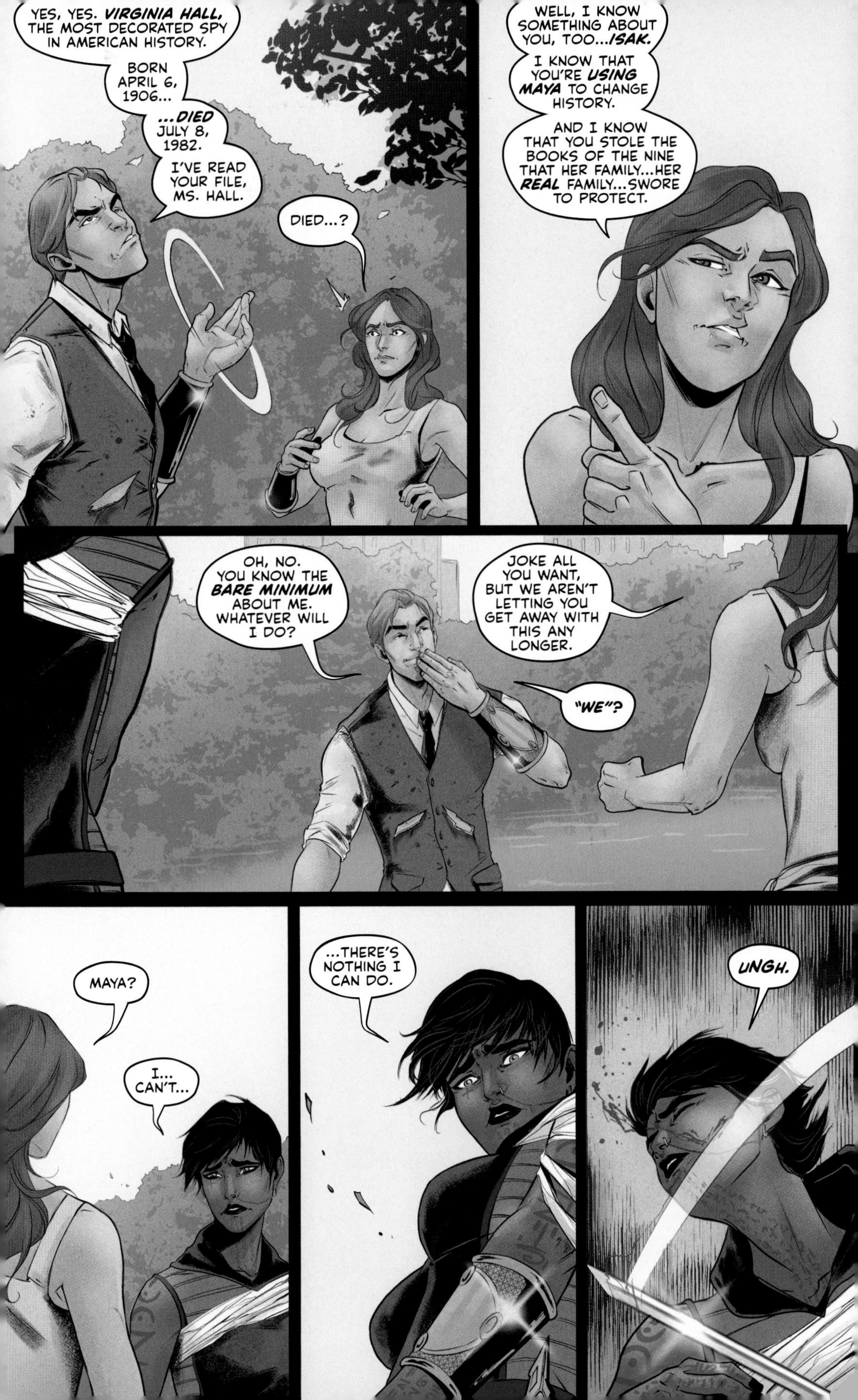

YES, YES. VIRGINIA HALL, THE MOST DECORATED SPY IN AMERICAN HISTORY.
BORN APRIL 6, 1906...
...DIED JULY 8, 1982.
I'VE READ YOUR FILE, MS. HALL.
DIED...?
WELL, I KNOW SOMETHING ABOUT YOU, TOO...ISAK.
I KNOW THAT YOU'RE USING MAYA TO CHANGE HISTORY.
AND I KNOW THAT YOU STOLE THE BOOKS OF THE NINE THAT HER FAMILY...HER REAL FAMILY...SWORE TO PROTECT.
OH, NO. YOU KNOW THE BARE MINIMUM ABOUT ME. WHATEVER WILL I DO?
JOKE ALL YOU WANT, BUT WE AREN'T LETTING YOU GET AWAY WITH THIS ANY LONGER.
"WE"?
MAYA?
I... CAN'T...
...THERE'S NOTHING I CAN DO.
UNGH.

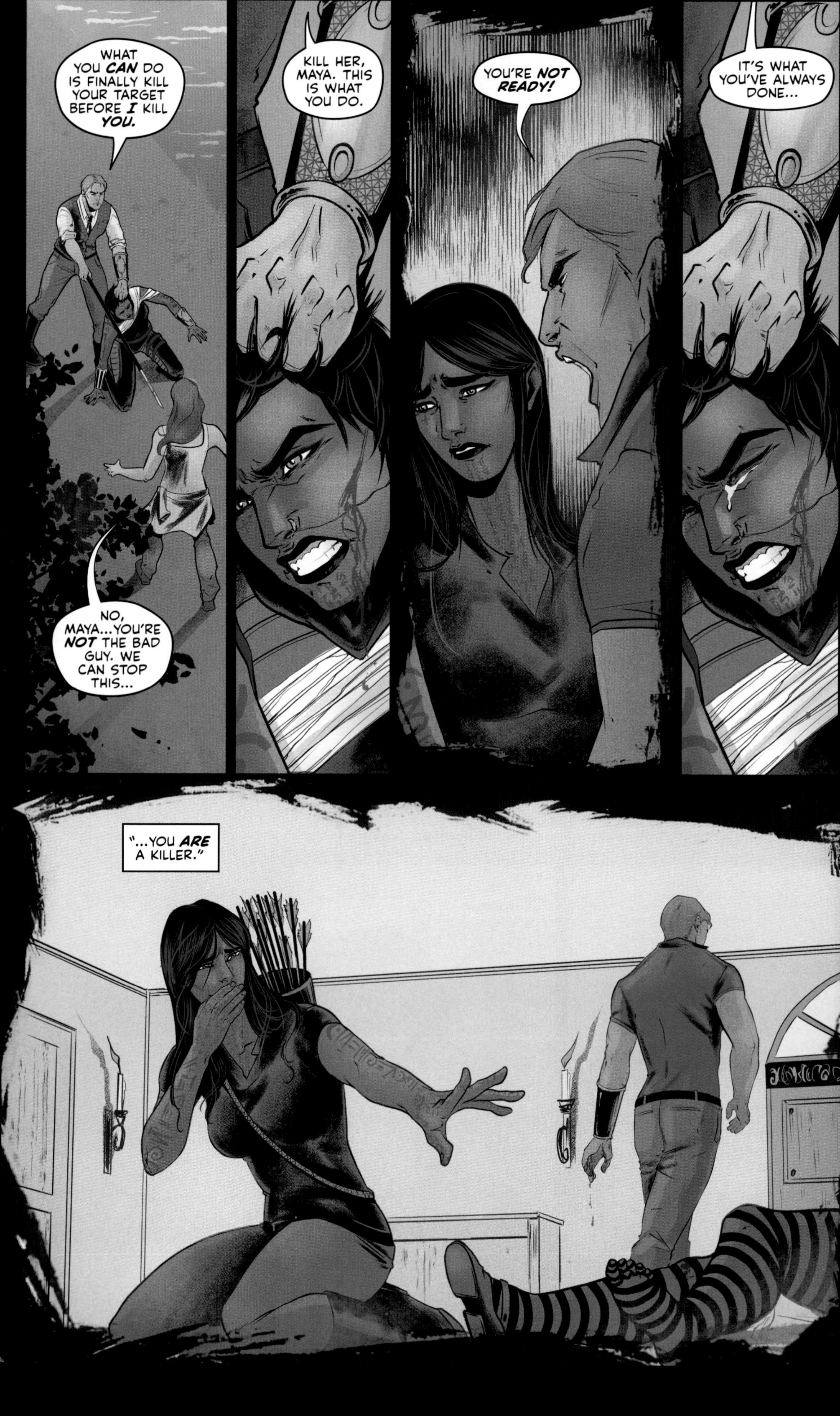
WHAT YOU CAN DO IS FINALLY KILL YOUR TARGET BEFORE I KILL YOU.
NO, MAYA...YOU'RE NOT THE BAD GUY. WE CAN STOP THIS...
KILL HER, MAYA. THIS IS WHAT YOU DO.
YOU'RE NOT READY!
IT'S WHAT YOU'VE ALWAYS DONE...
"...YOU ARE A KILLER."

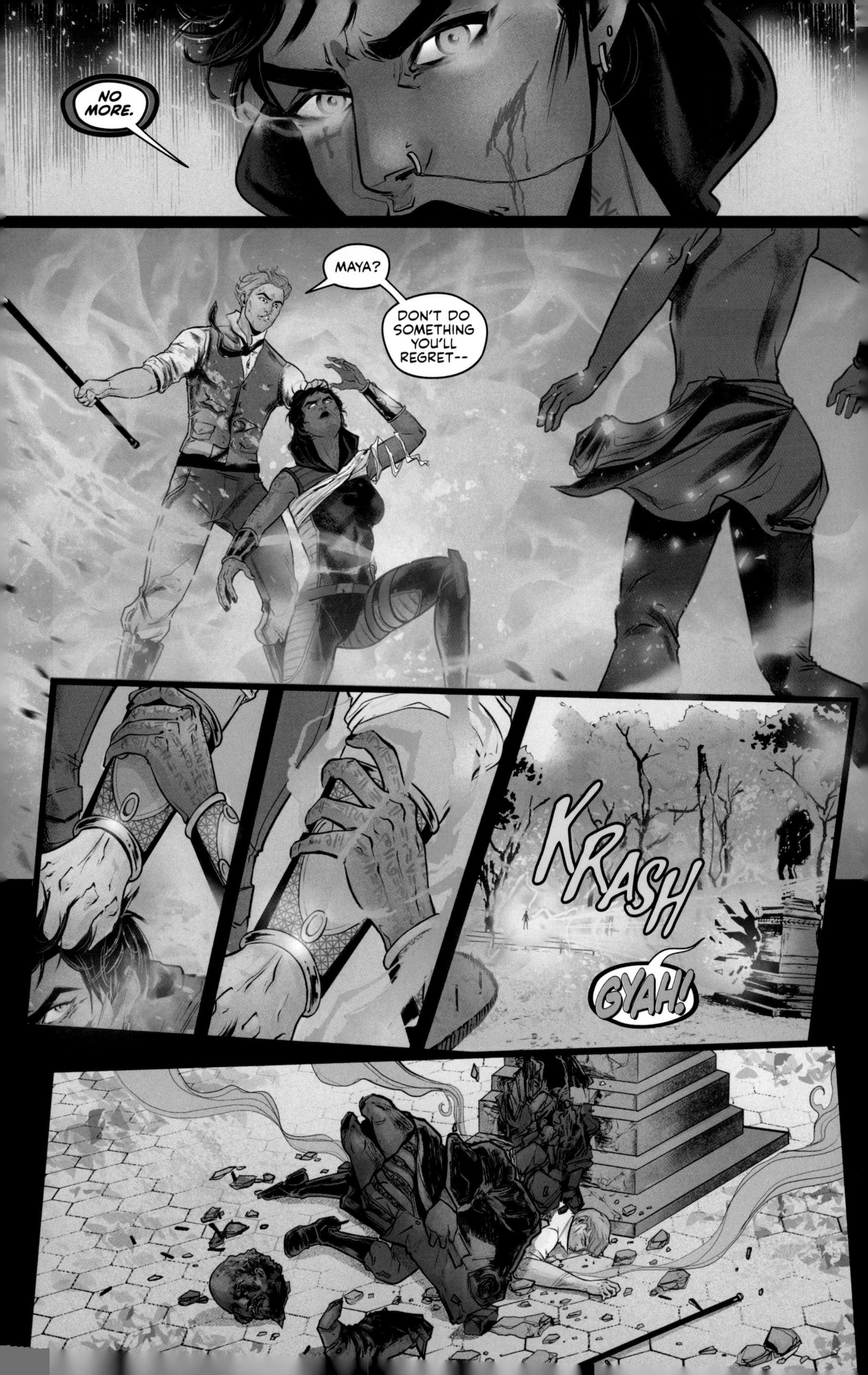
NO MORE.
MAYA?
DON'T DO SOMETHING YOU'LL REGRET--
KRASH
GYAH!

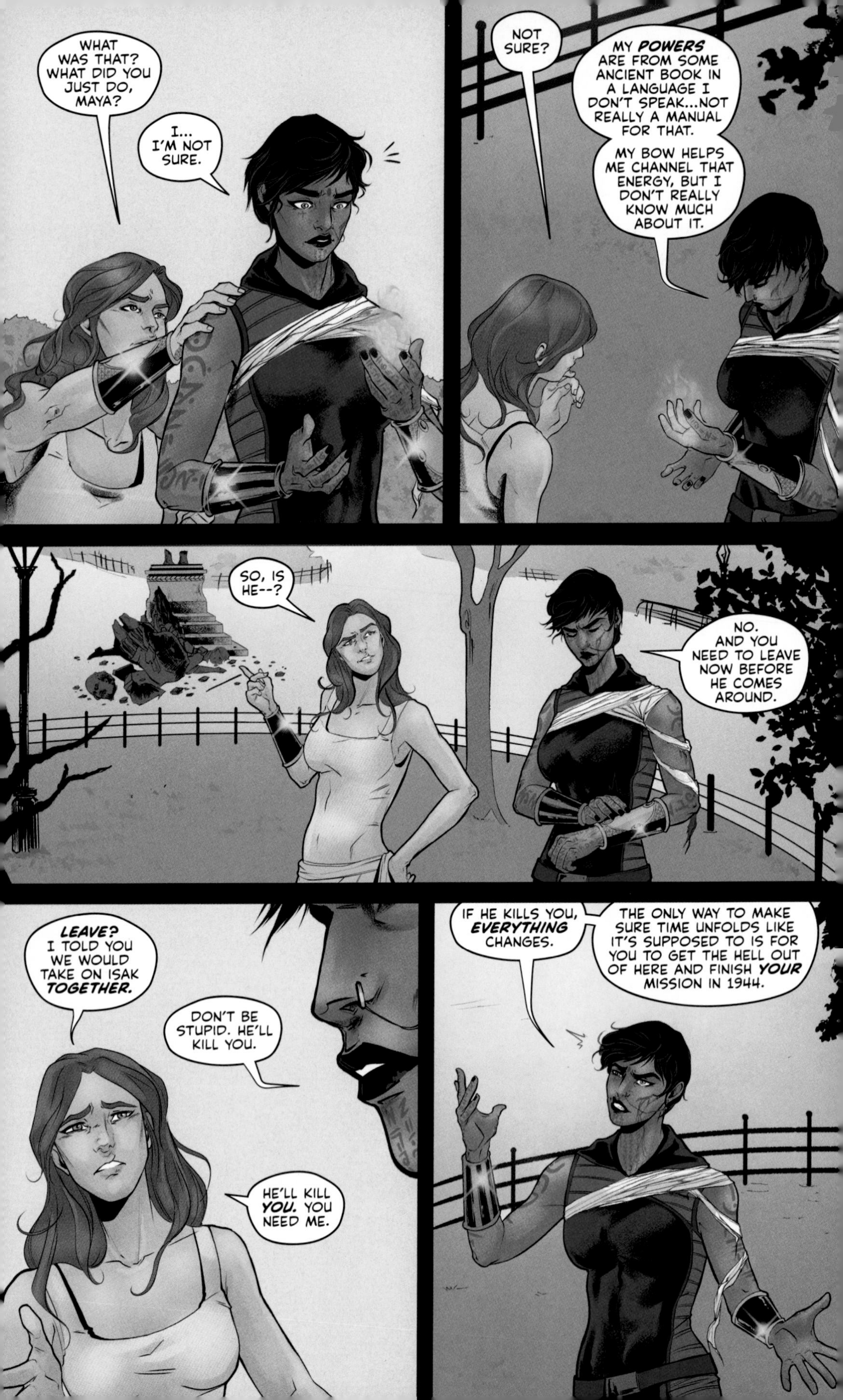

WHAT WAS THAT? WHAT DID YOU JUST DO, MAYA?
I... I'M NOT SURE.
NOT SURE?
MY **POWERS** ARE FROM SOME ANCIENT BOOK IN A LANGUAGE I DON'T SPEAK...NOT REALLY A MANUAL FOR THAT.
MY BOW HELPS ME CHANNEL THAT ENERGY, BUT I DON'T REALLY KNOW MUCH ABOUT IT.
SO, IS HE--?
NO. AND YOU NEED TO LEAVE NOW BEFORE HE COMES AROUND.
LEAVE? I TOLD YOU WE WOULD TAKE ON ISAK ***TOGETHER.***
DON'T BE STUPID. HE'LL KILL YOU.
HE'LL KILL ***YOU.*** YOU NEED ME.
IF HE KILLS YOU, ***EVERYTHING*** CHANGES.
THE ONLY WAY TO MAKE SURE TIME UNFOLDS LIKE IT'S SUPPOSED TO IS FOR YOU TO GET THE HELL OUT OF HERE AND FINISH ***YOUR*** MISSION IN 1944.

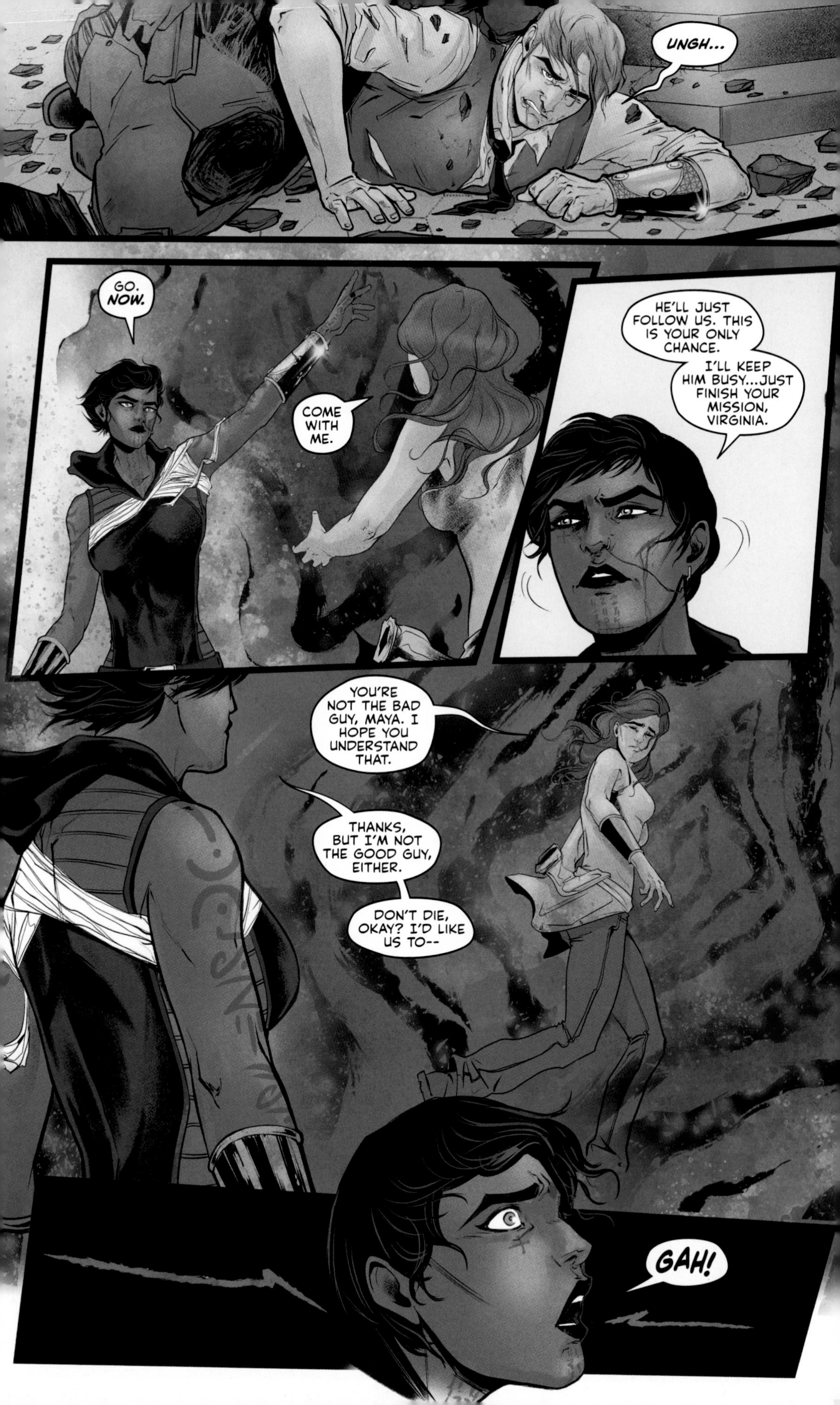
UNGH...
GO. NOW.
COME WITH ME.
HE'LL JUST FOLLOW US. THIS IS YOUR ONLY CHANCE.
I'LL KEEP HIM BUSY...JUST FINISH YOUR MISSION, VIRGINIA.
YOU'RE NOT THE BAD GUY, MAYA. I HOPE YOU UNDERSTAND THAT.
THANKS, BUT I'M NOT THE GOOD GUY, EITHER.
DON'T DIE, OKAY? I'D LIKE US TO--
GAH!

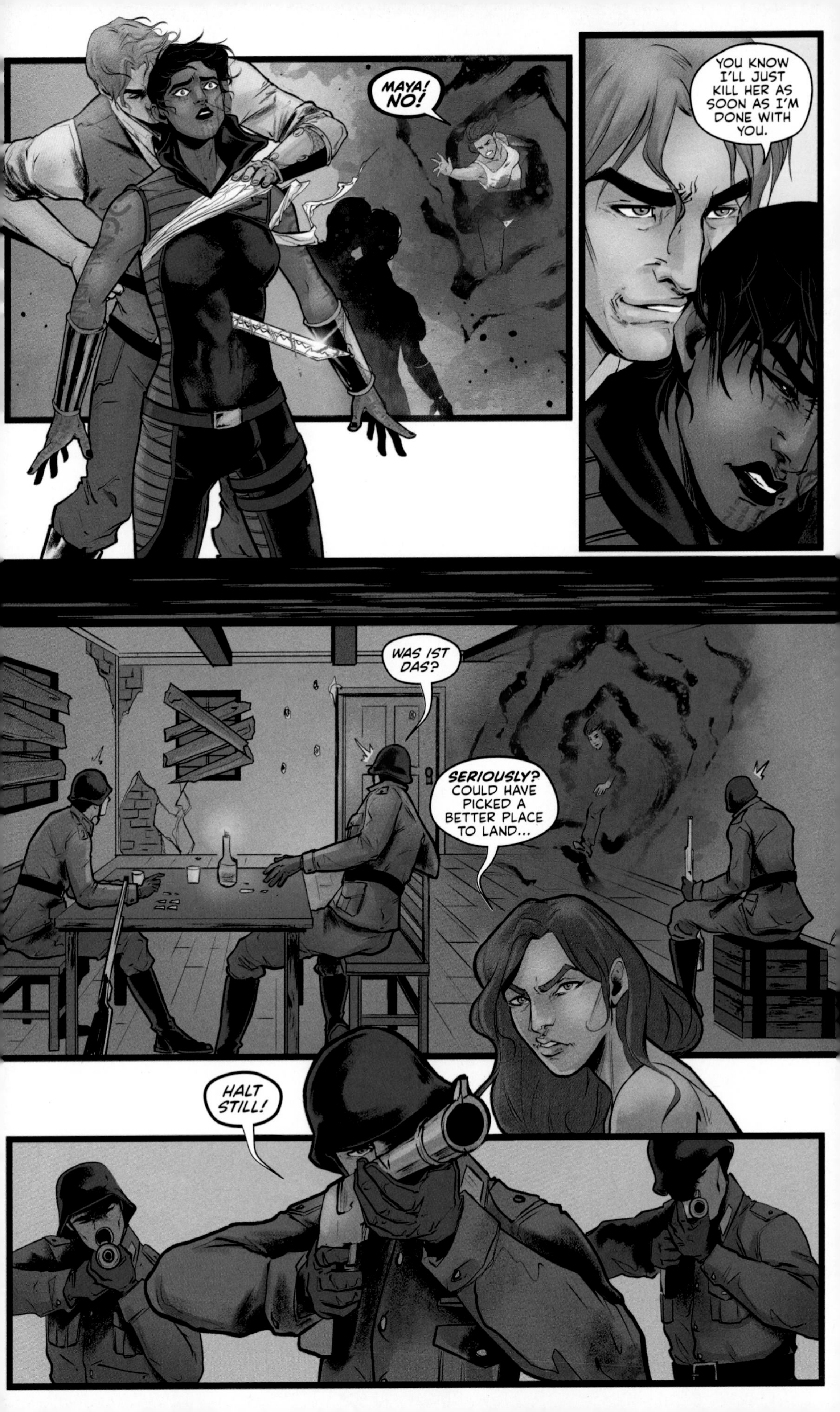
MAYA! NO!
YOU KNOW I'LL JUST KILL HER AS SOON AS I'M DONE WITH YOU.
WAS IST DAS?
SERIOUSLY? COULD HAVE PICKED A BETTER PLACE TO LAND...
HALT STILL!

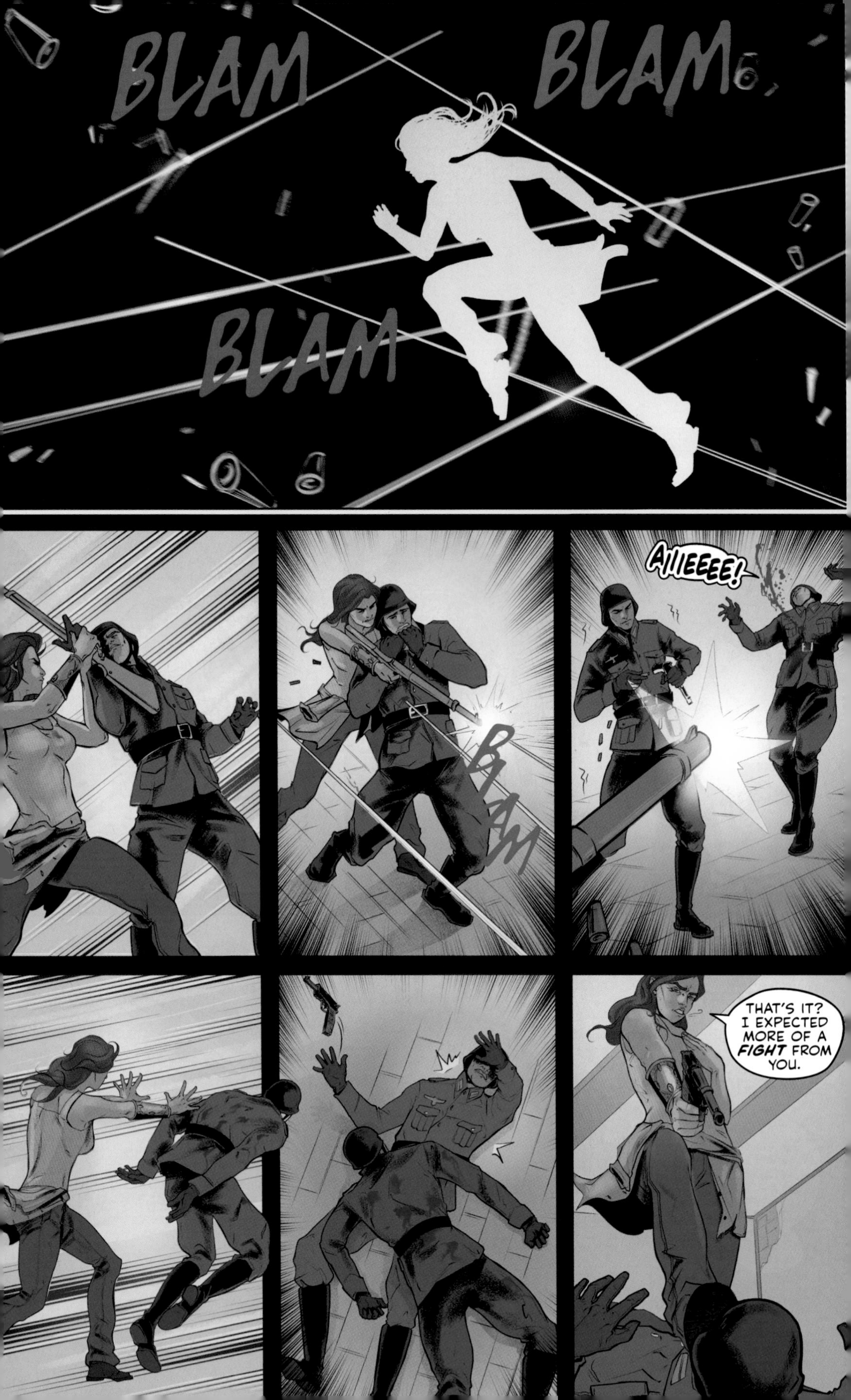
BLAM
BLAM
BLAM
BLAM
AIIIEEEE!
THAT'S IT? I EXPECTED MORE OF A *FIGHT* FROM YOU.

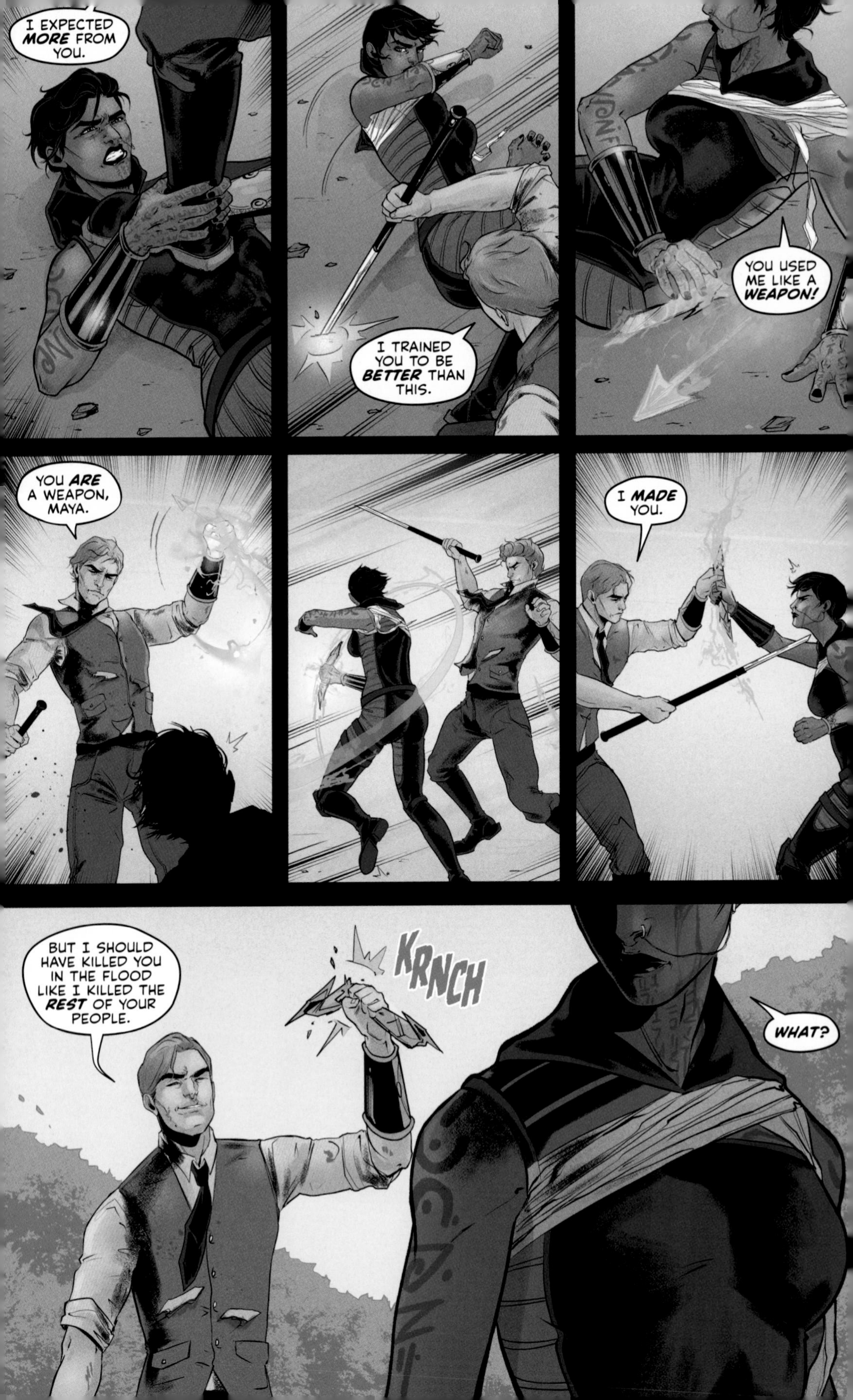
I EXPECTED MORE FROM YOU.
I TRAINED YOU TO BE BETTER THAN THIS.
YOU USED ME LIKE A WEAPON!
YOU ARE A WEAPON, MAYA.
I MADE YOU.
BUT I SHOULD HAVE KILLED YOU IN THE FLOOD LIKE I KILLED THE REST OF YOUR PEOPLE.
KRNCH
WHAT?

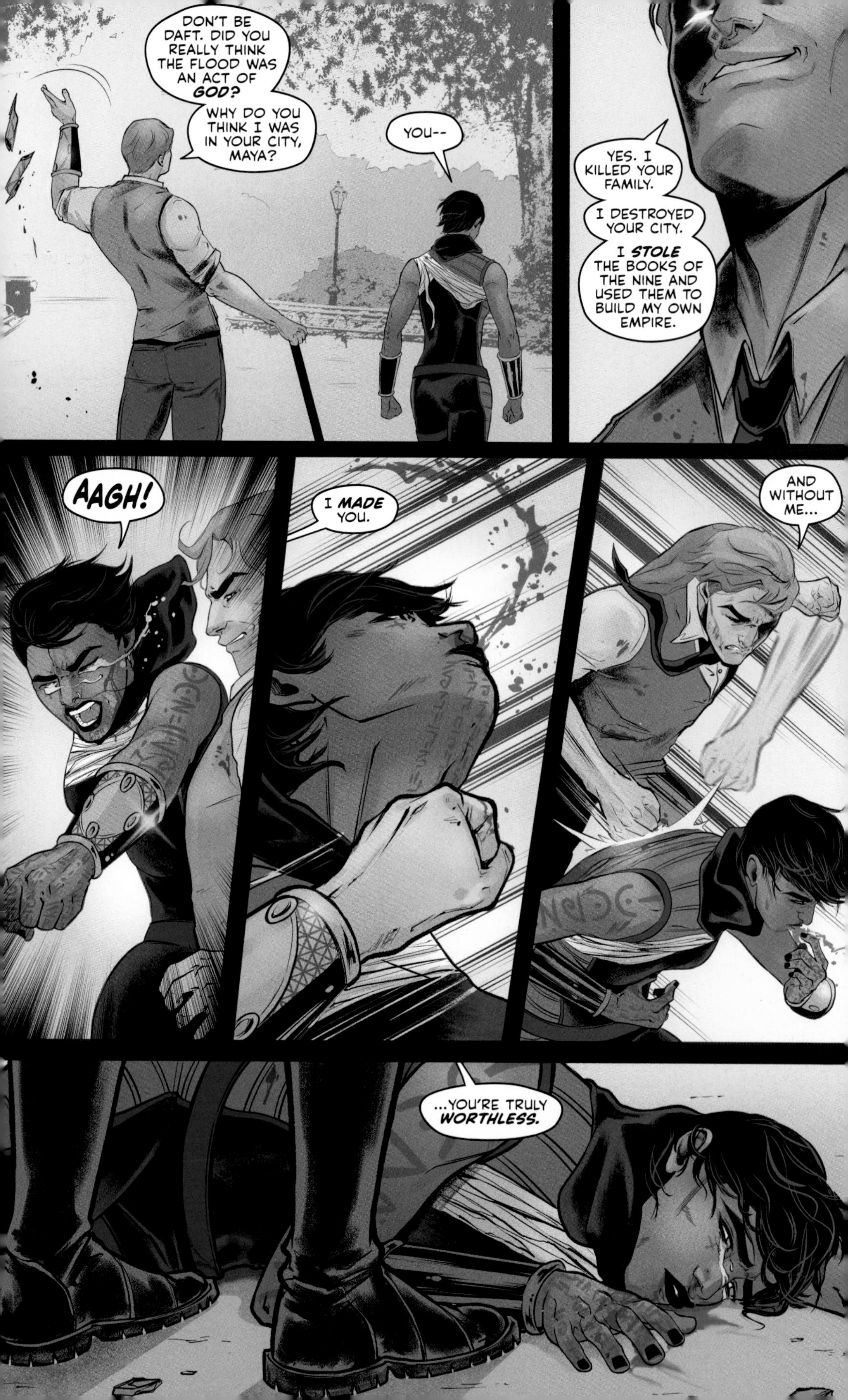
DON'T BE DAFT. DID YOU REALLY THINK THE FLOOD WAS AN ACT OF **GOD?**
WHY DO YOU THINK I WAS IN YOUR CITY, MAYA?
YOU--
YES. I KILLED YOUR FAMILY.
I DESTROYED YOUR CITY.
I **STOLE** THE BOOKS OF THE NINE AND USED THEM TO BUILD MY OWN EMPIRE.
AAGH!
I **MADE** YOU.
AND WITHOUT ME...
...YOU'RE TRULY **WORTHLESS.**

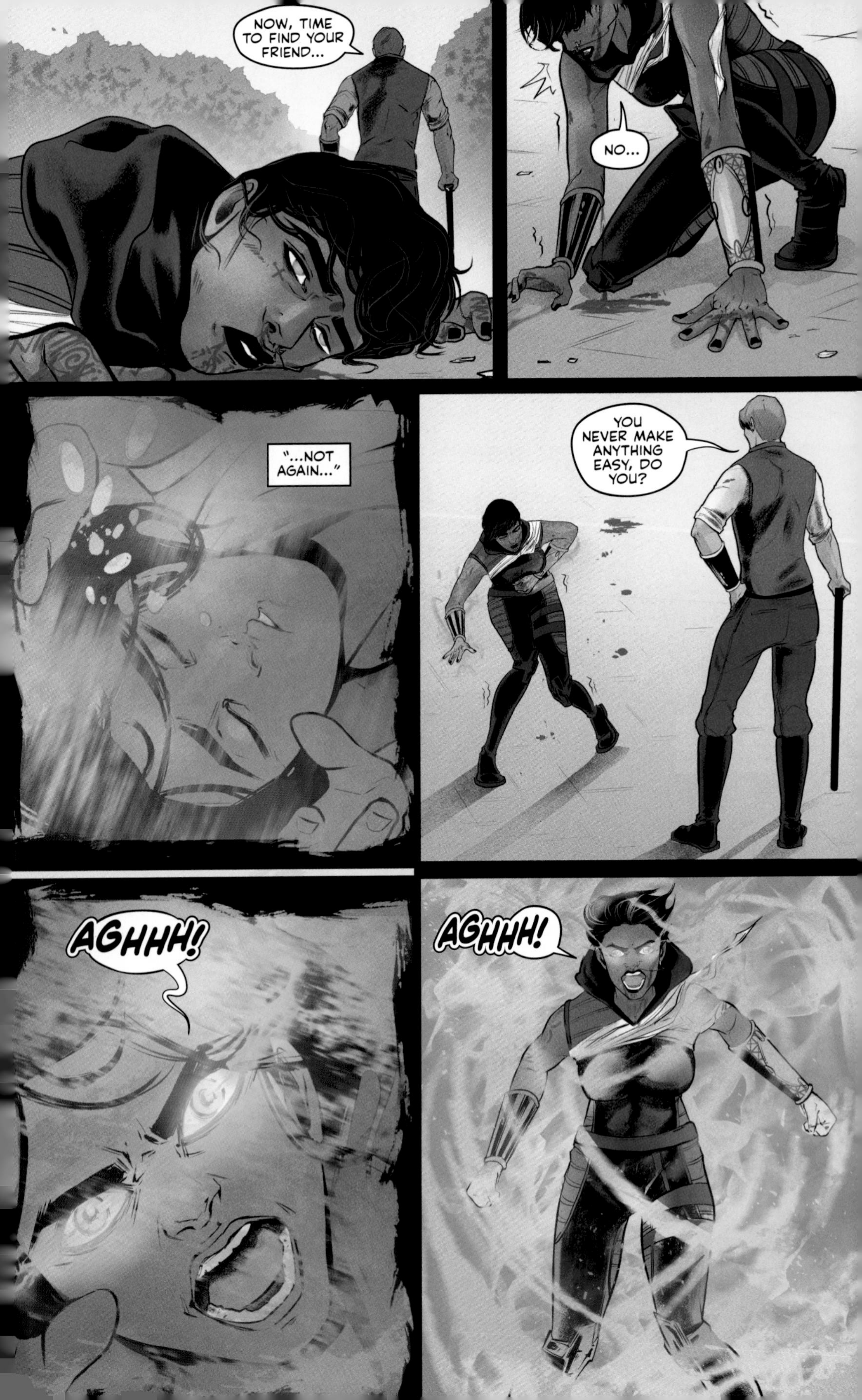
NOW, TIME TO FIND YOUR FRIEND...
NO...
"...NOT AGAIN..."
YOU NEVER MAKE ANYTHING EASY, DO YOU?
AGHHH!
AGHHH!

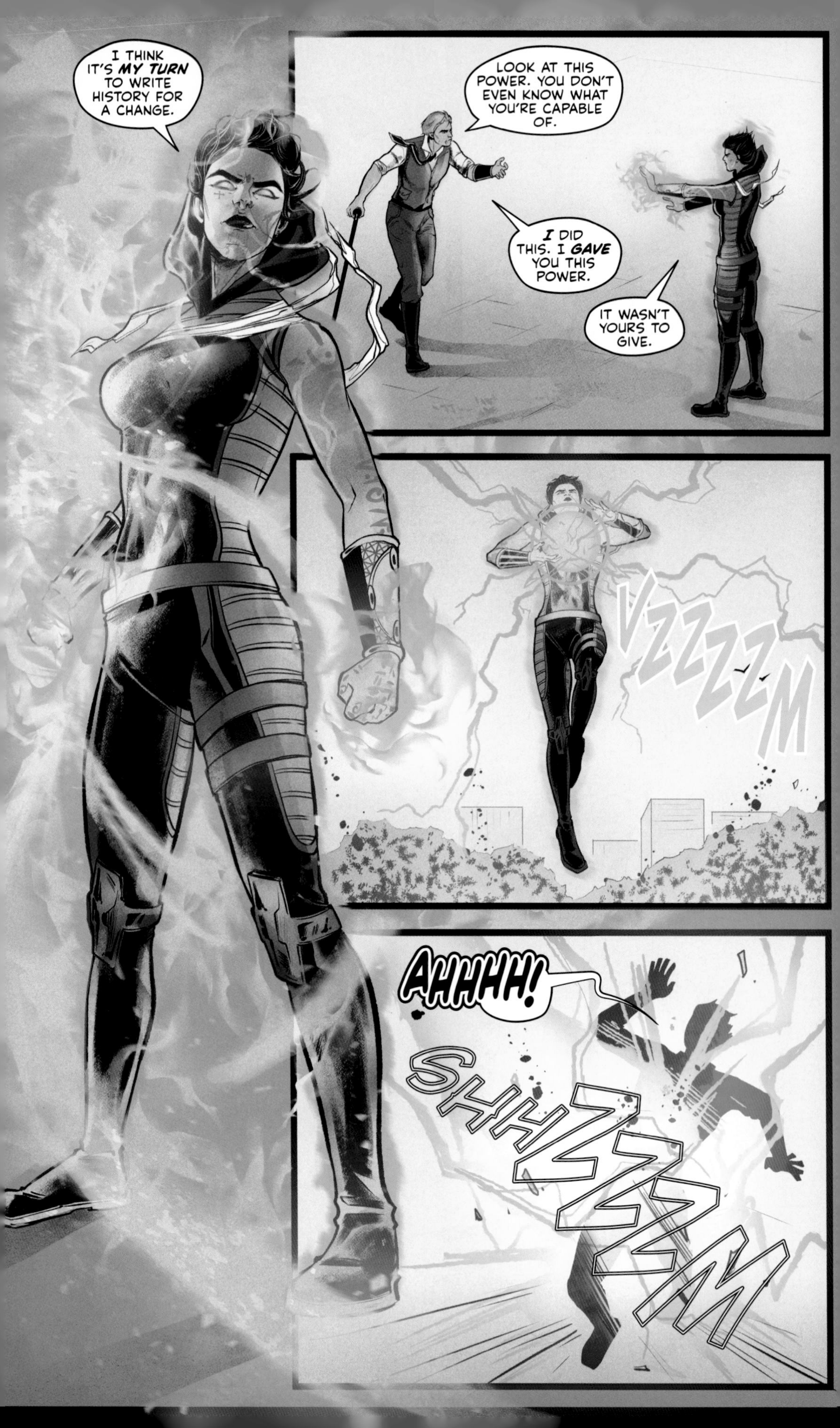
I THINK IT'S MY TURN TO WRITE HISTORY FOR A CHANGE.
LOOK AT THIS POWER. YOU DON'T EVEN KNOW WHAT YOU'RE CAPABLE OF.
I DID THIS. I GAVE YOU THIS POWER.
IT WASN'T YOURS TO GIVE.
VZZZZM
AHHHH!
SHHMMM

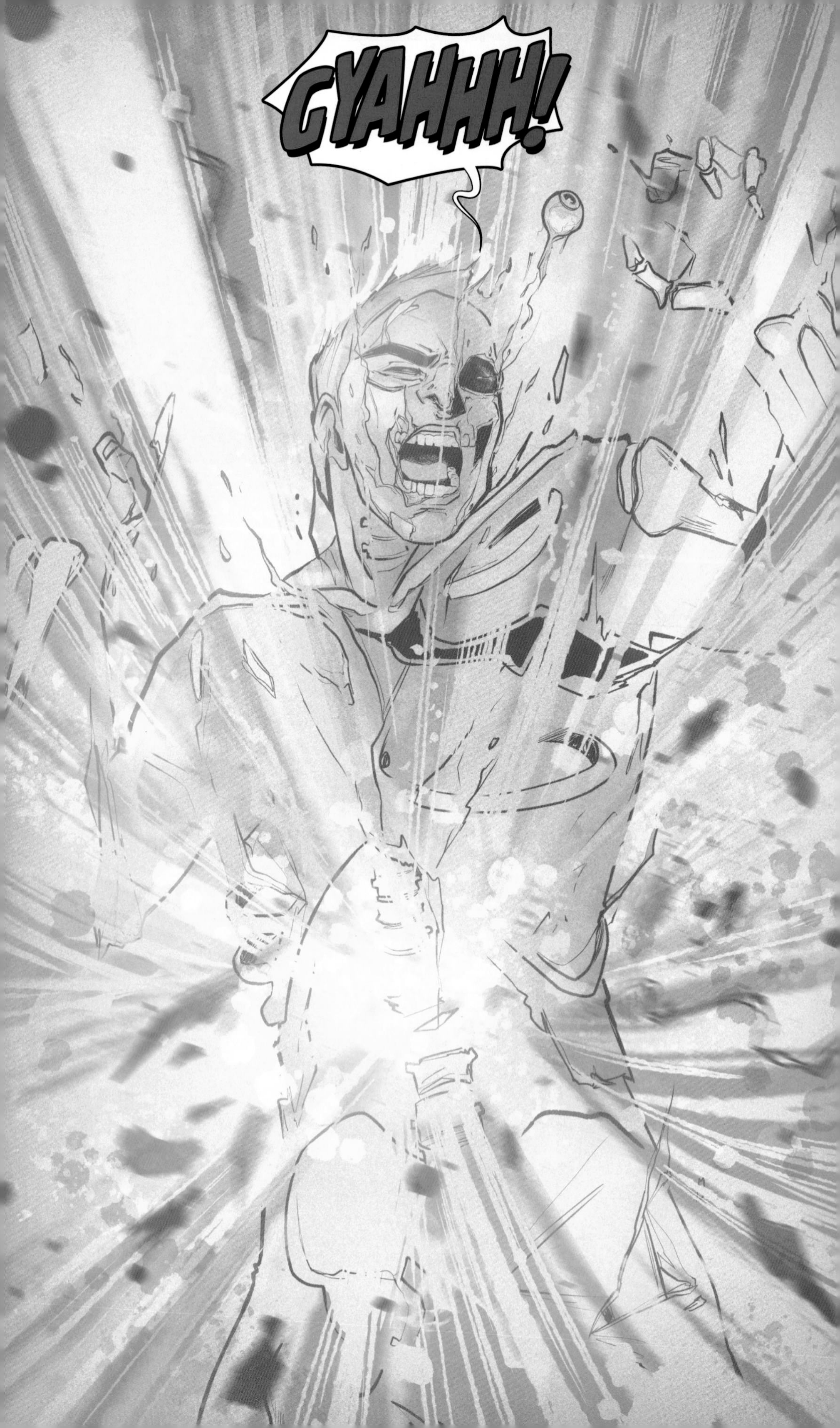
GYAHHH!

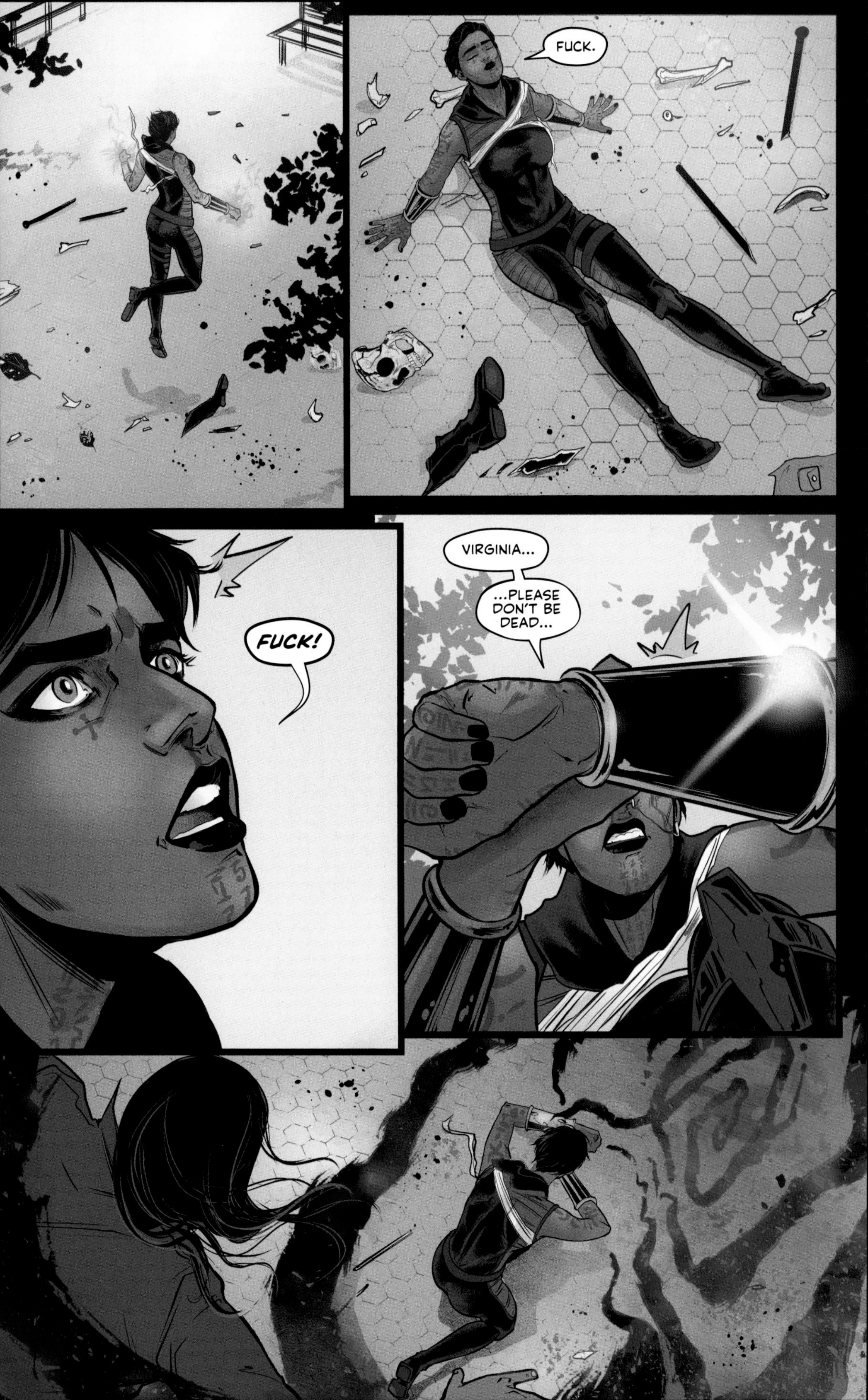
FUCK.
FUCK!
VIRGINIA...
...PLEASE DON'T BE DEAD...

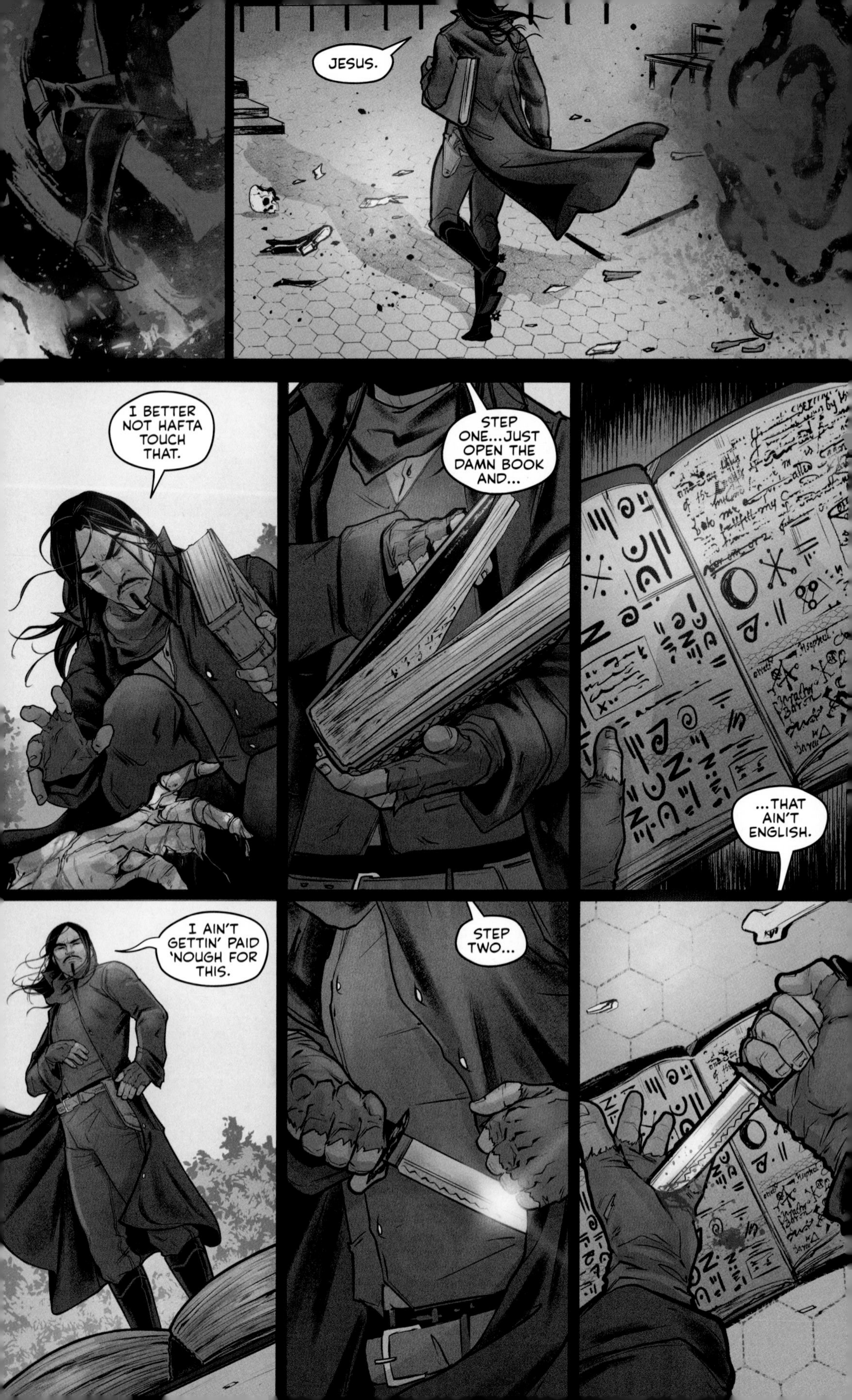
JESUS.
I BETTER NOT HAFTA TOUCH THAT.
STEP ONE...JUST OPEN THE DAMN BOOK AND...
...THAT AIN'T ENGLISH.
I AIN'T GETTIN' PAID 'NOUGH FOR THIS.
STEP TWO...

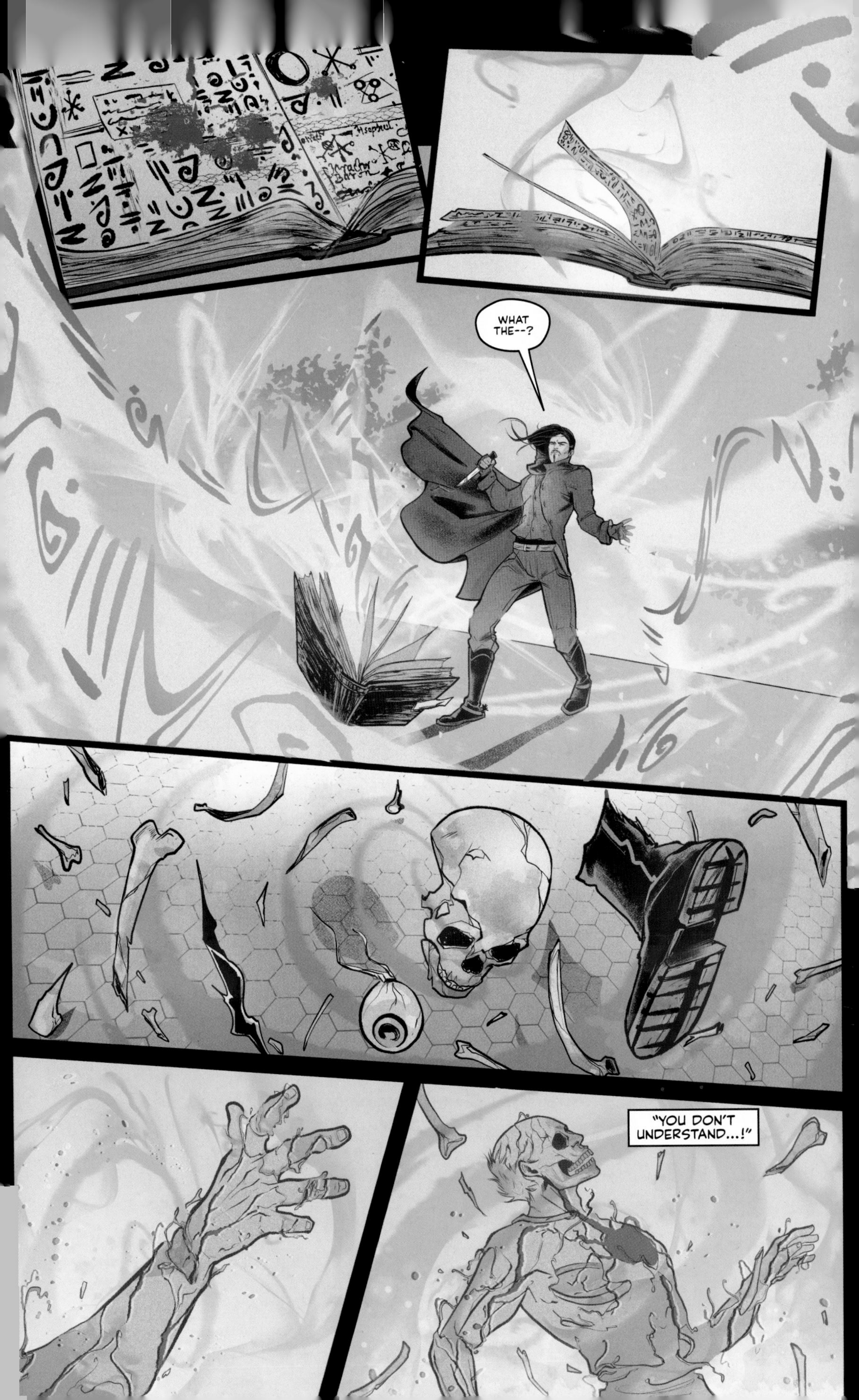
WHAT THE--?
"YOU DON'T UNDERSTAND...!"

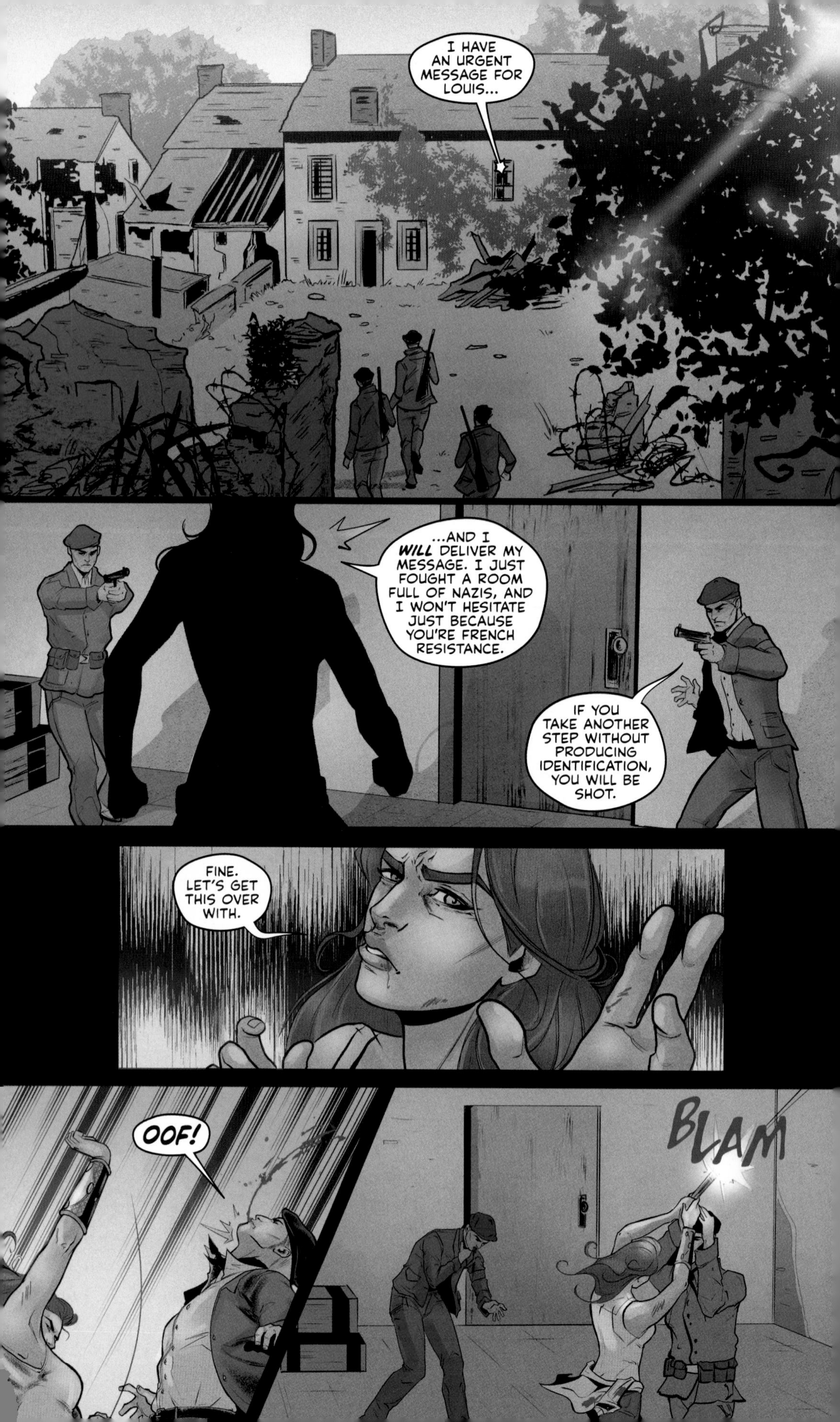
I HAVE AN URGENT MESSAGE FOR LOUIS...
...AND I *WILL* DELIVER MY MESSAGE. I JUST FOUGHT A ROOM FULL OF NAZIS, AND I WON'T HESITATE JUST BECAUSE YOU'RE FRENCH RESISTANCE.
IF YOU TAKE ANOTHER STEP WITHOUT PRODUCING IDENTIFICATION, YOU WILL BE SHOT.
FINE. LET'S GET THIS OVER WITH.
OOF!
BLAM

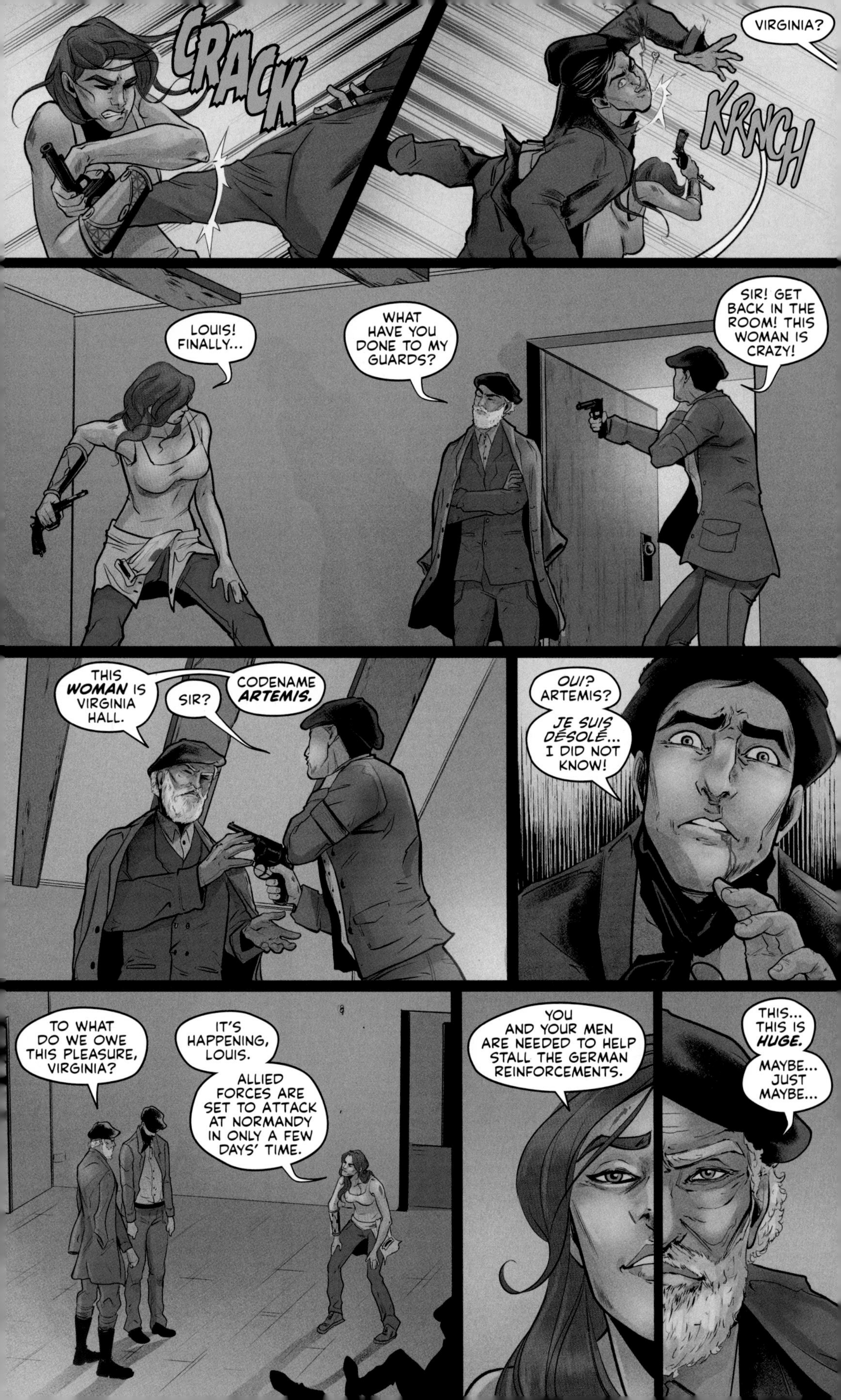
CRACK
VIRGINIA?
KRNCH
LOUIS! FINALLY...
WHAT HAVE YOU DONE TO MY GUARDS?
SIR! GET BACK IN THE ROOM! THIS WOMAN IS CRAZY!
THIS *WOMAN* IS VIRGINIA HALL.
SIR?
CODENAME *ARTEMIS.*
OUI? ARTEMIS?
JE SUIS DÉSOLÉ... I DID NOT KNOW!
TO WHAT DO WE OWE THIS PLEASURE, VIRGINIA?
IT'S HAPPENING, LOUIS.
ALLIED FORCES ARE SET TO ATTACK AT NORMANDY IN ONLY A FEW DAYS' TIME.
YOU AND YOUR MEN ARE NEEDED TO HELP STALL THE GERMAN REINFORCEMENTS.
THIS... THIS IS *HUGE.*
MAYBE... JUST MAYBE...

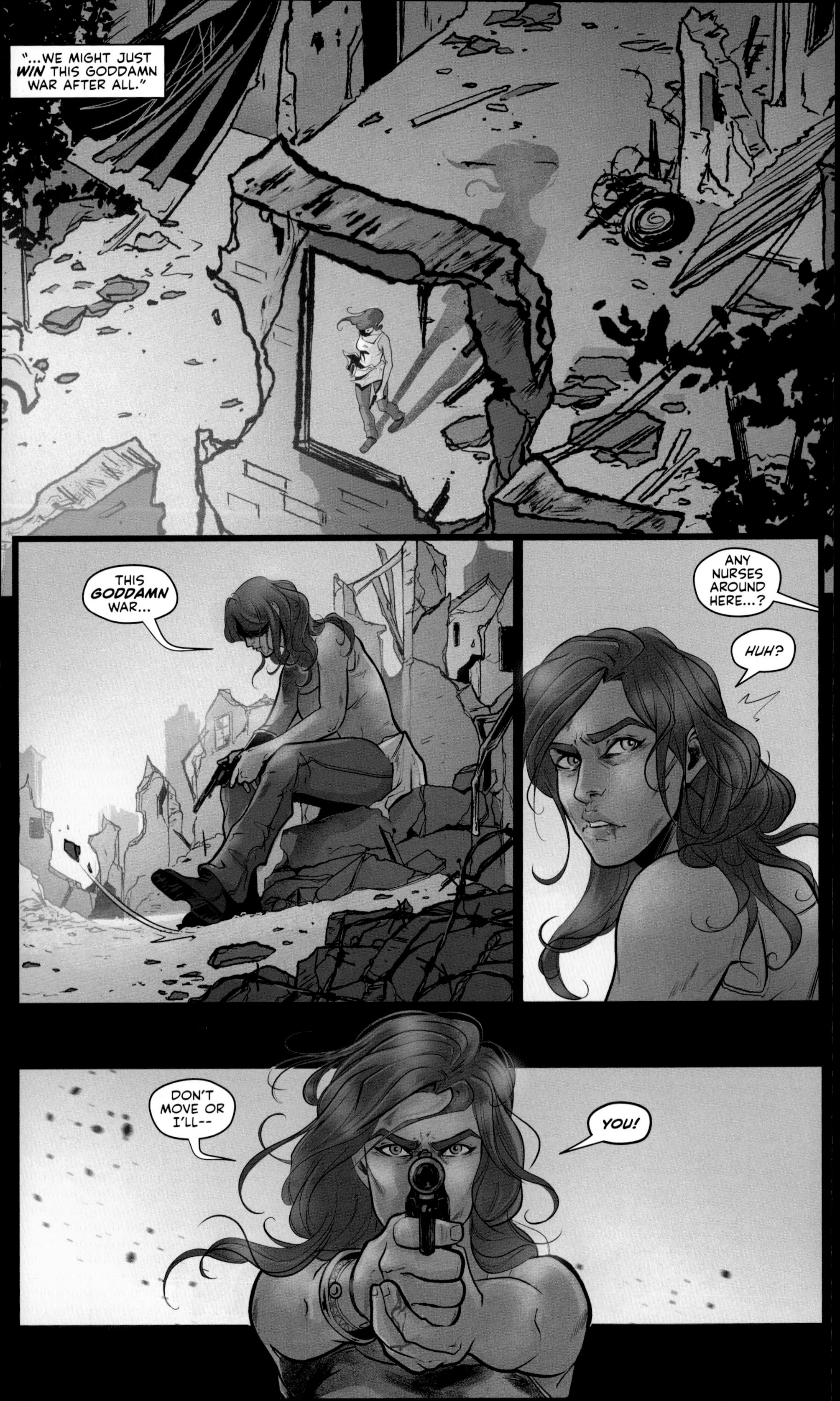
"...WE MIGHT JUST WIN THIS GODDAMN WAR AFTER ALL."
THIS GODDAMN WAR...
ANY NURSES AROUND HERE...?
HUH?
DON'T MOVE OR I'LL--
YOU!

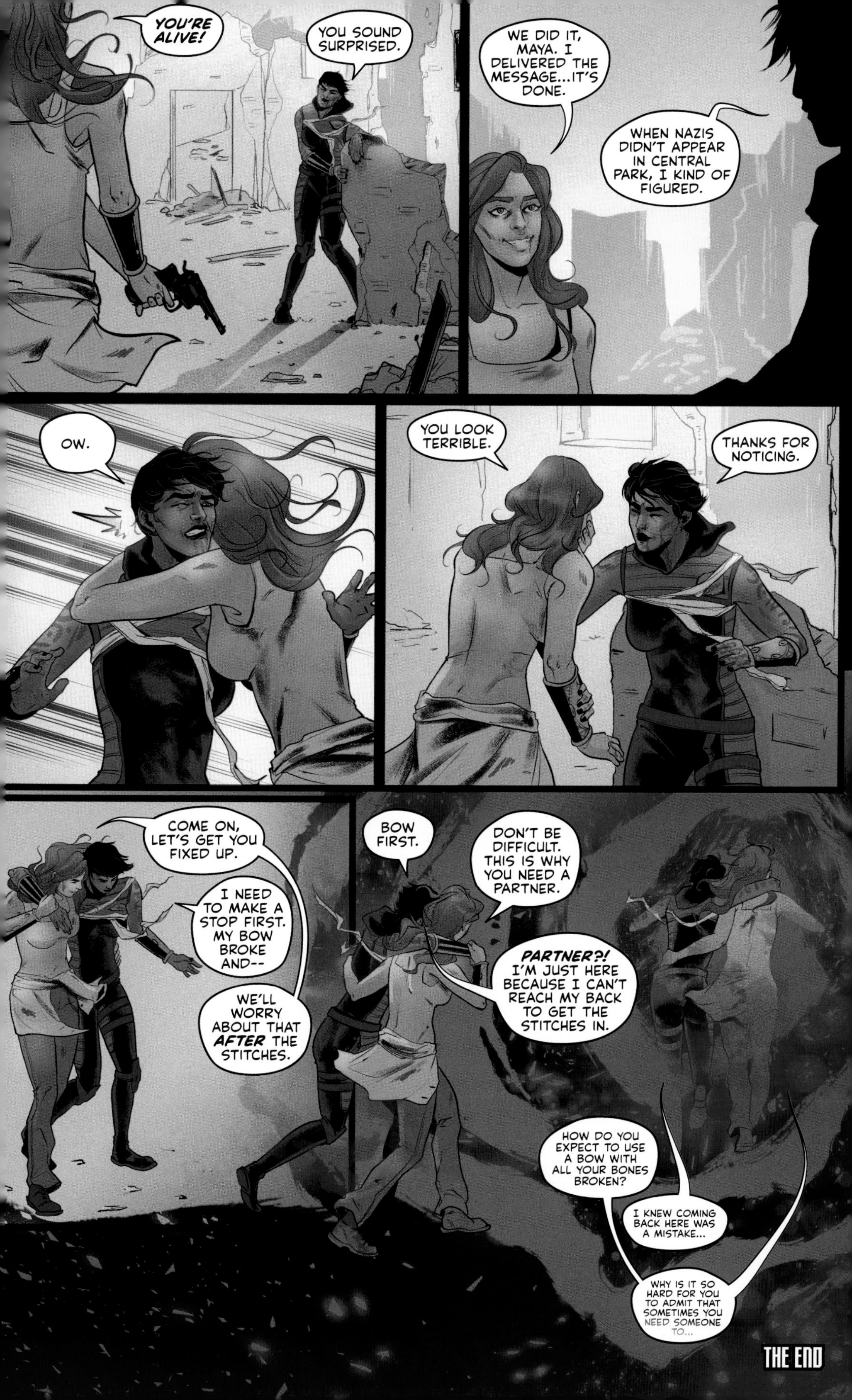
YOU'RE ALIVE!
YOU SOUND SURPRISED.
WE DID IT, MAYA. I DELIVERED THE MESSAGE...IT'S DONE.
WHEN NAZIS DIDN'T APPEAR IN CENTRAL PARK, I KIND OF FIGURED.
OW.
YOU LOOK TERRIBLE.
THANKS FOR NOTICING.
COME ON, LET'S GET YOU FIXED UP.
I NEED TO MAKE A STOP FIRST. MY BOW BROKE AND--
WE'LL WORRY ABOUT THAT AFTER THE STITCHES.
BOW FIRST.
DON'T BE DIFFICULT. THIS IS WHY YOU NEED A PARTNER.
PARTNER?! I'M JUST HERE BECAUSE I CAN'T REACH MY BACK TO GET THE STITCHES IN.
HOW DO YOU EXPECT TO USE A BOW WITH ALL YOUR BONES BROKEN?
I KNEW COMING BACK HERE WAS A MISTAKE...
WHY IS IT SO HARD FOR YOU TO ADMIT THAT SOMETIMES YOU NEED SOMEONE TO...
THE END

ARTEMIS

& THE ASSASSIN

BEHIND THE SCENES & EXTRAS

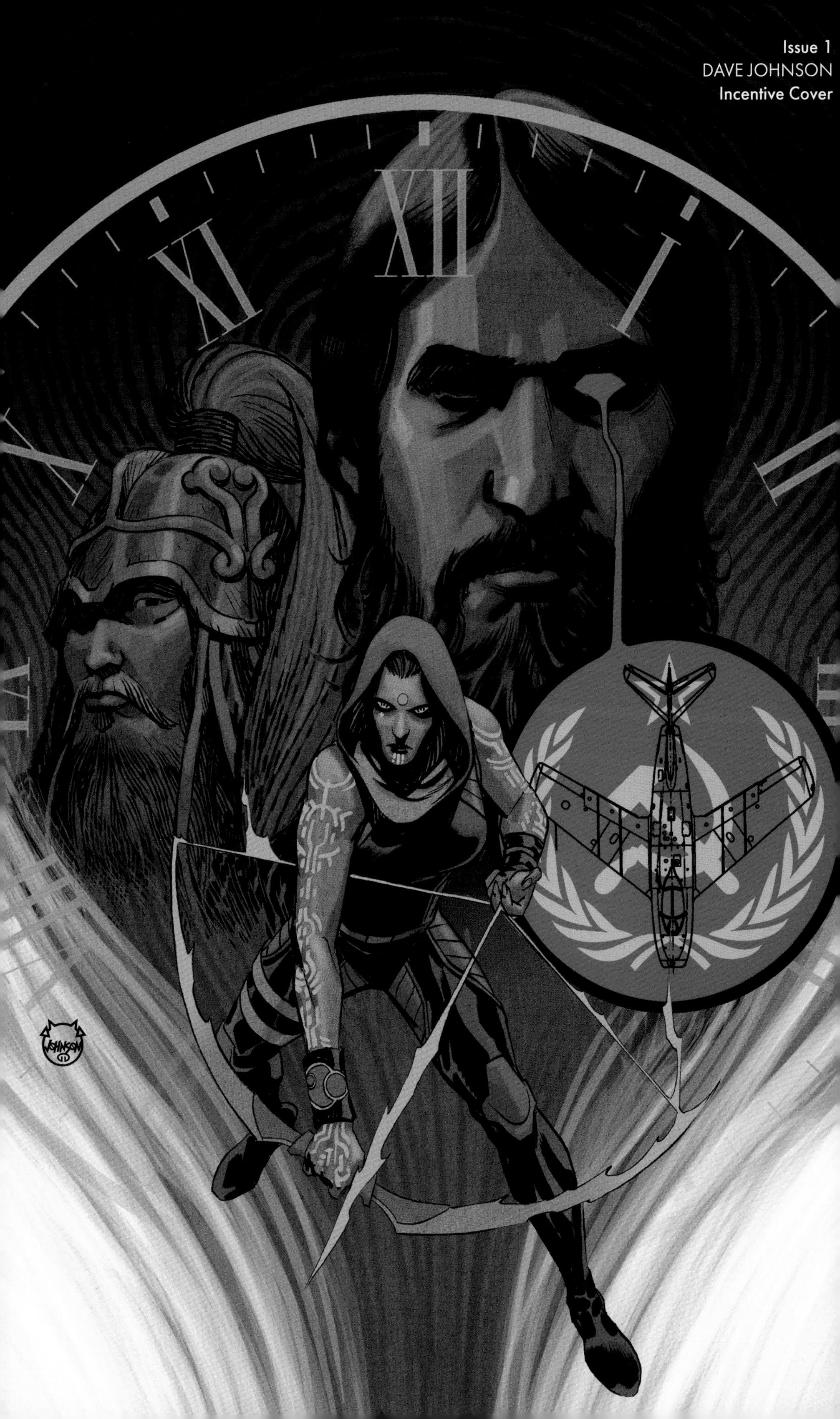

Issue 1
DAVE JOHNSON
Incentive Cover

Issue 1
TIM BRADSTREET
Corning Comics & Collectibles Exclusive Variant Cover

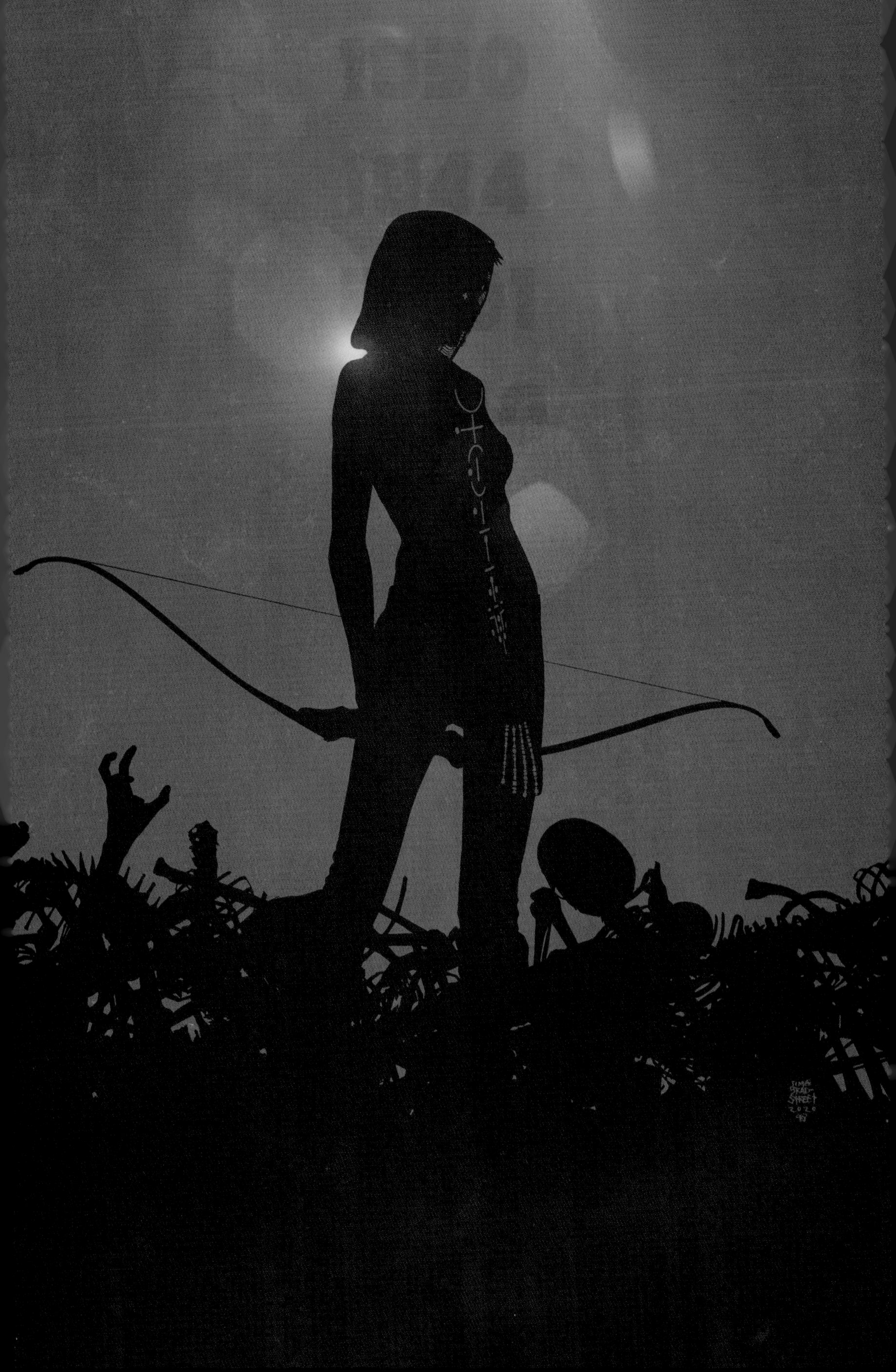

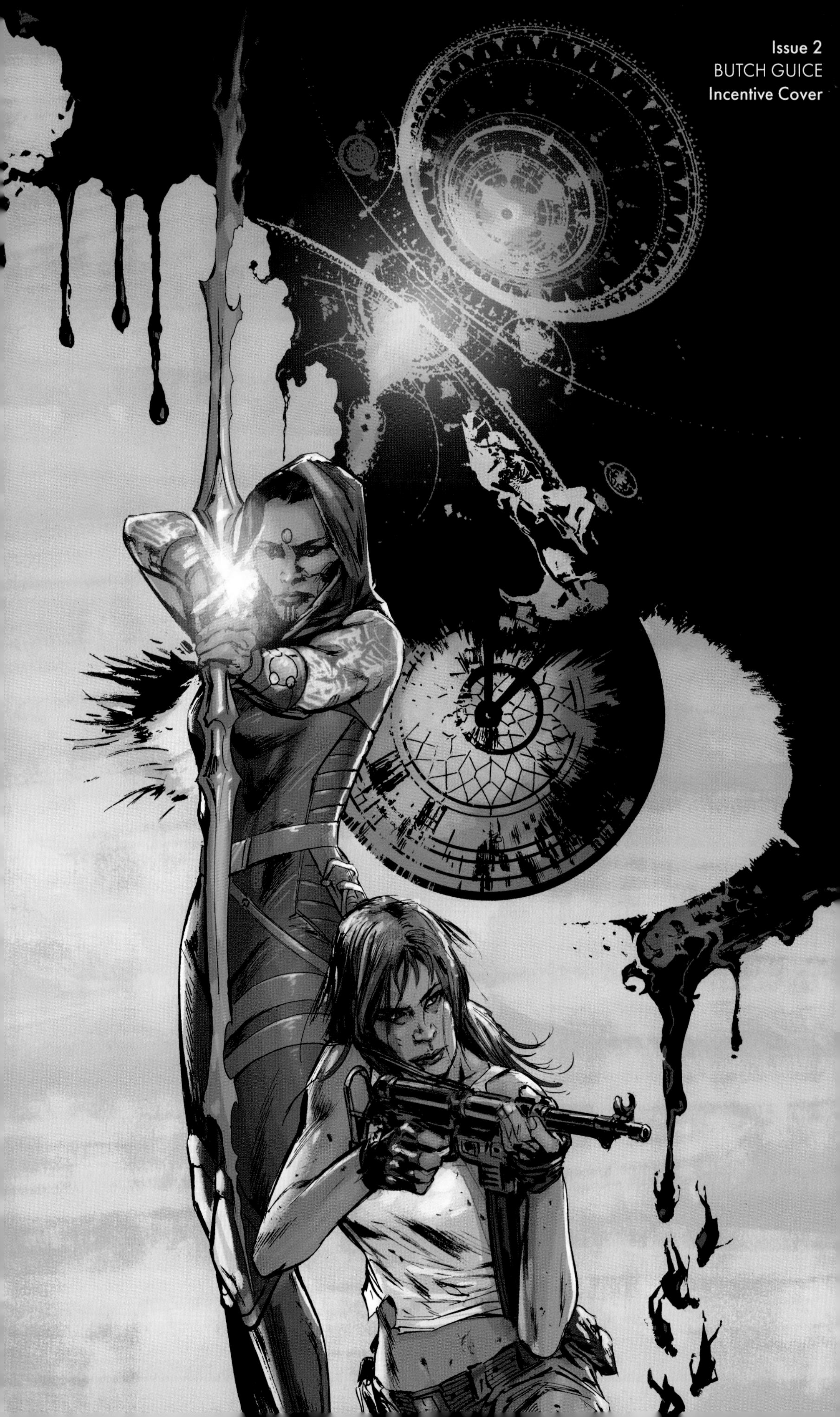

Issue 2
BUTCH GUICE
Incentive Cover

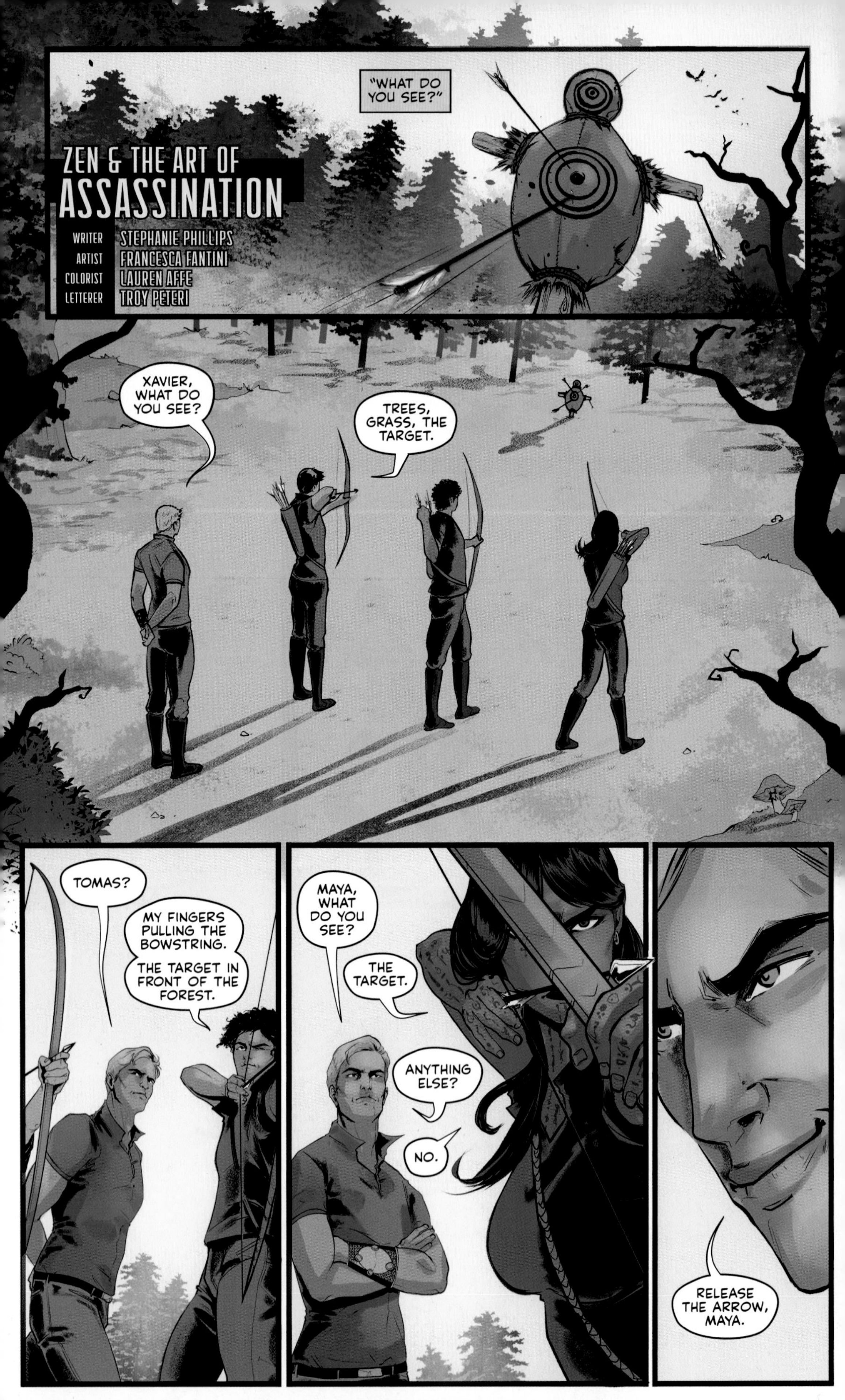
"WHAT DO YOU SEE?"
ZEN & THE ART OF ASSASSINATION
WRITER STEPHANIE PHILLIPS
ARTIST FRANCESCA FANTINI
COLORIST LAUREN AFFE
LETTERER TROY PETERI
XAVIER, WHAT DO YOU SEE?
TREES, GRASS, THE TARGET.
TOMAS?
MY FINGERS PULLING THE BOWSTRING.
THE TARGET IN FRONT OF THE FOREST.
MAYA, WHAT DO YOU SEE?
THE TARGET.
ANYTHING ELSE?
NO.
RELEASE THE ARROW, MAYA.

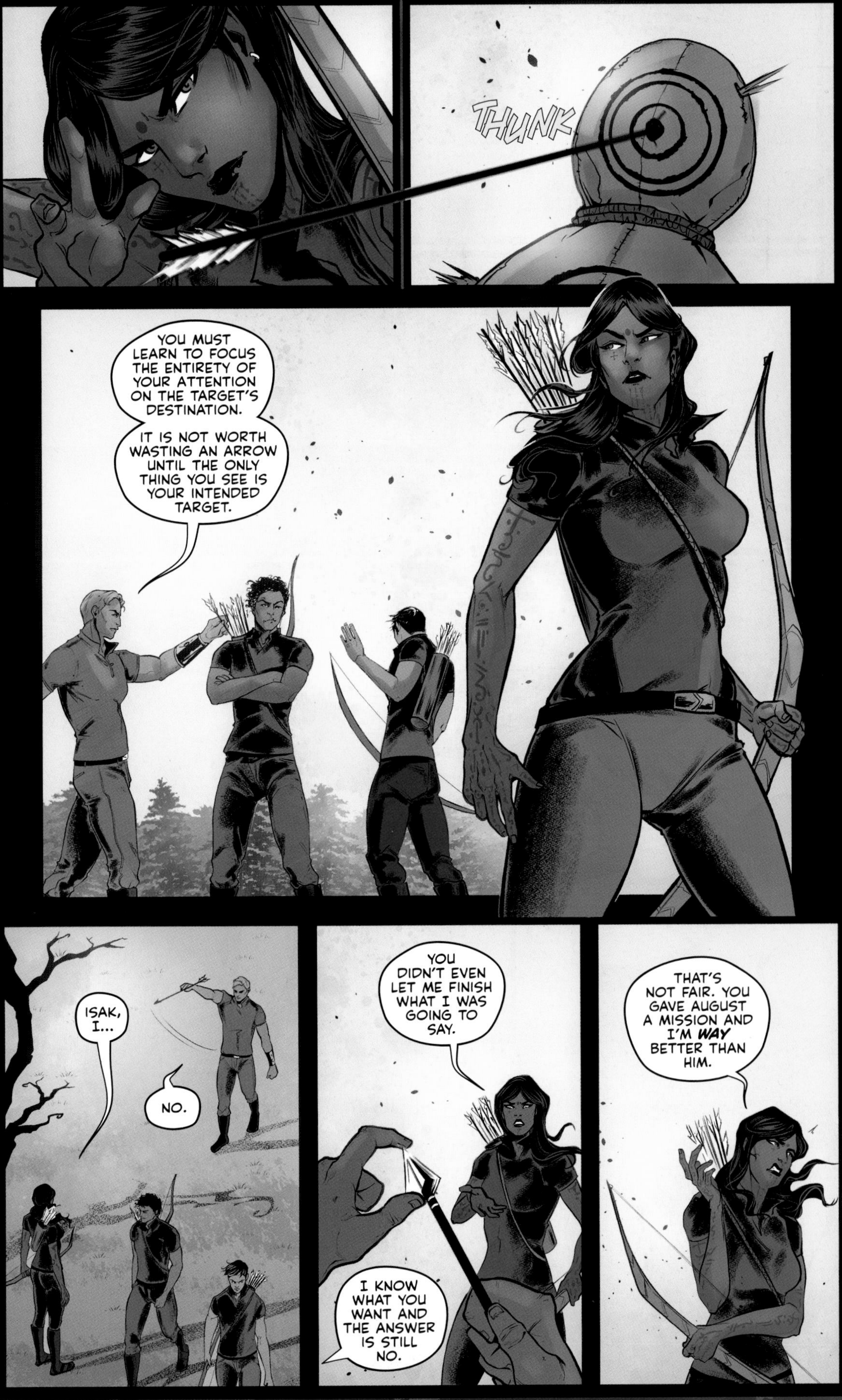
THUNK
YOU MUST LEARN TO FOCUS THE ENTIRETY OF YOUR ATTENTION ON THE TARGET'S DESTINATION.
IT IS NOT WORTH WASTING AN ARROW UNTIL THE ONLY THING YOU SEE IS YOUR INTENDED TARGET.
ISAK, I...
NO.
YOU DIDN'T EVEN LET ME FINISH WHAT I WAS GOING TO SAY.
I KNOW WHAT YOU WANT AND THE ANSWER IS STILL NO.
THAT'S NOT FAIR. YOU GAVE AUGUST A MISSION AND I'M *WAY* BETTER THAN HIM.

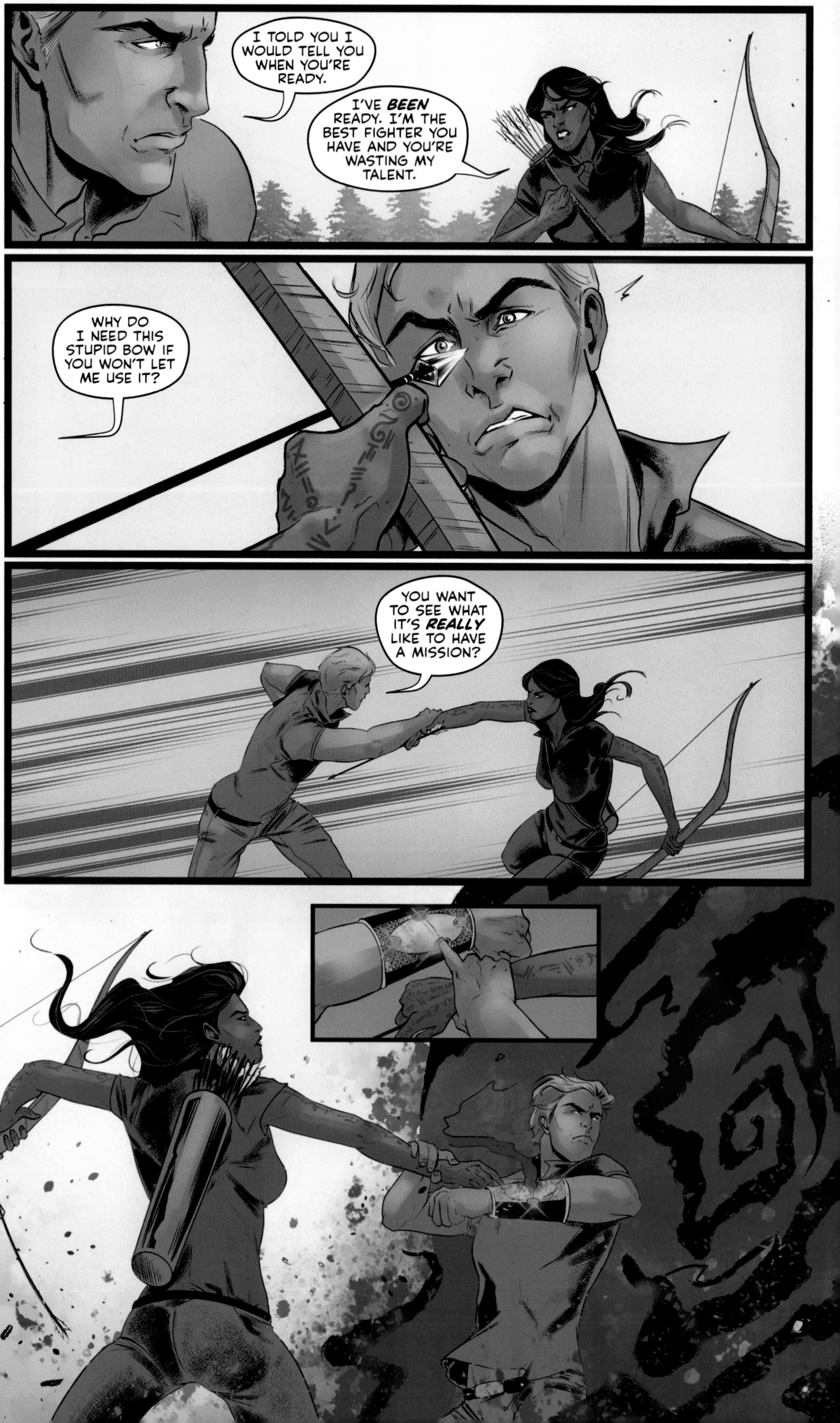
I TOLD YOU I WOULD TELL YOU WHEN YOU'RE READY.
I'VE **BEEN** READY. I'M THE BEST FIGHTER YOU HAVE AND YOU'RE WASTING MY TALENT.
WHY DO I NEED THIS STUPID BOW IF YOU WON'T LET ME USE IT?
YOU WANT TO SEE WHAT IT'S **REALLY** LIKE TO HAVE A MISSION?

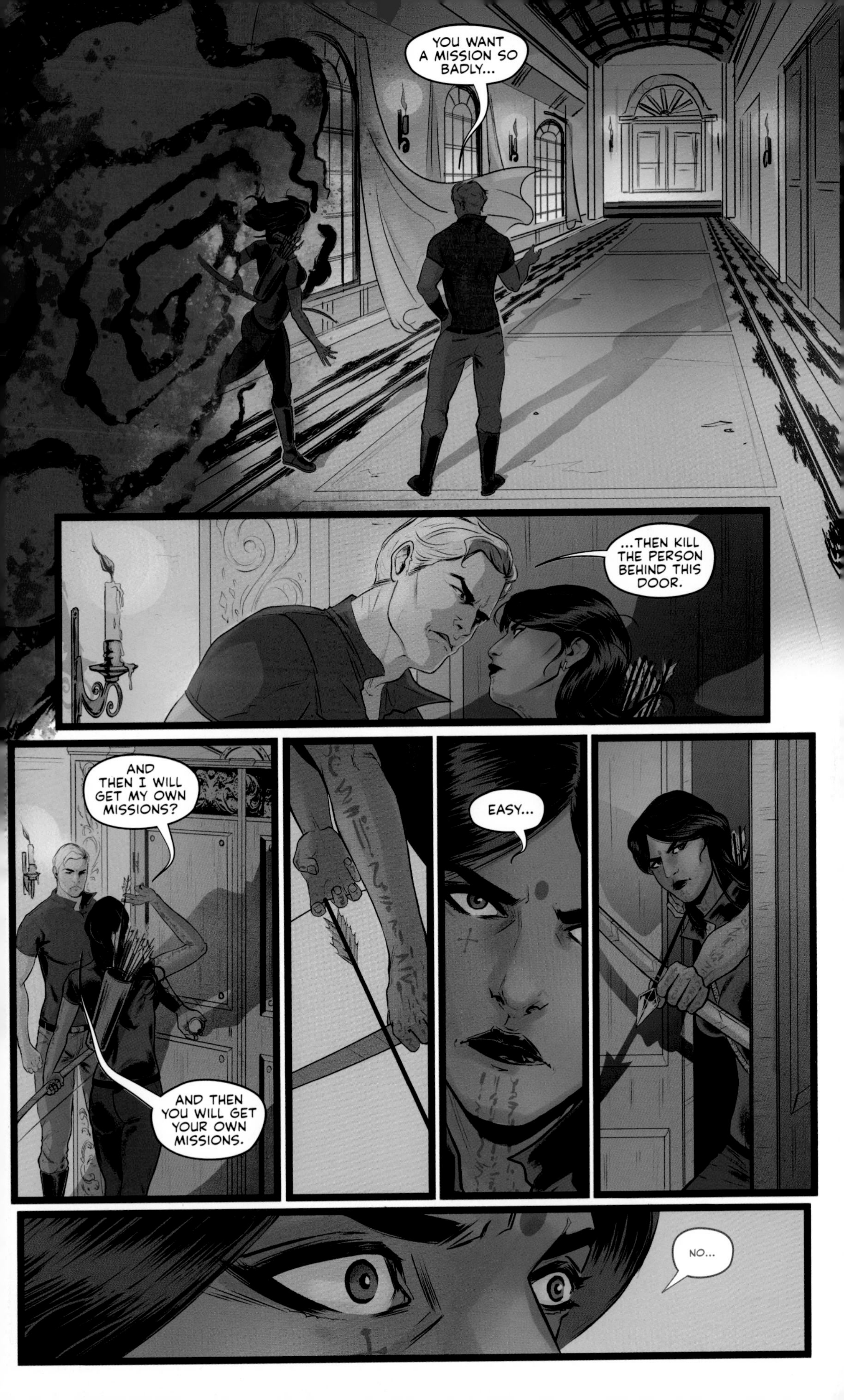
YOU WANT A MISSION SO BADLY...
...THEN KILL THE PERSON BEHIND THIS DOOR.
AND THEN I WILL GET MY OWN MISSIONS?
AND THEN YOU WILL GET YOUR OWN MISSIONS.
EASY...
NO...

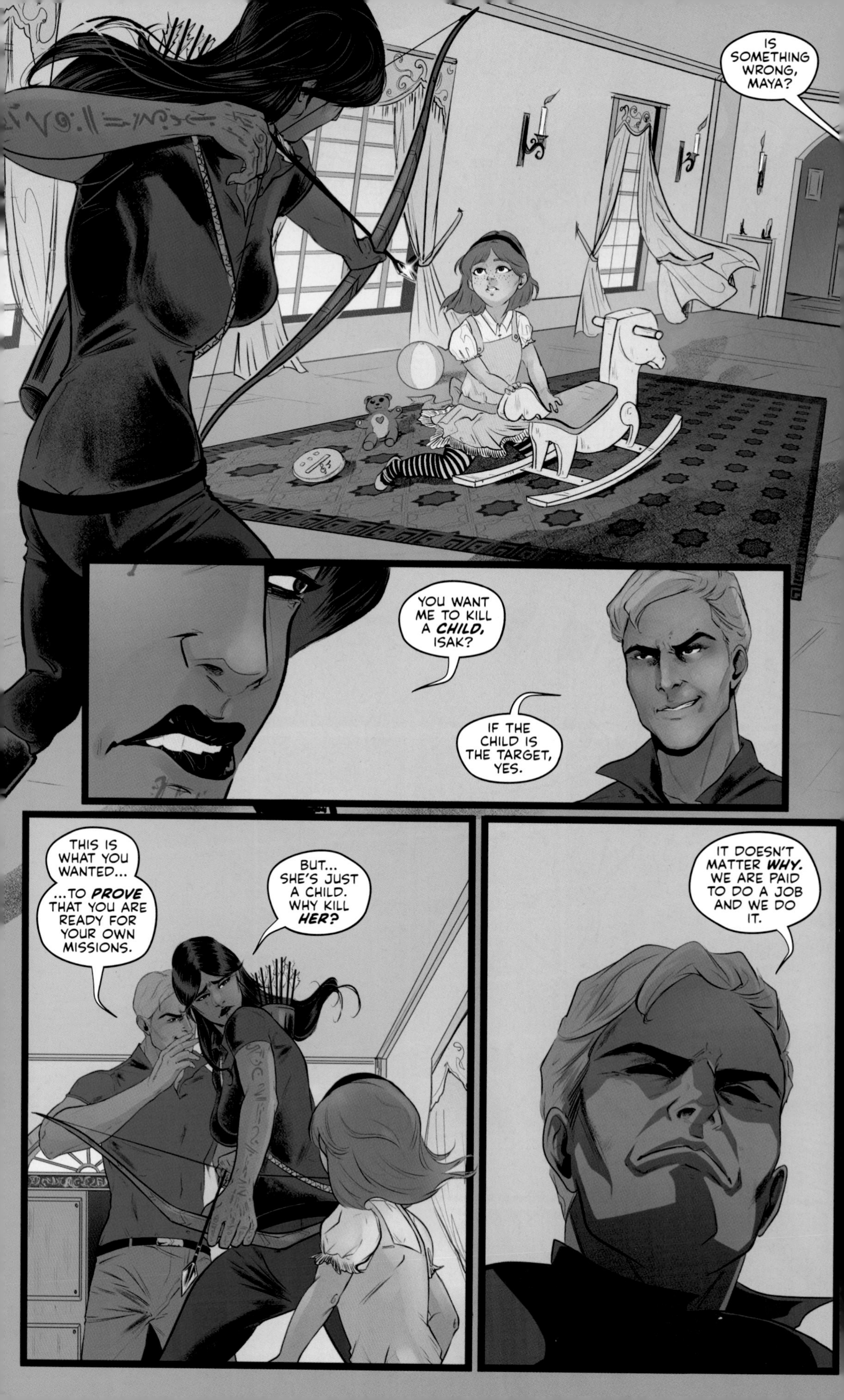
IS SOMETHING WRONG, MAYA?
YOU WANT ME TO KILL A *CHILD,* ISAK?
IF THE CHILD IS THE TARGET, YES.
THIS IS WHAT YOU WANTED...
...TO *PROVE* THAT YOU ARE READY FOR YOUR OWN MISSIONS.
BUT... SHE'S JUST A CHILD. WHY KILL *HER?*
IT DOESN'T MATTER *WHY.* WE ARE PAID TO DO A JOB AND WE DO IT.

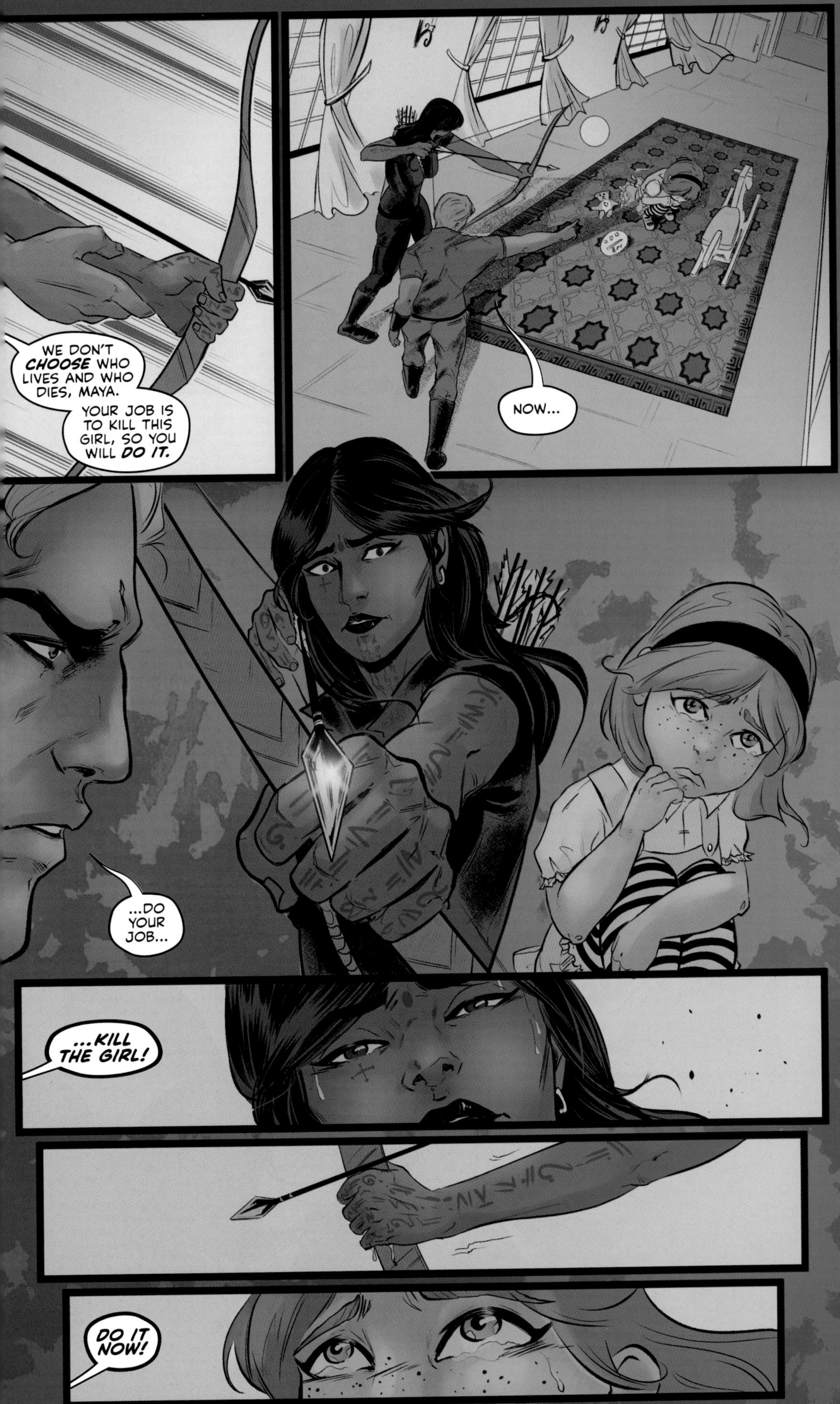
WE DON'T CHOOSE WHO LIVES AND WHO DIES, MAYA.
YOUR JOB IS TO KILL THIS GIRL, SO YOU WILL DO IT.
NOW...
...DO YOUR JOB...
...KILL THE GIRL!
DO IT NOW!

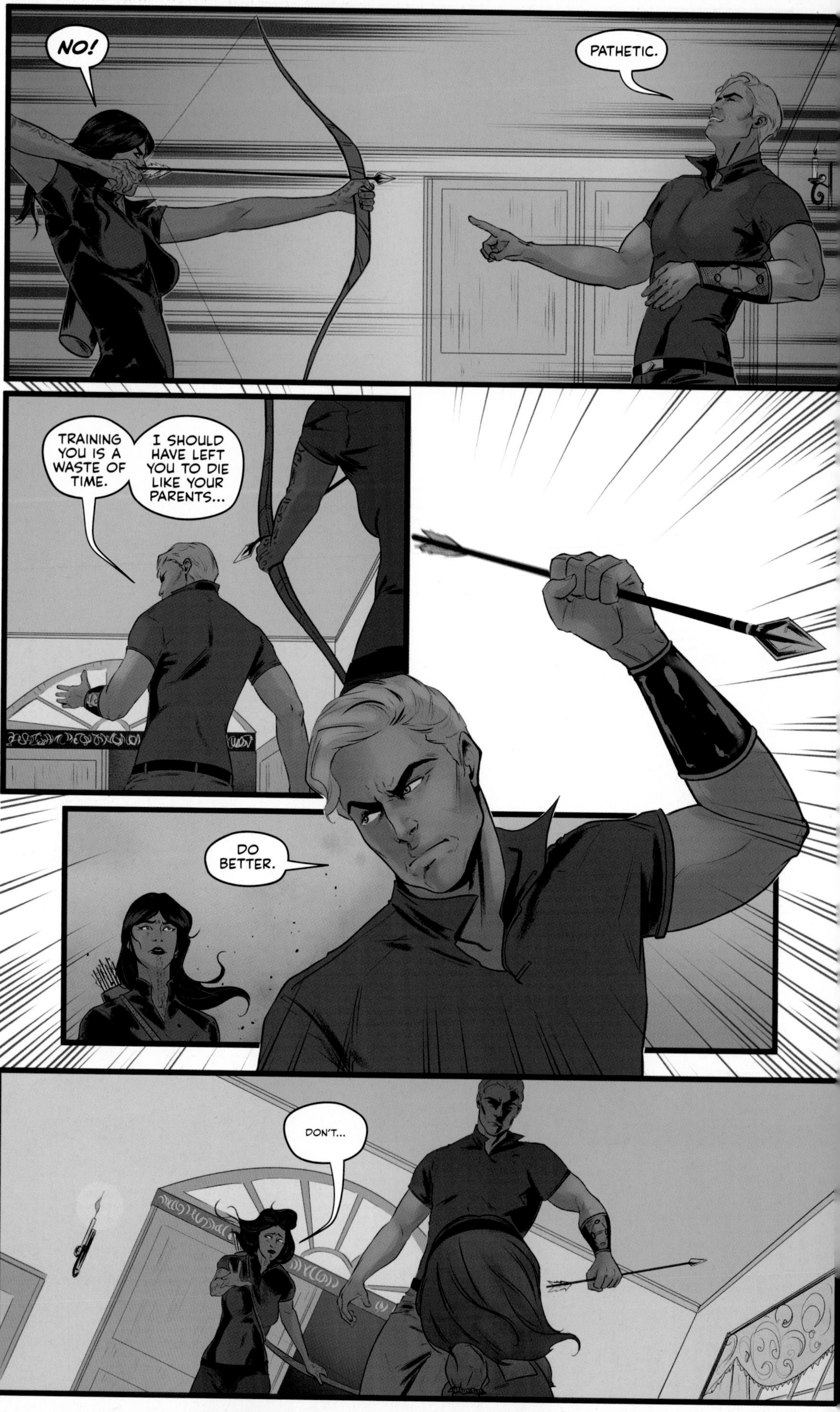
NO!
PATHETIC.
TRAINING YOU IS A WASTE OF TIME.
I SHOULD HAVE LEFT YOU TO DIE LIKE YOUR PARENTS...
DO BETTER.
DON'T...

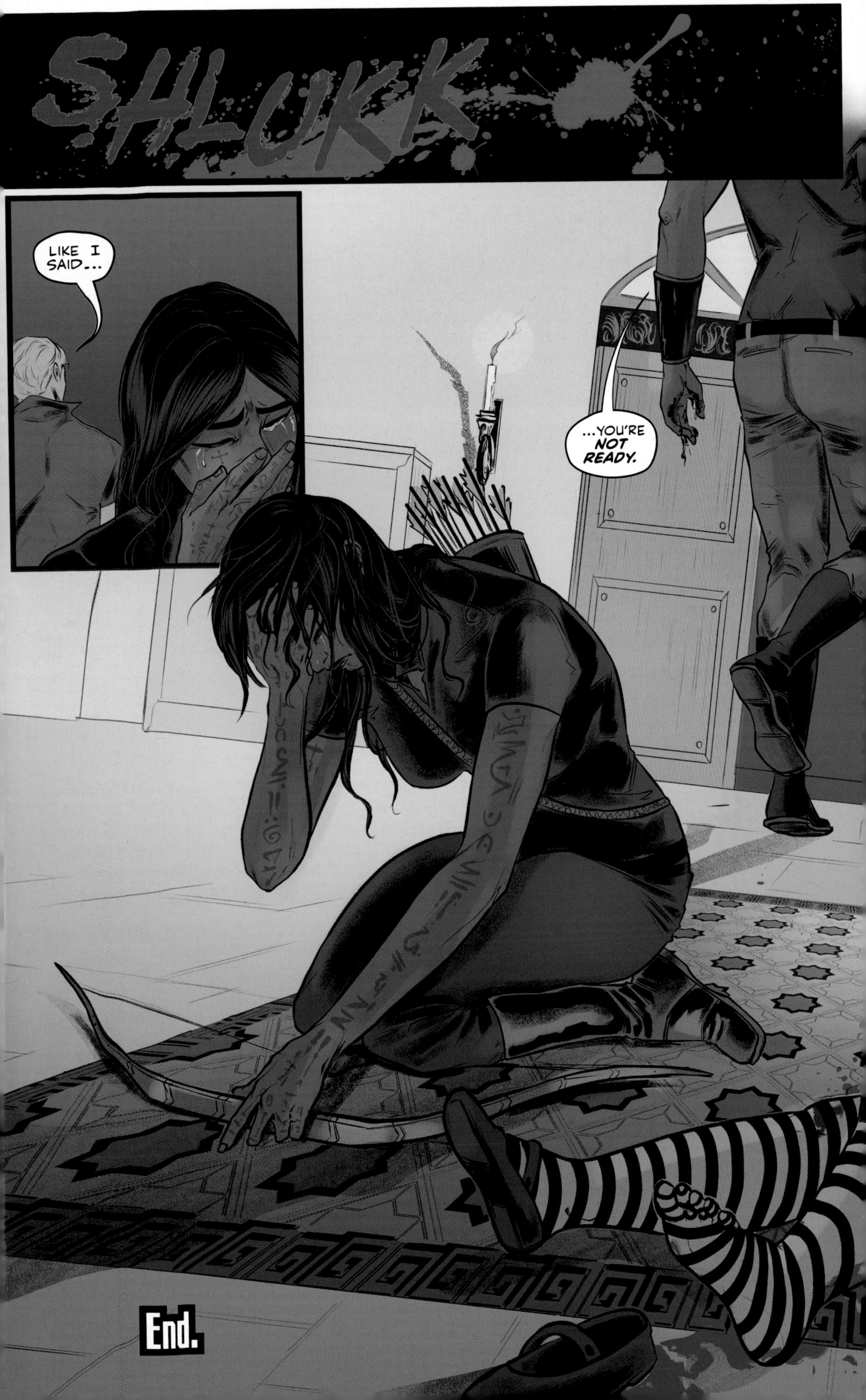
SHLUKK
LIKE I SAID...
...YOU'RE NOT READY.
End.

STEPHANIE PHILLIPS writer
🐦 @Steph_Smash

Stephanie Phillips is a comic book writer from Tampa, FL currently living in Buffalo, NY. Her work appears with AfterShock, Top Cow, Black Mask, Ominous Press and more. Along with comics, Stephanie is a writing professor at the University at Buffalo and a PhD candidate for English. She really likes pancakes and one time wore matching socks.

FRANCESCA FANTINI artist
🐦 @VioletArt22

Francesca Fantini is an Italian comic book artist, illustrator and painter. She grew up surrounded by art, as her father was a painter by profession. Her work has been displayed in galleries in Italy, and she has worked on comics for both Italian and American publishers. Her most recent work is ARTEMIS AND THE ASSASSIN with AfterShock Comics.

MEGHAN HETRICK artist
🐦 @MeghanHetrick

Meghan is an artist who has been drawing for as long as she could hold a crayon, much to the dismay of both her mother and the walls of her childhood homes. She lives outside of Atlanta, GA, with two slightly off-kilter boxer dogs, a dumb as bricks but adorable lab-hound mix, and four extremely attention seeking cats. When she tears herself away from her work long enough, she enjoys gaming, and working on her personal project, *Covenant*.

LAUREN AFFE colorist
🐦 @LaurenAffe

Lauren has been working in comics since graduating from SCAD in 2010. She has operated as color artist on many creator owned titles from Dark Horse Comics (*Buzzkill*, *The Ghost Fleet*, *The Paybacks*) and Image Comics (*Five Ghosts*). This has led to work on Dynamite Entertainment's *Turok: Dinosaur Hunter* relaunch as well as projects for Marvel Comics. In addition to THE REVISIONIST and DEAD KINGS for AfterShock, she is currently working on new projects for Stela, Random House and Image Comics.

TROY PETERI letterer
🐦 @A_Larger_World

Troy Peteri, Dave Lanphear and Joshua Cozine are collectively known as A Larger World Studios. They've lettered everything from *The Avengers*, *Iron Man*, *Wolverine*, *Amazing Spider-Man* and *X-Men* to more recent titles like *The Spirit*, *Batman & Robin Eternal* and *Pacific Rim*. They can be reached at studio@largerworld.com for your lettering and design needs.